A Da Capo Press Reprint Series

**FRANKLIN D. ROOSEVELT
AND THE ERA OF THE NEW DEAL**
GENERAL EDITOR: FRANK FREIDEL
Harvard University

RURAL MIGRATION
IN THE UNITED STATES

Division of Research
Work Projects Administration

Research Monographs

Works Progress Administration
Division of Social Research
Research Monograph XIX

RURAL MIGRATION IN THE UNITED STATES

By C. E. Lively
and Conrad Taeuber

DA CAPO PRESS • NEW YORK • 1971

A Da Capo Press Reprint Edition

This Da Capo Press edition of *Rural Migration in the United States* is an unabridged republication of the first edition published in Washington, D.C., in 1939. It is reprinted by permission from a copy of the original edition owned by the Harvard College Library.

Library of Congress Catalog Card Number 71-165601

ISBN 0-306-70351-3

Published by Da Capo Press, Inc.
A Subsidiary of Plenum Publishing Corporation
227 West 17th Street, New York, N.Y. 10011

Manufactured in the United States of America

RURAL MIGRATION
IN THE UNITED STATES

WORKS PROGRESS ADMINISTRATION

F. C. Harrington, *Administrator*

Corrington Gill, *Assistant Administrator*

DIVISION OF RESEARCH

Howard B. Myers, *Director*

RURAL MIGRATION

IN THE

UNITED STATES

By

C. E. Lively

University of Missouri

and

Conrad Taeuber

U. S. Department of Agriculture

Bureau of Agricultural Economics

•

RESEARCH MONOGRAPH XIX

1939

UNITED STATES GOVERNMENT PRINTING OFFICE, WASHINGTON

Letter of Transmittal

WORKS PROGRESS ADMINISTRATION,
Washington, D. C., May 1, 1939.

SIR: I have the honor to transmit a comprehensive analysis of rural migration in the United States. The effect of migration on the distribution of the rural population is important with respect to both the location and the extent of unemployment and relief needs and consequently affects the extent and distribution of employment under the Works Program. The depression of the early thirties markedly reduced the migration from rural areas. Since there was no corresponding decline in the excess of births over deaths, a rapid increase in farm population was inevitable. Moreover, the increase was most marked in the productive ages, especially among youth.

Not only have the reduced migration from rural areas and the back-to-the-land movement been important factors in intensifying rural relief needs but also residential requirements for public assistance have had the general effect of retarding needed migration from rural areas. Migration alone offers no panacea for the problems of rural areas. In combination with efforts to improve the social and economic conditions of rural people where they are and with a declining rural birth rate, however, guided migration for a limited number seems to offer one approach to solving the long-time problems of widespread need in rural areas.

By the use of census data this report presents a detailed analysis of the recent movements of the rural population. In addition data for approximately 22,000 rural families included in comparable field surveys conducted in 7 States make possible an intensive study of the characteristics of migrant and nonmigrant families in the same areas.

The study was made in the Division of Research under the direction of Howard B. Myers, Director of Research. The schedules and instructions used in the field surveys were prepared by C. E. Lively, now of the University of Missouri, and Conrad Taeuber, now of the U. S. Department of Agriculture, Bureau of Agricultural Economics, when they were members of the research staff of the Federal Emergency Relief Administration. The analysis of both the census and survey data was made under the supervision of T. J. Woofter, Jr., Chief, Rural Surveys Section, Division of Research, and Carl C.

Taylor, in charge, Division of Farm Population and Rural Life, Bureau of Agricultural Economics. The report was prepared by C. E. Lively and Conrad Taeuber with the assistance of Frances Foott, C. L. Folse, and Charles S. Hoffman. It was edited by Ellen Winston of the Division of Research. Special acknowledgment is due the State supervisors and assistant supervisors of rural research who conducted the field surveys and the staff of the Social Research Section, Farm Security Administration, who assisted with the field work and tabulations.

Respectfully submitted.

CORRINGTON GILL,
Assistant Administrator.

COL. F. C. HARRINGTON,
Works Progress Administrator.

Contents

ILLUSTRATIONS

Figures

Rural Migration in the United States

INTRODUCTION

THE PEOPLE of the United States are traditionally restless. The resultant redistribution of the population has signal influence on many of the Nation's basic programs, such as those concerned with land use, education, public health, public and private employment, and relief.

Before 1900 public interest in population movements was centered on foreign immigration, land settlement, and the westward movement. As the rush to the frontier died away and population turned toward the cities, such attention shifted to rural-urban migrations. During the World War, and subsequently, great interest was manifested in the northward migration of Negroes. Within the same period some attention was devoted to studies of the individual aspects of migration, including analyses of the types of people who moved. In the decade immediately preceding the economic depression of the early thirties, the suburban trend caught the fancy of persons concerned with population movements, and more recently urban-rural migrations have stimulated much discussion. At present the interest in migration shows definite indications of broadening to encompass the entire problem of the distribution of population in relation to resources and economic opportunity.

The urgency of the problem of conservation of natural, particularly agricultural, resources is becoming more and more apparent. Variations in the economic and social status of the population in different sections of the country are little short of startling. The natural increase of the population is so variable from section to section as to give rise to the pertinent remark of Rupert Vance that the most significant redistribution of population that could take place would result from cessation of migration. Failure of a large proportion of the rural population of many counties and States of high natural increase and relatively low economic opportunity to migrate elsewhere might precipitate these areas, and indeed the rural population generally, into an economic quagmire. This would place increased demands upon work programs, relief, and other forms of public assistance. Because of the residential requirements of public assistance

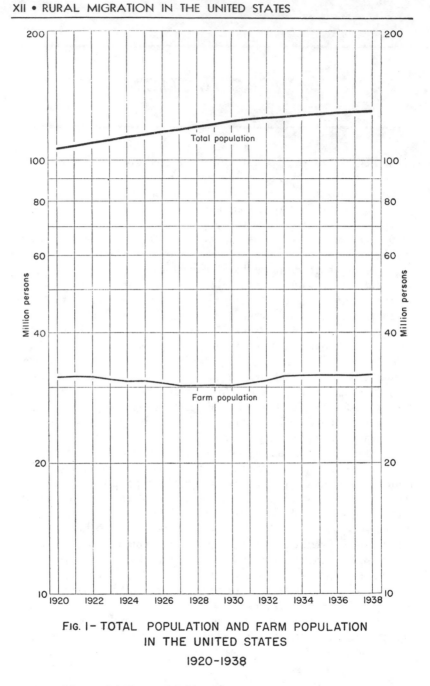

FIG. I— TOTAL POPULATION AND FARM POPULATION
IN THE UNITED STATES

1920-1938

Sources: Bureau of the Census, U.S. Department
of Commerce, and Bureau of Agricultural
Economics, U.S. Department of Agriculture,
Washington, D. C.

AF-2991,WPA.

programs, these demands might serve as deterrents to needed emigration. Yet, with the present state of the urban birth rate, the population of most large cities would soon begin to decline if rural-urban migrations were to cease. Thus, migration becomes an important phase of the entire problem of economic and social planning.

In spite of the growing interest in population movements, there does not now exist any comprehensive body of knowledge regarding the nature of migration and the migratory process. As a result, mistaken notions and theories regarding the occurrence and social significance of migration are widespread. Painstaking research alone can remedy this situation.

The present study was undertaken for the purpose of providing a better understanding of the extent and nature of rural population movements and of the relation of these movements to such significant social and economic factors as quality of land, economic status, population growth, depression, drought, unemployment, and the need for public work programs and relief. Because of such relationships movements of the rural population have bearing upon the welfare of the rural population and to some extent upon the welfare of the entire Nation. This volume summarizes the available data on broad movements of the rural population and reports on a field survey of the mobility of rural families.

The survey had its inception in 1934 when the authors were members of the staff of the Division of Research, Statistics, and Finance of the Federal Emergency Relief Administration. A project for the field study of rural population mobility launched at that time was subsequently used for the purpose of making studies in a number of States. The schedule has been used by the Works Progress Administration, Farm Security Administration, and Bureau of Agricultural Economics; and these agencies have collaborated in the analysis of the material. The mobility histories of approximately 22,000 families were secured through interviews in rural areas of Iowa, Kentucky, Maryland, North Carolina, North Dakota, Ohio, and South Dakota.[1]

---

[1] For methodology see appendix B, p. 168.

New Lands Ahead.

SUMMARY

THE EXTENT and direction of the movements of the rural population of the United States are significant not only with respect to rural areas but also with respect to the population of the Nation as a whole, since there is a constant exchange of people between rural and urban areas. Because the study of internal migration is comparatively recent, detailed data are often lacking. On the basis of the materials which are available, however, it is possible to analyze the general trends in rural migration and to evaluate their social significance. Sufficient data on the migrants are also at hand to indicate important characteristics of rural population mobility.

While data on rural population change in each State give the general aspects of the situation, it is only when rural migration is studied county by county that the wide variations from area to area are directly observable. The rural population of the United States as a whole increased 9.2 percent during the decade 1900–1910, but nearly 40 percent of all counties decreased in rural population. Population readjustments incident to the growth of cities and to a maturing rural civilization were already under way in this period.

During the following decade, 1910–1920, the rate of rural increase fell to 3.2 percent while more than one-half of the counties experienced a decrease in rural population. The trends evident in this decade were continued from 1920 to 1930 with only minor changes. Although the average rate of growth of the rural population increased to 4.7 percent, again more than one-half of the counties lost rural population. In general, however, a definite tendency toward greater stability in rural population growth was noticeable.

Since few if any counties have more deaths than births, such population losses as have been experienced must be attributed to migration. During the decade 1920–1930 the net loss in total rural population through migration to urban areas amounted to 11.1 percent of the 1920 population. Thus, had there been no net loss from rural migration, the gain to the total rural population would probably have been approximately 16 percent instead of less than 5 percent. The net loss from migration was not evenly distributed. The rural-farm loss amounted to 19.3 percent, but there was a rural-nonfarm gain of 1.7 percent. The white population in rural areas lost more heavily through migration than the colored population. More than three-fourths of the net rural migrants were less than 25 years of age in 1920. Females predominated among migrants in both the younger and the older age groups.

The net effect of migration between 1920 and 1930 varied greatly among geographic divisions with the net loss in rural population through migration ranging from 7.9 percent in the Middle Atlantic Division to 15.8 percent in the East South Central Division. Only the Pacific Division experienced an actual increase in rural population through migration. All except eight States had decreases with the losses heaviest in the North Central States and in the South. Although far greater changes resulting from migration occurred in the rural-farm than in the rural-nonfarm population, there was virtually no relation among the States between the rate of gain or loss from migration in the rural-farm population and the corresponding gain or loss in the rural-nonfarm population.

Analysis of net migration on a county basis showed that 517 counties gained and 2,542 lost rural population through migration during the decade. The largest proportion of counties gaining rural population in this manner was found in the Pacific Division (55 percent). Conversely, in the East South Central Division 95 percent of all counties experienced a net loss through migration.

Since 1930 Nation-wide data are available only for the farm segment of the rural population. During the period 1930–1932, when urban employment opportunities were rapidly decreasing, many persons were moving to farms in various parts of the country. Beginning in 1933, this migration to farms was sharply reduced and once more there was an important net movement from farms. Even so, the annual net migration from farms for the period 1930 through 1934 averaged only 120,000 in comparison with an annual average of 600,000 during the decade preceding 1930.

Widespread variations in migration to and from farms occurred among the various geographic divisions of the country. The areas reporting net migration from farms during the 5-year period 1930–1934 were, broadly speaking, the major agricultural regions—the areas producing cotton and wheat together with a section of the Corn Belt. Areas receiving a relatively large net migration to farms included the northeastern portion of the United States, the Appalachian Mountains, the Lake States Cut-Over Region, and the far Northwest as well as scattered smaller areas. Although the total net movement from farms to villages, towns, and cities from 1930 through 1934 was only 600,000 persons, approximately 8 times as many persons actually moved to achieve this result, reflecting the constant interchange of farm and nonfarm population.

When the net migration from farms was reduced after 1930 without a correspondingly sharp decline in the excess of births over deaths, a marked growth in farm population was inevitable. Moreover, the age groups which normally would have contributed the largest proportion of the migrants from farms naturally had the greatest increases, resulting in a tremendous "piling up" of persons in the productive ages.

Persons who have moved to farms since 1930 have shown a definite tendency to locate near cities. This indicates that the movement has not been primarily a return movement to areas from which migrants to cities had come between 1920 and 1930. Nor have the migrants gone disproportionately to the poorest agricultural areas. In fact, the data indicate that recent migrants were not primarily responsible for the high relief rates in the poorer or so-called "problem areas."

Since pressure of population upon available resources is generally regarded as a fundamental factor affecting migration, the sharp differentials in the rate of rural reproduction among the subdivisions of the United States are important. The rate of reproduction as measured by the number of children under 5 years of age per 1,000 women 20–44 years of age is higher in rural than in urban areas and higher in the rural-farm than in the rural-nonfarm population. The highest rural-farm fertility ratios in 1930 prevailed generally throughout most of the Southern States, the Western Plains area, parts of the Rocky Mountain section, and northern Michigan, Minnesota, and Wisconsin. Rural-farm fertility ratios were lowest in the older, more urbanized New England area, in the farm areas of the Middle West, and on the Pacific coast. Approximately the same general picture prevailed in the rural-nonfarm population except that fertility ratios were distinctly below those of the rural-farm population.

In no State as a whole was the rural population failing to replace itself in 1930, although in 22 counties the rural fertility ratio was already below replacement requirements. At the other extreme there were more than 200 counties in which the surplus of children above actual replacement needs was equal to 100 percent or more.

Rural reproduction as measured by the fertility ratio was only slightly related to the rate of gain or loss of population through migration from 1920 to 1930; i. e., there was a slight tendency for counties losing rural population through migration to have higher fertility ratios than the counties which gained by migration.

Consideration of selected factors other than fertility which supposedly are related to migration indicates that no one of them is of primary significance in determining variations in migration. While mechanization of agriculture is generally considered a cause of migration from rural areas, it may also have been a result of such movements. The quality of land appears to be only indirectly related to

migration trends, and slow changes resulting from erosion and depletion are not likely to produce widespread migration. Also, little
direct relationship has been found to exist between migration and per
capita agricultural income. The extent of educational facilities is
another factor which is probably not of primary importance in determining the rate of migration.

Measures of the economic well-being of the population suggest that
there is no simple relationship between the rate of migration and the
presence or absence of a given level of living. However, it does appear
that measured in terms of the rural plane of living index, migration
during 1920–1930 was disproportionately greater from the less prosperous areas.

As far as distance to cities is concerned, the effect of urban centers
upon the rate of rural migration appears to be localized since only a
slight influence was noted beyond a distance of 100 miles. On the
other hand, the suburban trend, which has been an important element
in the growth of cities, promises to continue to be of major importance.

Counties with the highest average relief rates from July 1934 through
June 1935 had experienced a greater net migration from rural areas between 1920 and 1930 than any group of counties in which the relief rates
were lower. In the areas with high relief rates the relatively heavy
migration had apparently been insufficient to effect basic readjustments of numbers to natural resources.

Factors dependent on individual evaluations of conflicting alternatives often determine whether or not a migration actually occurs.
For this reason migration takes place not only from rural areas of
relatively little opportunity but also from areas which appear to offer
better opportunities. Likewise, this accounts for the important crosscurrents of migration which constantly occur.

While the importance of data on the volume and direction of rural
population mobility and the interrelationships of such data with
various social and economic factors are basic, it is also significant to
analyze the characteristics of the migrants themselves and their successive movements, as revealed by special surveys. Relatively few
changes in residence were reported by the heads of the rural families
surveyed, especially in those areas which had been settled longest.
Within rural areas village residents had moved almost as infrequently
as open country residents. Of those heads of households who had
changed residence at some time, the great majority had moved only
once. Almost one-half of the heads of families who had moved had
come from another residence within the same county. Range of
migration was also related to the frequency with which changes of
residence were made. As the frequency of change of residence increased, the proportion which had moved from places within the
survey area or from adjoining counties generally decreased. A

larger proportion of village than of open country residents in the survey areas had come from cities. Moreover, there was more movement from open country to village than from village to open country.

Since the onset of the depression of the early thirties there have been some noticeable changes in mobility in the rural areas surveyed. There was a marked retardation of migration of children 16–24 years of age from the parental home, which affected both boys and girls. A slightly greater increase in the proportion of young women remaining at home in relief than in nonrelief households occurred, but no difference in rate of migration from the two types of households was observed for young men. When young people did migrate during the depression period, they were more likely to move short distances and to the open country than were those who migrated prior to January 1, 1929. The most distant migrations of adult children from both open country and village homes were principally to cities.

Young adults are the most mobile groups among both men and women, and their mobility is closely related to marriage and the beginning of an occupational career. Women leave the parental home at somewhat younger ages than men, but in the survey areas the proportions of persons 25 years of age and over of either sex who were living in the parental homes were comparatively small. Family heads who were under 35 years of age were more mobile than those who were older. Families consisting of husband and wife with or without children were more mobile than other family types. The presence in the household of more than one gainful worker tended to retard mobility. Special circumstances were also found to influence the mobility of family groups; for example, families with female heads were slightly more stable than those with male heads.

Different occupational groups showed varying rates of mobility. Within both the farm and nonfarm groups unskilled workers were highly mobile, but their migrations were primarily for short distances. Professional persons had traveled the greatest distances of any occupational group. Farm owners showed the greatest degree of stability among the farm groups and proprietors, managers, and officials among the nonfarm groups.

There was some shifting in occupations within the survey areas. Those areas in which the number of farms and the farm population increased most sharply experienced some changes from nonagricultural occupations to agriculture. Newcomers to agriculture were more likely to become tenants than owners, but farm owners by usual occupation were able to maintain their status more frequently than were tenants.

On the average, families on relief had moved more frequently than those not on relief. The migrations of nonrelief families were more likely to be for longer distances, however, with the migrations of families on relief more frequently confined to the immediate vicinity of the survey areas.

Although the effects of net migration from country to city have generally been regarded as beneficial to both in terms of population redistribution and plane of living, whether the quality of the residual rural population is lowered has not been satisfactorily settled. Migration seriously depletes the wealth of rural communities which bear the cost of rearing children for the cities, while the payment of inheritance claims to migrants offers another channel through which rural wealth is lost to urban areas. Moreover, where rural migration is both rapid and severe, it causes maladjustments in rural organizations and institutions.

The most obvious effect of rural-urban migration upon cities has been the contribution to urban growth. That the future growth of cities is dependent largely upon the volume of rural-urban migration can scarcely be doubted.

Three types of mobility are especially characteristic of agriculture: the tendency for farm-reared youth to enter agriculture; the movement of families from farm to farm; and the movement of farm operators and their families up and down the socio-economic scale. In spite of large-scale migration, however, the farm population has not been distributed in a manner determined by productivity of the land resources. For the great majority of people farming on mediocre or poor land, it appears that programs for economic and social improvement must be developed on the basis of local situations as the prospects for planned large-scale migration and resettlement are slight. This will necessarily involve greater emphasis on noncommercial production. Even so, emigration should be definitely encouraged from the poorer rural areas where the birth rate is markedly higher than is necessary for maintaining a stationary population. By such means it may be possible to improve, or at least to maintain, the status of the large number of people who live upon the land but who have little or no chance of success as commercial farmers.

Large-scale population movements, both planned and unplanned, are inextricably associated with problems of relief. The reduced migration from rural areas and the back-to-the-land movement have been important factors in intensifying rural relief needs. Areas receiving large-scale migrations, such as the far West, have found the migrants a burden with which the relief agencies have been unable to cope adequately.

Development of a Nation-wide relief and work program has had significant, though unmeasurable, effects upon the volume of rural migration as residential requirements for public assistance have retarded the flow of population. Differences in policies of distributing relief have also undoubtedly affected currents of migration. Failure of sufficient numbers to migrate from the South and from the Plains States has complicated the programs of both the Works Progress Administration and the Farm Security Administration.

Experience indicates that migration offers no general panacea for the problems of rural areas. Unguided migration has not been effective in preventing the need for relief, and planned resettlement must necessarily be on a small scale in terms of the large numbers of poverty-stricken rural people. Rather, a combination of directed migration, reduced birth rates, and improvement of social and economic conditions in general within overpopulated areas seems to offer the soundest approach to solving the long-time problems of widespread need in rural areas.

Chapter I

RURAL POPULATION MOVEMENTS BEFORE 1930

BECAUSE THE attempt at detailed study of internal migration in the United States is comparatively recent, the factual materials necessary for such study have been only partially assembled. Furthermore, the most complete data cover only recent years. The student who would analyze trends in rural migration before 1920 must content himself with information relative to differential increases and decreases in the rural population, which are the result both of the excess of births over deaths and the balance of in-and-out movements. Migration for the decade 1920–1930 may be dealt with directly. On the basis of the data which are available, it is possible to present the general trends of migration for the rural population of the United States before 1930 and to suggest their implications with respect to future trends.

GROWTH OF THE RURAL POPULATION

The rural population of the United States increased from a total of 8,961,000 persons in 1820 to 53,820,000 persons in 1930.[1] [2] Had it not been for the exceptionally rapid rate of growth of the urban population during the latter half of the same period, the rural population would scarcely have been regarded as slow-growing. With the exception of the decade following the Civil War the decennial increase in the rural population did not fall below 25 percent until the decade 1880–1890, and it was not until after 1900 that the 10-year increase fell below 10 percent.

---

[1] Thompson, Warren S. and Whelpton, P. K., *Population Trends in the United States,* New York: McGraw-Hill Book Company, Inc., 1933, p. 20.

[2] Assuming the line of trend to be that determined by the compound interest formula, the rate was 1.5 percent per year.

1

FIG. 2 - DENSITY OF POPULATION IN THE UNITED STATES

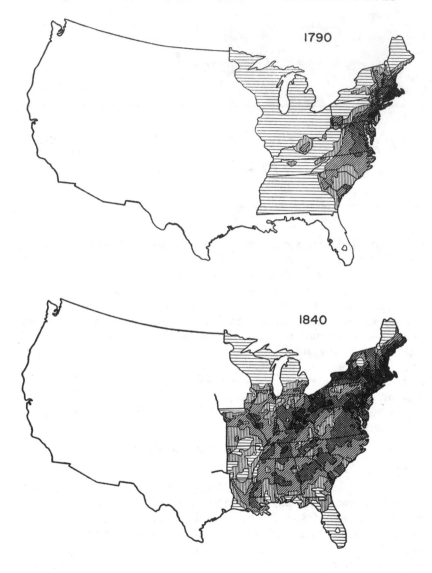

Source: Paullin, Charles O., *Atlas of the Historical Geography of the United States*, published jointly by Carnegie Institution of Washington and American Geographical Society of New York, 1932, Plates 76B and 76G.

Persons per square mile

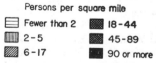

FIG. 2– DENSITY OF POPULATION IN THE UNITED STATES (Continued)

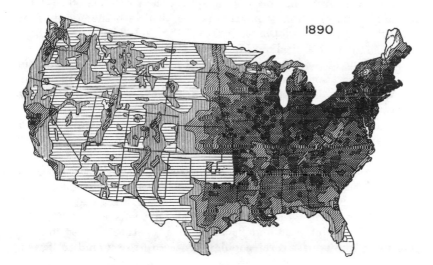

1890

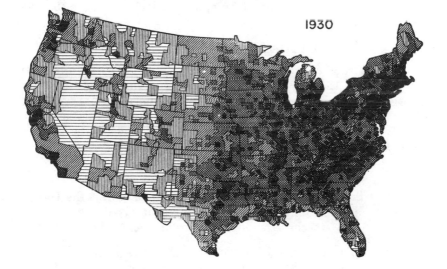

1930

Source: Paullin, Charles O., *Atlas of the Historical Geography of the United States*, published jointly by Carnegie Institution of Washington and American Geographical Society of New York, 1932, Plates 78B and 79D.

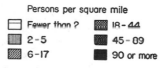

Persons per square mile

☐ Fewer than 2	▨ 18–44
▨ 2–5	▨ 45–89
▨ 6–17	■ 90 or more

AF–2967A, WPA

The decrease in the rate of growth of the rural population, particularly in recent years, has been the result of the combined effects of a declining birth rate and of migration, together with the cessation of immigration. Although the birth rate of the United States as a whole has apparently been declining for more than a hundred years,[3] a lag in the decline of the rural birth rate and the addition of considerable foreign immigration, particularly before 1900, tended to postpone the day when the rate of rural population increase would turn sharply downward.

Since 1790, when the first Federal Census was taken, profound changes have occurred in the regional distribution of the population [4] (fig. 2). By 1930, 37.9 percent of the rural population lived west of the Mississippi River. At that time the South Atlantic Division claimed the largest proportion (18.8 percent) of rural dwellers, followed by the East North Central Division with 15.8 percent and the West North Central and West South Central Divisions each with 14.4 percent. The Mountain and Pacific States together claimed but 9.1 percent.[5] The largest rural populations were to be found in Texas, Pennsylvania, and North Carolina, in the order named, but the greatest density of rural population occurred in Connecticut, Maryland, New Jersey, and Pennsylvania, all of which had more than 60 persons per square mile.

RURAL POPULATION CHANGE BY COUNTIES

Data on rural population change on a State basis as presented above conceal the extensive variations which occur within the larger political units. Hence, it is more satisfactory for present purposes to analyze the average rate of increase of the rural population on a county basis. This more detailed analysis is made for the decades 1900–1910, 1910–1920, and 1920–1930.

1900–1910

During the decade 1900–1910 the rural population of the United States as a whole increased 9.2 percent. Of the 2,797 counties (exclusive of Massachusetts, New Hampshire, and Rhode Island) [6]

[3] Whelpton, P. K., "Geographic and Economic Differentials in Fertility," *The Annals of the American Academy of Political and Social Science*, Vol. 188, November 1936, p. 41.

[4] Paullin, Charles O., *Atlas of the Historical Geography of the United States*, published jointly by Carnegie Institution of Washington and American Geographical Society of New York, 1932, Plate 76B.

[5] Bureau of the Census, *Fifteenth Census of the United States: 1930*, Population Vol. II, U. S. Department of Commerce, Washington, D. C., 1933.

[6] Rural population of these States not available by counties.

existing at that time, more than 40 percent gained at a rate equal to or greater than the national average, nearly 20 percent gained at a rate less than the average, and nearly 40 percent decreased in rural population (fig. 3 and appendix table 1).

The location of the counties experiencing these changes is of interest. The largest numbers of counties showing increases equal to or greater than the average were to be found in the West North Central, the South Atlantic, and the West South Central Divisions. The highest proportion of counties experiencing such increases, however, was to be found in the Mountain Division where 74 percent of the counties increased 9.2 percent or more. High percentages of increase also occurred in the West South Central and Pacific Divisions and in scattered areas throughout the remainder of the United States.

The largest numbers of counties with decreases in population were in the East North Central, West North Central, South Atlantic, and East South Central Divisions. The largest proportions of counties showing decreases, however, occurred in the New England, Middle Atlantic, East North Central, and West North Central Divisions. In all of these geographic divisions more than 50 percent of all counties decreased in rural population during the decade. The counties of decrease were concentrated in a triangular area from Ohio to central Kansas and from Missouri to central Minnesota, with prominent areas in Vermont, New York, Pennsylvania, Tennessee, and Texas. Few decreases occurred west of the 100th meridian.

The picture may be conveyed in a slightly different manner by classifying the counties of the United States upon the basis of change greater or less than 10 percent (table 1). This classification shows that 47 percent of all counties changed less than 10 percent in rural population during the decade. A total of 40 percent gained 10 percent or more while 13 percent lost 10 percent or more. Only in the Middle Atlantic and East North Central Divisions were the counties losing 10 percent or more approximately equal in number to those gaining 10 percent or more.

During the decade a total of 357 counties gained rural population at a rate of 50 percent or more. The Dakotas, northern Minnesota, and western Nebraska, Kansas, and Texas claimed most of these counties, which were still largely of the pioneer type. Only six counties lost rural population to the extent of 50 percent or more during the decade, and they were widely scattered.

Thus, the decade 1900–1910 was characterized by: (1) a slower rate of rural population growth than previous decades; (2) a marked extension of the rural population into the West (beyond the 100th meridian) and into Florida, increases throughout most of the Southern States, and heavy increases in the Appalachian Highlands; (3) an extension

Table 1.—Counties of the United States by Percent Change in the Rural Population, by Geographic Division, 1900–1910, 1910–1920, and 1920–1930

Geographic division	1900–1910				1910–1920				1920–1930			
	Total	Lost 10 percent or more	Changed less than 10 percent	Gained 10 percent or more	Total	Lost 10 percent or more	Changed less than 10 percent	Gained 10 percent or more	Total	Lost 10 percent or more	Changed less than 10 percent	Gained 10 percent or more
	Number of counties											
United States	2,797	369	1,312	1,116	2,887	576	1,598	713	3,002	613	1,635	754
New England [1]	38	3	30	5	38	4	31	3	38	2	33	3
Middle Atlantic	143	25	90	28	143	40	82	21	143	22	77	44
East North Central	435	71	295	69	436	102	284	50	436	105	271	60
West North Central	582	100	285	197	606	86	387	133	618	104	423	91
South Atlantic	500	41	256	203	515	65	304	146	536	121	264	151
East South Central	355	50	180	125	360	69	235	56	364	71	223	70
West South Central	431	37	129	265	455	111	190	154	468	91	196	181
Mountain	188	28	23	137	205	62	50	93	267	78	112	77
Pacific	125	14	24	87	129	37	35	57	132	19	36	77
	Percent distribution											
United States	100	13	47	40	100	20	55	25	100	20	55	25
New England [1]	100	8	79	13	100	11	81	8	100	5	87	8
Middle Atlantic	100	17	63	20	100	28	57	15	100	15	54	31
East North Central	100	16	68	16	100	23	66	11	100	24	62	14
West North Central	100	17	49	34	100	14	64	22	100	17	68	15
South Atlantic	100	8	51	41	100	13	59	28	100	23	49	28
East South Central	100	14	51	35	100	19	65	16	100	20	61	19
West South Central	100	9	30	61	100	24	42	34	100	19	42	39
Mountain	100	15	12	73	100	30	24	46	100	29	42	29
Pacific	100	11	19	70	100	29	27	44	100	14	27	59

[1] Exclusive of Massachusetts, New Hampshire, and Rhode Island.

Sources: Bureau of the Census, *Fourteenth Census of the United States: 1920*, Population Vol. I, tables 49 and 50, and *Fifteenth Census of the United States: 1930*, Population Vol. III, table 13, U. S. Department of Commerce, Washington, D. C.

of the areas with a decrease in population to include almost two-fifths of all counties, located chiefly in the good farming areas of the North Central States and in the Middle Atlantic Division; and (4) the appearance of minor areas of declining rural population in the Southern States, which heralded a broader base for such decreases during subsequent decades. Some land pioneering was still going on in the West, in Florida, in the Appalachian Highlands, and in the Northern States of the Great Lakes Region. It was over in most of the eastern half of the United States, and readjustments were occurring incident to the growth of cities and a maturing rural civilization.

1910–1920

By the decade 1910–1920 certain changes suggested by the trend of rural population during the previous decade had become apparent.

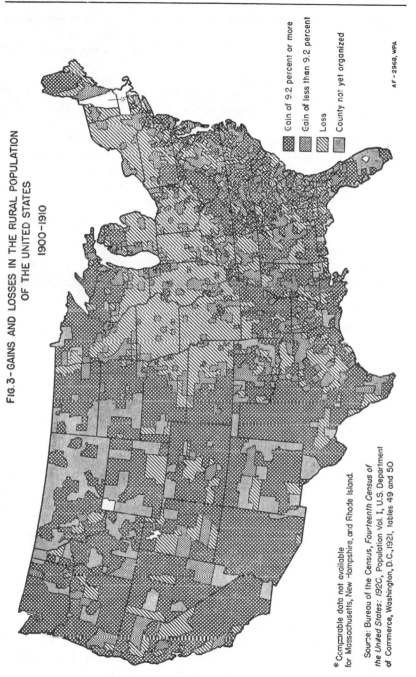

FIG. 3-GAINS AND LOSSES IN THE RURAL POPULATION OF THE UNITED STATES 1900-1910

Gain of 9.2 percent or more

Gain of less than 9.2 percent

Loss

County not yet organized

AF - 2968, WPA

*Comparable data not available for Massachusetts, New Hampshire, and Rhode Island.

Source: Bureau of the Census, *Fourteenth Census of the United States: 1920,* Population Vol. I, U.S. Department of Commerce, Washington, D.C., 1921, tables 49 and 50

During this period the average rate of growth of the rural population of the United States fell to 3.2 percent, only one-third the rate of increase during the previous decade. While 39 percent of the total number of counties (exclusive of Massachusetts, New Hampshire, and Rhode Island) increased as much as or more than that amount, 9 percent increased at a slower rate and 52 percent decreased in rural population (fig. 4 and appendix table 1). For the first time in the history of the United States more than one-half of the counties decreased in rural population. Owing partly to the creation of new counties, the number showing an average increase or more nearly equaled the number showing such increase during the previous decade. The number showing less than the average increase shrank more than 50 percent, however, and the number showing a loss increased by 37 percent over the previous decade. Among the geographic divisions the largest numbers of counties increasing at an average rate or more were found in the West North Central, South Atlantic, and West South Central Divisions. The proportion of counties showing such increase was highest in the Mountain Division, followed by the Pacific, South Atlantic, and West South Central Divisions. There was a definite tendency for the proportion of counties showing more than average increase to decline in the Western States, however, and to increase in the Eastern States. In the New England, Middle Atlantic, and East North Central Divisions the proportions of counties increasing at the average rate, or better, showed definite gains. In the West North Central, South Atlantic, and East South Central Divisions there was little change, while in the remaining divisions the proportions definitely declined. While the growth of rural population was slowing down in the West, processes of readjustment were getting under way in parts of the East. Changes in type of farming, the influence of the automobile, suburbanization, part-time farming, and the like were beginning to influence rural population trends. Also, the expansion of agriculture incident to the World War made it profitable for the time being to farm land which under other circumstances would have proved unprofitable. It is not surprising, therefore, that the number of counties showing more than average growth in the rural population should increase in such States as Pennsylvania, Ohio, Wisconsin, Minnesota, and Iowa.

Geographically, the picture for the decade ending in 1920 differed sharply from that of the preceding decade. The major characteristics of the picture were as follows: First, areas of decrease had become rather generally distributed throughout the United States. Large areas of decrease in the rural population had appeared in all of the Western States, and areas of decrease were widespread throughout the South. Second, only minor areas, such as northern Minnesota

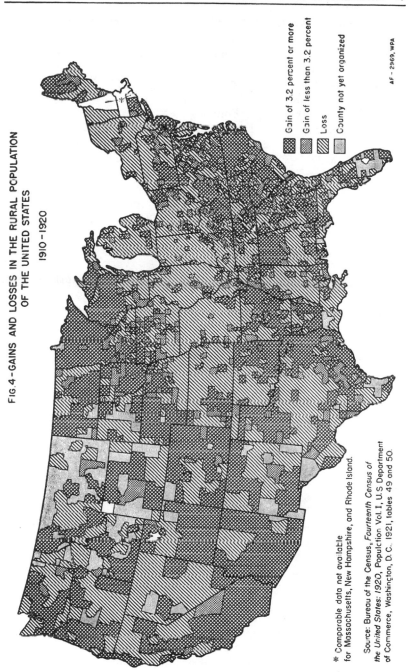

FIG. 4 – GAINS AND LOSSES IN THE RURAL POPULATION OF THE UNITED STATES

1910 – 1920

Gain of 3.2 percent or more

Gain of less than 3.2 percent

Loss

County not yet organized

AF - 2969, WPA

* Comparable data not available
for Massachusetts, New Hampshire, and Rhode Island.

Source: Bureau of the Census, *Fourteenth Census of the United States: 1920,* Population Vol. I, U.S. Department of Commerce, Washington, D.C.: 1921, tables 49 and 50.

and Wisconsin, southern California, Arizona, Utah, and portions of Colorado, Maine, Nebraska, North Carolina, and North Dakota were so uniform with respect to rural population growth as to suggest frontier development. Third, the proportion of all counties gaining 10 percent or more in rural population had dropped from 40 to 25 percent, and the proportion losing 10 percent or more had risen from 13 to 20 percent (table 1). Fourth, the number of counties displaying marked changes in the rural population showed a definite decrease when compared with the previous decade. Whereas a total of 555 counties gained 30 percent or more in rural population from 1900 to 1910, only 248 counties experienced such gains during the subsequent decade. Also, while only 31 counties lost 30 percent or more of their rural population between 1900 and 1910, a total of 83 counties experienced such losses between 1910 and 1920. Extreme gains were concentrated in the West South Central and Mountain Divisions, but many such cases occurred also in West Virginia, Florida, Wisconsin, Minnesota, the Dakotas, Nebraska, Kansas, Washington, and California. Extreme losses were concentrated in the West South Central, Mountain, and Pacific Divisions, with a substantial number of such counties in the West North Central and South Atlantic Divisions. A total of 116 counties gained rural population to the extent of 50 percent or more, while 34 counties lost rural population at the same rate. With the exception of scattered cases the counties gaining at this rate were located west of a line drawn south from the western boundary of Minnesota to the western boundary of Louisiana. Those experiencing losses of 50 percent or more were, for the most part, scattered throughout the same territory.

1920–1930

During the period 1920–1930 the rural population trends noted for the previous decade continued with only minor changes. The rate of growth of the rural population increased slightly, the average for the United States being 4.7 percent for the decade. While 34 percent of all counties increased by that percentage or more, 14 percent increased at a slower rate and 52 percent decreased in rural population (appendix table 1). Thus, for the second successive decade more than one-half of the counties of the Nation lost rural population. The largest numbers of counties with more than average increases were located in the South Atlantic and West South Central Divisions. The highest proportions of counties increasing at the average rate or more were located in the Middle Atlantic, West South Central, and Pacific Divisions.

The largest numbers of counties showing decreases in the rural population were found in the East North Central, West North Central, and South Atlantic Divisions. The largest proportions of counties losing rural population were to be found in the East North Central, West North Central, South Atlantic, East South Central, and Mountain Divisions, each of which had more than 50 percent of its counties in the group showing a decrease. In a number of Midwestern and Southern States more than 60 percent of all counties decreased in rural population during the decade.

Of the 3,002 counties extant during the decade 1920–1930, 25 percent gained as much as 10 percent or more; 55 percent changed less than 10 percent; and 20 percent lost 10 percent or more of their rural population (table 1). Among the divisions the proportion of counties gaining 10 percent or more in rural population varied from 8 percent in New England to 59 percent in the Pacific Division. The proportion of counties losing 10 percent or more of their rural population ranged from 5 percent in New England to 29 percent in the Mountain Division.

Extreme gains and losses in rural population continued as in previous decades. Between 1920 and 1930, 306 counties gained in rural population to the extent of 30 percent or more, and of these 145 counties gained to the extent of 50 percent or more. These counties were distributed in all divisions except New England. Approximately one-half of the counties gaining 50 percent or more were located in the West South Central Division, chiefly in the western half of Texas. Many were located in California also. There was a notable increase in the number of rapidly growing counties east of the Mississippi River, particularly in southern Michigan, Florida. and the Appalachian Highlands.

The number of counties losing 30 percent or more of their rural population fell slightly during the decade following 1920 to 63. These counties were concentrated in the South Atlantic, Mountain, and West South Central Divisions Only nine counties experienced losses of 50 percent or more. Two were located in Florida and two in Nevada, while the other five were scattered in as many States.

The general picture for the decade 1920–1930 included, in the first place, a slightly greater average gain in rural population than the preceding 10-year period. In the second place, there was reduction of the broad areas of more than average increase. The northern portions of Minnesota, Wisconsin, and Michigan shifted from areas of more than average increase to areas of decrease as did also most of Montana and Idaho and much of Oklahoma, New Mexico, and Utah. The areas of marked gain in North Carolina, Florida, Arkansas, and the Appalachian Highlands also became dotted with counties of decrease. In the third place, areas like western Maine, Vermont, New York, Ohio, and southern Michigan, in which the rural population decreased almost uniformly during the previous decade, showed a definite tendency to recover. The effects of industrial development, the automobile, and electricity were reflected perhaps in a growing rural population in many counties. Finally, a definite tendency toward greater stability in rural population growth was noticeable.

The evidence presented indicates that since about 1910, and perhaps before, there has been a definite slowing down in the rate of change in the rural population of the various counties. Without doubt part of this has resulted from a reduced rate of natural increase. Even so, high rates of gain could scarcely have been the result of natural increase alone. Gains of 30 percent or more during a decade must be attributed largely to migration. There has been a definite tendency since 1910 for the number of counties experiencing such heavy gains to decrease and a corresponding tendency for the number experiencing only slight changes to increase. On the other hand, the number of counties showing a loss in total population has increased. Since few if any counties actually have more deaths than births, such losses must be attributed to migration. Although the volume of migration from one rural area to another has probably decreased during the last three decades, the volume of migration away from rural territory has greatly increased.

NET RURAL MIGRATION, 1920–1930

The net migration from farms of the United States during the decade 1920–1930 has been estimated on more than one occasion and perhaps with sufficient accuracy for ordinary purposes. There is no disposition to criticize these estimates although the estimates in this monograph differ slightly from them. Rather the aim is to extend the range of these estimates to cover both the rural-farm and rural-nonfarm population. The 1930 Census provided for the first time the essential data for making such estimates.

For a comprehensive picture of net rural migration in the United States it is necessary to analyze trends in migration on a county basis in order to delineate those areas in which profound population changes resulting from migration are taking place. Not all rural migration occurs between city and country. Shifts are constantly occurring within the rural population. Analysis of net rural migration by counties tends to reveal not only the net volume of rural-urban migration but also the areas of dispersion and concentration within the rural population itself.

If there is no emigration, a population will grow by the amount of its natural increase plus whatever population it has acquired through immigration. If the volume of emigration is smaller than the volume of immigration, the population will grow by the amount of its natural increase plus the surplus of immigrants over emigrants. But, if the volume of emigration exceeds the volume of immigration, the population will grow by an amount equal to the natural increase minus the net emigration as long as the latter does not exceed the former. When the volume of net emigration exceeds the natural increase there is, of course, a decrease in the base population. This explains why a population may possess a considerable natural increase and show no gain, or even a loss, at each succeeding census.

In lieu of dependable vital statistics for rural areas in the past net rural migration must be calculated on the basis of the population living at the beginning of the period, in this case 1920–1930, with life tables used to determine how much of the observed change in the population during the period was the result of deaths occurring in the resident population and how much was the result of net migration into or out of the area under consideration. Following this technique estimates of the net migration to and from rural territory during the decade 1920–1930 have been made for the continental United States, for the rural-farm and rural-nonfarm populations, for whites and Negroes, and for males and females. Estimates have also been made for the rural-farm and rural-nonfarm populations by geographic divisions and States and for the total rural population of all counties.[7] In these estimates only the population living in 1920 is included since no satisfactory technique for estimating the net migration of children born after the 1920 Census has been developed. This means that all persons referred to as migrants in this chapter were 10 years of age and over in 1930.

Number of Migrants

The total estimated net migration[8] from rural areas of the United States during the decade 1920–1930 amounted to 5,734,200 persons[9] (table 2). Of this number 5,099,900 were white and 634,300 were colored. Colored persons, mostly Negroes, thus composed 11.1 percent of the total net migration from the rural districts. Of the total

[7] Because the age distributions of the rural-farm and rural-nonfarm populations for 1920 are not available by counties, it is possible to estimate net migration for the total rural population only.

[8] In estimating net rural migration a correction was made for the underenumeration of children in both the 1920 and the 1930 Censuses. For 1920 and 1930 the number of white children enumerated was increased by 5 percent and that of colored children by 11 percent in the North, 13.5 percent in the South, 8 percent in the West, and 13 percent in the United States as a whole. These are the corrections suggested by Whelpton, P. K., op. cit., p. 41. The suggested corrections for Negro children are used here for all colored children.

[9] No attempt was made in these estimates to hold the territory of 1920 constant. It is well known that the territory designated as rural varies from census to census because of changes in the incorporated area of towns and cities. Gillette estimated that during the decade 1910–1920 the rural population lost 990,000 persons by incorporation. Such losses are included in the estimates of this monograph. See Gillette, John Morris, Rural Sociology, Revised Edition, New York: The Macmillan Company, 1928, p. 94.

net migration 55 percent were females. Thus, for every 100 males who were lost to the rural districts during the decade, 123 females were also lost. The rural-farm population lost 6,084,600 persons,[10] but a small part of this loss was offset by the fact that the rural-nonfarm population gained 350,400 persons.[11]

Table 2.—Net Gain or Loss [1] Through Migration to the Rural Population [2] of the United States, by Residence, Color, and Sex, 1920–1930 [3] (Estimated)

Residence, color, and sex	Rural population, 1920		Net rural migration, 1920–1930	
	Enumerated	Corrected for underenumeration [4]	Number	Percent of corrected 1920 population
Total	51,356,200	51,742,600	−5,734,200	−11.1
Rural-farm	31,340,100	31,594,300	−6,084,600	−19.3
Rural-nonfarm	20,016,100	20,148,300	+350,400	+1.7
White	44,162,100	44,477,900	−5,099,900	−11.5
Colored	7,194,100	7,264,700	−634,300	−8.7
Male	26,666,400	26,867,000	−2,574,100	−9.6
Female	24,689,800	24,875,600	−3,160,100	−12.7

[1] Minus (−) indicates a loss.
[2] Includes only persons living in 1920 whose ages were reported.
[3] For method of computation see appendix B.
[4] Of children under 5 years of age.

When the net rural migration was calculated as a percent of the 1920 rural population, it was found that a total equal to 11.1 percent of the population living in the rural districts at the beginning of the decade was lost through migration during the period. The rural population actually increased by 4.7 percent [12] during the same period, but had there been no net loss from rural migration, the gain would probably have been approximately 16 percent. Thus, more than two-thirds of the expected natural increase was lost through migration.

This net loss from migration during the decade was not evenly distributed throughout the rural population. The white population lost a total equal to 11.5 percent of the 1920 population, while the corresponding loss to the colored population was only 8.7 percent. The loss to the rural male population by migration was only 9.6 percent of the 1920 population in comparison with 12.7 percent for the rural female population. Finally, 19.3 percent of the persons living on

[10] See O. E. Baker's estimate of 5,897,810 persons in "Rural-Urban Migration and the National Welfare," *Annals of the Association of American Geographers*, Vol. XXIII, No. 2, 1933, p. 69. See also Hamilton, C. Horace, *Rural-Urban Migration in North Carolina, 1920 to 1930*, Bulletin No. 295, North Carolina Agricultural Experiment Station, Raleigh, N. C., February 1934; and Thornthwaite, C. Warren, *Internal Migration in the United States*, Philadelphia: University of Pennsylvania Press, 1934.

[11] A portion of this gain was the result of a change in the definition of rural territory.

[12] Corrected for underenumeration. The census figure is also 4.7 percent.

farms in 1920 were lost by migration, while the rural-nonfarm population gained 1.7 percent as a result of migration.

Age of Migrants

Almost 45 percent of the net rural migrants from 1920 to 1930 were 10–19 years of age in 1920 (table 3 and fig. 5). More than 75 percent of the migrants were persons who were less than 25 years of age in 1920. Only 17.3 percent of the male migrants were under 10 years of age in 1920, but 21.5 percent of the female migrants were in this age group. This is a reflection of the well-known fact that females migrate at an earlier age than males. On the other hand, females also predominated in the net migration of older people. While 21.0 percent of the net migration of females from farms were composed of persons aged 35 years and over, 19.0 percent of the males were in the older ages.

Of the net colored migration 28.1 percent of all persons were 35 years of age and over in 1920. The corresponding percent for the net white migration was 19.1. This racial difference in the age of migrants is probably a reflection of the fact that, during the decade in question, the migration of Negroes was principally from the country to large cities. Adults aged 35 and over who left the country went directly to cities, chiefly northern ones, instead of moving to villages as many whites did. In addition to that, it is possible that since the Negro migration more nearly resembled mass depopulation of an area, the movement was less selective with respect to age.

Table 3.—Net Gain or Loss[1] Through Migration to the Rural Population[2] of the United States, by Age, Residence, Color, and Sex, 1920–1930[3] (Estimated)

Age, 1920	Net gain or loss through migration, 1920-1930						
	Total rural	Rural-farm	Rural-nonfarm	White	Colored	Male	Female
Total	−5,734,200	−6,084,600	+350,400	−5,099,900	−634,300	−2,574,100	−3,160,100
Under 5 years	−413,100	−356,500	−56,600	−494,600	+81,500	−154,900	−258,200
5–9 years	−709,500	−624,000	−85,500	−639,500	−70,000	−289,700	−419,800
10–14 years	−1,385,700	−1,449,900	+64,200	−1,210,400	−175,300	−673,500	−712,200
15–19 years	−1,158,000	−1,341,100	+183,100	−989,400	−168,600	−593,000	−565,000
20–24 years	−658,800	−715,400	+56,600	−496,500	−162,300	−318,600	−340,200
25–29 years	151,700	238,000	+86,300	−156,200	+4,500	−43,400	−108,300
30–34 years	−104,100	−132,000	+27,900	−138,400	+34,300	−11,600	−92,500
35–39 years	−282,400	−216,400	−66,000	−268,900	−13,500	−117,100	−165,300
40–44 years	−21,100	−60,500	+39,400	+24,900	−46,000	+61,400	−82,500
45–49 years	−312,600	−267,100	−45,500	−241,100	−71,500	−167,100	−145,500
50–54 years	−176,700	−192,900	+16,200	−151,600	−25,100	−89,700	−87,000
55–59 years	−56,700	−126,000	+69,300	−61,300	+4,600	−17,200	−39,500
60–64 years	−101,100	−148,700	+47,600	−81,400	−19,700	−47,900	−53,200
65–69 years	−70,300	−102,200	+31,900	−57,700	−12,600	−36,200	−34,100
70–74 years	−44,900	−53,300	+8,400	−43,200	−1,700	−27,000	−17,900
75 years and over	−87,500	−60,600	−26,900	−94,600	+7,100	−48,600	−38,900

[1] Minus ( ) indicates a loss.
[2] Includes only persons living in 1920.
[3] For method of computation see appendix B.

Among the colored migrants who were 35 years of age and over in 1920, seven-eighths were 35–54 years of age. In comparison only two-thirds of the white migrants 35 years of age and over were less

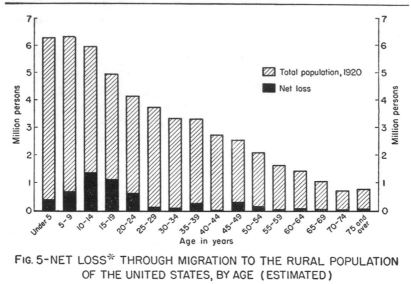

FIG. 5–NET LOSS* THROUGH MIGRATION TO THE RURAL POPULATION
OF THE UNITED STATES, BY AGE (ESTIMATED)
1920–1930

*For method of computation see appendix B.   AF-2970, WPA

than 55 years of age. It seems probable, therefore, that the proportion of migrants retiring on account of age was nearly three times as
high among white as among colored persons. Thus, the difference in
age, as well as the comparative economic status of the rural residents
of the two groups, suggests that a much higher proportion of the net
loss of the white population than of the colored population represented retirement from the rural districts to towns and cities.

Although a number equal to 11.1 percent of the rural population of
1920 was lost by migration during the decade, the loss was unequally
distributed throughout the various age groups (table 4). In the
group aged 10–19 years in 1920 the loss was equal to 23 out of every
100 persons. Losses of 10 percent or more occurred also in the groups
aged 5–9, 20–24, and 45–54 years in 1920. Losses of less than 5 percent occurred in the groups 25–29 and 30–34 years of age in 1920.

In the rural-farm population losses were still heavier. The net
loss reached 41 percent in the group aged 15–19 years, 37 percent in the
group aged 10–14 years, and 29 percent in the group aged 20–24 years.
All other age groups lost less than the average for the rural-farm
population as a whole. As a result primarily of retirement, losses of
15 percent or more occurred in the age groups above 44 years.

Net gains in rural-nonfarm population from migration occurred
chiefly among persons aged 10–34 years in 1920, although a gain also
occurred in the group aged 55 years and over. The latter was undoubtedly composed primarily of persons retiring from farms to villages.

Table 4.—Percent Net Gain or Loss [1] Through Migration to the Rural Population [2] of the United States, by Age, Residence, Color, and Sex, 1920–1930 [3] (Estimated)

Age, 1920	Percent net gain or loss through migration, 1920–1930						
	Total rural	Rural-farm	Rural-nonfarm	White	Colored	Male	Female
Total	−11.1	−19.3	+1.7	−11.5	−8.7	−9.6	−12.7
Under 5 years	−6.2	−8.4	−0.2	−8.8	+7.8	−4.6	−7.8
5–9 years	−11.2	−15.2	−3.8	−12.0	−6.9	−9.0	−13.4
10–14 years	−23.2	−36.5	+3.2	−24.2	−18.0	−22.0	−24.4
15–19 years	−23.2	−41.1	+10.6	−23.6	−21.1	−23.3	−23.1
20–24 years	−15.8	−28.8	+3.4	−14.1	−24.5	−15.1	−16.4
25–29 years	−4.0	−11.2	+5.3	−4.8	+0.9	−2.3	−5.8
30–34 years	3.1	7.0	11.0	1.7	18.7	0.7	5.7
35–44 years	−5.0	−7.9	−1.0	−4.6	−7.7	−1.8	−8.6
45–54 years	−10.4	−16.4	−1.5	−9.6	−16.0	−9.8	−11.2
55–64 years	−5.1	−15.1	+9.1	−5.1	−5.1	−3.7	−6.8
65 years and over	−7.8	−15.6	+1.1	−8.3	−3.0	−8.0	−7.6

[1] Minus (−) indicates a loss.
[2] Includes only persons living in 1920.
[3] For method of computation see appendix B.

Losses were heavier for females than for males in the rural population at all ages except 15–19 years and 65 years and over. An important difference in the group aged 5–9 years in 1920 reflects the earlier age of migration among females. Important differences also occurred in the age groups above 24 years. This reflects the migration of females who had not married up to that time and also the migration of farm widows who are less likely to remain on the farm after the death of their husbands than are operators who lose their wives.

NET RURAL MIGRATION, 1920–1930, BY STATES

The net effect of migration during the decade 1920–1930 varied greatly among both geographic divisions and States (appendix table 2). All divisions but two, the New England and Pacific Divisions, lost rural population through migration. The West North Central, South Atlantic, and East South Central Divisions each lost more than a million persons. The East North Central and West South Central Divisions lost approximately nine hundred thousand each. The Middle Atlantic group of States lost nearly a half million, and had it not been for the change in definition of rural territory for three New England States in the 1930 Census that division also would have suffered a net loss.[13] While the net loss from rural migration, 1920–1930,

---

[13] In 1920 all towns in Massachusetts, New Hampshire, and Rhode Island "which had a population of 2,500 or more were classified as urban. This resulted in including a considerable number of places that were mainly rural in their general characteristics. In 1930, the special rule for these States has been modified so as to place in the urban classification, in addition to the regularly incorporated cities, only those towns in which there is a village or thickly settled area having more than 2,500 inhabitants and comprising, either by itself or when combined with other villages within the same town, more than 50 percent of the total population of the town." Bureau of the Census, *Fifteenth Census of the United States: 1930*, Population Vol. I, U. S. Department of Commerce, Washington, D. C., 1931, p. 7.

amounted to 11.1 percent of the total rural population in 1920, the relative losses ranged from 7.9 percent in the Middle Atlantic Division to 15.8 percent in the East South Central Division.

Among the States losses tended to be general with only eight States (New Hampshire, Massachusetts, Rhode Island, New York, Delaware, Arizona, Oregon, and California) gaining rural population by means of migration. In general, State increases were moderate except in California where more than 250,000 people were added to the rural population by migration during the decade, an increase of 23.3 percent. Heaviest losses from migration occurred in Georgia and Pennsylvania both of which had net losses of approximately 500,000 persons. Proportionately, decreases ranged from less than 1 percent in Washington to 23.3 percent in Georgia. Although the losses from migration were distributed generally throughout the States, they were heaviest in the North Central States and in the South.

The relation between net gain or loss from migration and the actual change in rural population recorded by the census for the decade is of interest. Of the 48 States 35 actually gained rural population during the decade while 13 lost rural population. On the other hand, 40 of the States experienced a net loss from migration while only 8 gained rural population by this means. No State that actually lost rural population between 1920 and 1930 failed also to lose rural population because of migration. The most conspicuous cases of States experiencing increases in rural population and yet having a net loss as a result of migration were those possessing relatively high rates of natural increase and also important net losses from migration. Such States as Mississippi, New Mexico, North Carolina, North Dakota, Oklahoma, South Dakota, Texas, Utah, and West Virginia are good illustrations. Thus, in spite of comparisons which show actual increases in total population in the face of net decreases through migration, a close relation between actual change and change resulting from net migration existed among the States for the period in question.

Rural-Farm and Rural-Nonfarm

Although the preceding analysis was for the rural population as a whole, far greater changes resulting from migration occurred in the rural-farm than in the rural-nonfarm population. Between 1920 and 1930 the farm population of the United States suffered an estimated net loss of 6,084,600 persons through migration (appendix table 3). Most of this loss occurred in the two North Central and three Southern Divisions.[14]

Apparently California was the only State, exclusive of Massachusetts and Rhode Island, in which the farm population increased as a result of migration. Heaviest total losses from migration occurred in South Carolina, Georgia, Kentucky, and Texas, each of which lost more than

---

[14] See also Baker, O. E., *op. cit.*, pp. 68–69.

Home by the Highway!

300,000 rural-farm population. So concentrated were the losses in the rural-farm population through migration that one-fourth of the States [15] accounted for 59 percent of the total.

When considered as a percent of the 1920 rural farm population, these losses from migration assume still greater significance. Although the average loss for the United States amounted to −19.3 percent of the 1920 rural-farm population, a total of 25 States lost less than that percent and only 20 States lost that percent of persons or more. Percentage losses were above 30 in Georgia, South Carolina, and Utah. Losses of less than 10 percent occurred only in Wyoming, Nevada, Washington, and Oregon.[16]

By way of contrast with the heavy losses from migration occurring in the rural-farm population, the rural-nonfarm population gained an estimated 350,400 persons, or a number equal to 1.7 percent of the 1920 population. By virtue of the changes in definition employed by the 1930 Census a net total of 284,708 persons was classified as urban in 1930 who would have been classified as rural under the 1920 definition. Assuming that these persons belonged chiefly to the rural-nonfarm population, the continued use of the 1920 definition of rural would probably have shown the rural-nonfarm population to have gained more than 3 percent from migration.

Aside from the New England States which were especially affected by the change in definition, five of the divisions lost rural-nonfarm population by migration and three divisions gained. The loss was heaviest in the West North Central Division, while the gain was heaviest in the Pacific Division. By States the largest gain through migration occurred in California which increased her rural-nonfarm population during the decade by a number equal to 38.9 percent of her 1920 population.

Most of the losses were slight. Only six States lost more than 10 percent of their rural-nonfarm population through migration. With no change in definition of rural territory in 1930, one of these—Pennsylvania—would certainly have lost less than 10 percent.

Among the States there was virtually no relation between the rate of gain or loss from migration of the rural-farm population and the corresponding gain or loss of the rural-nonfarm population. For example, in both the East North Central and South Atlantic Divisions heavy emigration from farms occurred, but the rural-nonfarm population gained consistently.

---

[15] Alabama, Arkansas, Georgia, Illinois, Kentucky, Missouri, North Carolina, Ohio, South Carolina, Tennessee, Texas, and Virginia.

[16] It seems probable that the influence of the changed definition of rural territory employed by the Bureau of the Census in 1930 was slight as far as the farm population was concerned except in Massachusetts and Rhode Island. Most of the effect of this change of definition is reflected in the changes in the rural-nonfarm population.

NET RURAL MIGRATION, 1920–1930, BY COUNTIES

By considering net migration on a county basis it is possible to determine marked changes which have resulted from migration. With the exception of a few counties, estimates of the total change resulting from net migration are sufficiently accurate to contribute to a national picture of the migration tendencies of the rural population for the decade 1920–1930.[17]

For the period under consideration 83 percent of all counties [18] suffered a net loss in rural population through migration (table 5), while 17 percent had a net gain. Of the counties that increased in population, almost 40 percent gained fewer than 1,000 persons and about 70 percent gained fewer than 3,000 persons. Approximately 12 percent gained 6,000 persons or more. Of the counties that suffered a net loss of rural population, less than 18 percent lost fewer than 1,000 persons, 65 percent lost fewer than 3,000, and 9 percent lost 6,000 persons or more. Thus, the variation in number of persons gained was greater than in number of persons lost. Although the proportion of counties gaining fewer than 1,000 persons was more than twice as great as the proportion losing by that amount, the proportion gaining as many as 8,000 persons was also more than twice the proportion losing by that amount. Many of the gains were extreme. For the 44 counties gaining 8,000 persons or more, the average gain was 16,000; for the 87 counties losing by that number, the average loss was 9,200 persons.[19]

---

[17] For a comparison of the results obtained by State and county estimates, see appendix table 19.

[18] Of the 3,072 counties in the United States in 1930, 13 had no rural population. Hence, only 3,059 counties figured in these computations.

[19] Counties gaining or losing rural population through migration, 1920–1930, were as follows:

517 counties gaining rural population through migration

		Total gain
a.	44 counties gaining 8,000 persons or more	700, 000
b.	69 counties gaining 4,000–7,999 persons	370, 000
c.	94 counties gaining 2,000–3,999 persons	270, 000
d.	107 counties gaining 1,000–1,999 persons	160, 000
e.	203 counties gaining fewer than 1,000 persons	100, 000
	Total	1, 600, 000

2,542 counties losing rural population through migration

		Total loss
a.	450 counties losing fewer than 1,000 persons	200, 000
b.	639 counties losing 1,000–1,999 persons	900, 000
c.	564 counties losing 2,000–2,999 persons	1, 400, 000
d.	329 counties losing 3,000–3,999 persons	1, 100, 000
e.	331 counties losing 4,000–5,999 persons	1, 600, 000
f.	142 counties losing 6,000–7,999 persons	1, 200, 000
g.	87 counties losing 8,000 persons or more	800, 000
	Total	7, 200, 000

Table 5.—Counties of the United States by Net Gain or Loss Through Migration to the Rural Population, 1920–1930 [1] (Estimated)

Number of persons gained or lost	Number of counties					
	Total		Gained rural population, 1920–1930		Lost rural population, 1920–1930	
	Number	Percent	Number	Percent	Number	Percent
Total	3,059	100.0	517	100.0	2,542	100.0
Fewer than 500	334	10.9	135	26.1	199	7.8
500–999	319	10.4	68	13.1	251	9.9
1,000–1,999	746	24.4	107	20.7	639	25.2
2,000–2,999	610	20.1	52	10.1	561	22.2
3,000–3,999	371	12.1	42	8.1	329	12.9
4,000–5,999	381	12.5	50	9.7	331	13.0
6,000–7,999	161	5.3	19	3.7	142	5.6
8,000 or more	131	4.3	44	8.5	87	3.4

[1] For method of computation see appendix B.

The concentration of the counties showing gains as a result of migration may be indicated by the fact that 41 percent of the 517 counties with gains were located in New York, Florida, Kansas, Texas, and California (appendix table 4). More than 35 percent of the 113 counties gaining 4,000 persons or more by means of net migration were located in New York, Texas, and California.

With respect to losses through migration notable concentration of counties occurred in the West North Central and South Atlantic Divisions. In the former division were located 22 percent and in the latter division 19 percent of all counties losing rural population through migration. If to these divisions are added the East North Central, East South Central, and West South Central Divisions, 83 percent of all counties experiencing losses through migration are included.

The largest proportion of counties gaining rural population by migration was found in the Pacific Division where 55 percent of all counties showed some gain. No other division was a close competitor. Conversely, the highest proportion of counties showing losses was found in the East South Central Division where 95 percent of all counties experienced a net loss from migration. There were 12 States in which more than 95 percent of all counties lost rural population by migration.

Although the number of persons gained or lost by counties through net migration is of interest, the rate at which population was gained or lost is perhaps of greater significance. When the gain or loss to the rural population, 1920–1930, was computed with the 1920 rural population as the base, more than one-fifth of all counties were found to have experienced a net change of less than 10 percent in the rural population as the result of net migration (appendix table 5). Of the 517 counties gaining rural population as a result of net migration, about two-fifths gained less than 10 percent and more than seven-

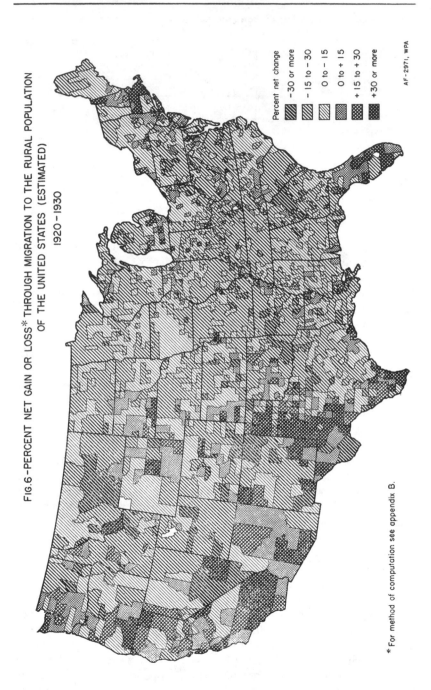

FIG. 6 – PERCENT NET GAIN OR LOSS* THROUGH MIGRATION TO THE RURAL POPULATION OF THE UNITED STATES (ESTIMATED)

1920–1930

Percent net change

- −30 or more
- −15 to −30
- 0 to −15
- 0 to +15
- +15 to +30
- +30 or more

AF−2971, WPA

* For method of computation see appendix B.

tenths gained less than 30 percent. However, more than 15 out of 100 gained 50 percent or more. Of the 2,542 counties that lost rural population as a net result of migration, the modal loss was 10–19 percent. Approximately 8 counties in 100 lost as much as 30 percent of their rural population.

Counties with low gains tended to be concentrated in the South Atlantic and West South Central Divisions (fig. 6). Counties gaining 30–49 percent were located chiefly in the West South Central and Mountain Divisions, while counties gaining 50 percent or more were located chiefly in Texas and Florida.

Counties losing by migration a number that equaled less than 10 percent of their rural population in 1920 were well distributed, although more than one-third of them were in the East North Central and South Atlantic Divisions and more than three-fifths in these two divisions plus the West North Central and West South Central Divisions. Counties losing by migration a number equal to 30 percent or more of their rural population in 1920 were concentrated in the South Atlantic, West South Central, and Mountain Divisions.

The data cited in preceding paragraphs represent the net result of migration, but the total amount of migration that occurred was far larger than they indicate. It was estimated by the Bureau of Agricultural Economics that a net migration of 6,296,000 persons [20] from the farms of the Nation during the period 1920–1930 was obtained by 13,140,000 moves to farms and 19,436,000 moves from farms. Thus, there was a total of 32,576,000 moves between farms and villages, towns, and cities during the decade. If each person who was involved in these migrations had moved only once during the decade, it would mean that the number of migrants was approximately equal to the number of persons living on farms, or to one-fourth of the entire population of the United States. Unfortunately, migrations to and from rural-nonfarm areas cannot be estimated, but their number likewise must be very large in terms of the population concerned.

[20] Bureau of Agricultural Economics, *Farm Population Estimates, January 1, 1938*, U. S. Department of Agriculture, Washington, D. C., June 16, 1938. The estimate is slightly higher than the estimate of 6,084,600 used in this chapter, but the BAE figure includes all ages and is based upon annual estimates.

Chapter II

MOVEMENTS OF THE FARM POPULATION SINCE 1930

CHANGES IN the farm population during any given period occur as a result of the balance of births and deaths and of migrations to and from farms. In recent years migrations to and from farms have involved many more persons than are added to the population through the excess of births over deaths. The numbers of births and deaths change slowly from year to year. Although the estimated excess of births over deaths in the farm population dropped from 485,000 in 1920 to 398,000 in 1930 and 394,000 in 1935,[1] the trends in the farm population do not directly reflect such changes as the number of migrants is much greater. Furthermore, the volume of migration is sensitive to changing employment and income opportunities so that the net movement may be to farms during one year and away from farms during the following year. Therefore, the basis of major annual changes in the number of persons living on farms must be sought in the shifting balance of migrations.

The farm population of the United States was estimated to total 31,729,000 persons [2] on January 1, 1937, or only 115,000 more than in 1920. During the 17-year period the natural increase on farms was more than 7,600,000 persons or almost 450,000 persons per year. The small increase in the total farm population was the direct result of the tremendous movement from farms to villages, towns, and cities. The net movement from farms during the decade preceding 1930 amounted to about 600,000 annually. As a result of depression the average for 1930 through 1934 was reduced to approximately one-fifth of that total, or 120,000 per year. In 1932 the trend was actually reversed, and 266,000 more persons moved to farms than left farms (table 6 and fig. 7).

---

[1] Bureau of Agricultural Economics, *Farm Population Estimates, January 1, 1938*, U. S. Department of Agriculture, Washington, D. C., June 16, 1938.
[2] *Ibid.*

Table 6.—Movement to and From Farms, 1920–1937

Year	Persons arriving at farms from cities, towns, and villages	Persons leaving farms for cities, towns, and villages	Net movement from—	
			Cities, towns, and villages to farms	Farms to cities, towns, and villages
1920	560, 000	896, 000	—	336, 000
1921	759, 000	1, 323, 000	—	564, 000
1922	1, 115, 000	2, 252, 000	—	1, 137, 000
1923	1, 355, 000	2, 162, 000	—	807, 000
1924	1, 581, 000	2, 068, 000	—	487, 000
1925	1, 336, 000	2, 038, 000	—	702, 000
1926	1, 427, 000	2, 334, 000	—	907, 000
1927	1, 705, 000	2, 162, 000	—	457, 000
1928	1, 698, 000	2, 120, 000	—	422, 000
1929	1, 604, 000	2, 081, 000	—	477, 000
1930	1, 611, 000	1, 823, 000	—	212, 000
1931	1, 546, 000	1, 566, 000	—	20, 000
1932	1, 777, 000	1, 511, 000	266, 000	—
1933	944, 000	1, 225, 000	—	281, 000
1934	700, 000	1, 051, 000	—	351, 000
1935	825, 000	1, 211, 000	—	386, 000
1936	719, 000	1, 166, 000	—	447, 000
1937	872, 000	1, 160, 000	—	288, 000
1920–1924	5, 370, 000	8, 701, 000	—	3, 331, 000
1925–1929	7, 770, 000	10, 735, 000	—	2, 965, 000
1930–1934	6, 578, 000	7, 176, 000	—	598, 000

Source: Bureau of Agricultural Economics, *Farm Population Estimates, January 1, 1938*, U. S. Department of Agriculture, Washington, D. C., June 16, 1938.

On the basis of farm population movements the period since 1930 may be divided into two parts. During the first years, 1930–1932, urban employment opportunities were decreasing and in some parts of the country many persons were moving to farms from villages, towns, and cities. Some returned to the farm homes which they had left only a few years previously. Some moved to abandoned farmsteads or looked for other places where they could secure cheap housing and perhaps provide subsistence for themselves and their families.

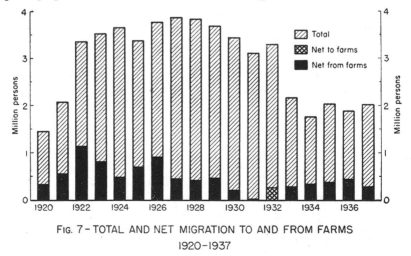

Fig. 7 – TOTAL AND NET MIGRATION TO AND FROM FARMS

1920–1937

Source: Adapted from Bureau of Agricultural
Economics, U.S. Department of Agriculture.

AF– 2973, WPA

Beginning in 1933 there was a revival in urban employment and a revival of hope of employment prospects. The latter may be as significant for migration as an actual increase in jobs. The migration from villages, towns, and cities to farms was sharply reduced, and once more there was a net movement from farms, as there had been annually during the 1920's.[3]

A comparison of the movements of farm population between 1930 and 1935 and of net rural migration between 1920 and 1930 suggests that the changes which occurred between 1930 and 1935 were to some extent a continuation of trends begun in the earlier period. The rural areas which reported net gains by migration between 1920 and 1930 and those counties which lost only slightly received a disproportionately large share of the migrants to farms after 1930 (table 7).

Table 7.—Farm Population, 1930, and Changes in Farm Population, 1930–1934, in Counties With Specified Rates of Net Rural Migration, 1920–1930 [1]

Net rural migration, 1920–1930	Percent of total farm population, 1930	Percent of migrants to farms, 1930–1934	Percent increase in farm population, 1930–1934	Percent increase in 1930 farm population because of migrants from nonfarm territory, 1930–1934	Percent change in farm population, exclusive of migrants from nonfarm territory, 1930–1934
Total [2]	100.0	100.0	+4.5	+6.6	−2.1
From rural territory:					
Less than 10 percent	17.6	19.7	+3.7	+7.3	−3.6
10–19 percent	40.3	33.6	+2.9	+5.4	−2.5
20–29 percent	22.3	18.7	+5.9	+5.5	+0.4
30 percent or more	4.9	4.4	+4.8	+5.9	−1.1
To rural territory	14.9	23.6	+7.1	+10.4	−3.3

[1] For method of computation see appendix B.
[2] Includes figures for farm population in counties which had no rural population: 8,483 persons in 1930 and 1,005 migrants to farms, 1930–1934.

Source: Bureau of the Census, *United States Census of Agriculture: 1935*, Vol. II, U. S. Department of Commerce, Washington, D. C., 1936, county table IV.

Total increases in farm population after 1930, however, were no directly related to gains or losses before 1930. This again illustrates the necessity for taking into account all factors that contribute to a change in population, i. e., migration to an area, natural increase, and migration from the area. In the case of the counties which had a net gain by migration before 1930, the large increase in farm population after 1930 was due primarily to the migration to farms, which was only partially offset by migration from farms. In the counties losing most heavily before 1930, there was much less movement from farms

[3] The available data on population of cities since 1930 give further support to the interpretation that there was no wholesale migration from cities to farms. While some cities decreased in population between 1930 and 1935, others maintained their numbers or reported slight increases. For a summary of some of the data see Bureau of the Census, *State and Special Censuses Since 1930*, release of the U. S. Department of Commerce, Washington, D. C., May 29, 1937.

after that date. The increases in such counties are explained by migration to farms plus a retardation of the movement from farms.

NET MIGRATION TO AND FROM FARMS

Widespread variations in migration occurred among the different geographic divisions of the country during the 5-year period 1930–1934. The number of persons moving to farms exceeded the number leaving farms during each of the years 1930–1933 in the New England States, 1930–1934 in the Middle Atlantic States, and 1930–1932 in the East North Central States.[4] In the South Atlantic States, where the reverse type of flow occurred, the movements from farms exceeded the movements to farms during each of the 5 years, though the difference was as little as 2,000 in 1932. In the other divisions the number moving to farms was generally greater than the number moving from farms before 1932 and less after 1932, except in the Pacific States where more persons were arriving on farms than were leaving farms during 1933 and 1934. The individual States in each division showed much diversity with respect to these movements.[5]

By taking into account the natural increase in the farm population during the 5 years, 1930–1934, it is possible to estimate the extent of the net migration to and from farms (fig. 8).[6] Several areas which received a relatively large net migration stand out. The largest area is that extending from the northeastern seaboard to the Appalachian Mountains, and even farther west into Ohio. Another area which received large numbers of migrants is the Lake States Cut-Over Region. The States of the far Northwest received a proportionately heavy migration, while the wide diversity of conditions in California is reflected by the irregular patterns of migration. Other areas of immigration are found in southwestern Utah, the Rio Grande Valley in Colorado and New Mexico, the Ozark Region of Missouri, and the industrialized areas near the Great Lakes. Florida generally received migrants to her farms.

---

[4] Bureau of Agricultural Economics, *Farm Population Estimates, January 1, 1938, op. cit.*

[5] Data on file in the U. S. Department of Agriculture, Bureau of Agricultural Economics, Washington, D. C.

[6] Fig. 8 was constructed by relating natural increase to the total increase as reported in the *United States Census of Agriculture: 1935.* The areas for which the comparability of the census figures may be called into question are generally the areas which are here shown as having a large migration to farms. But Connecticut and West Virginia, where it is most difficult to account for the total increase reported by the census, also reported a large proportion of persons "who lived in a nonfarm residence five years earlier" and are therefore classified correctly. For methodology see Taeuber, Conrad and Taylor, Carl C., *The People of the Drought States*, Research Bulletin Series V, No. 2, Division of Social Research, Works Progress Administration, Washington, D. C., 1937, pp. 61–63.

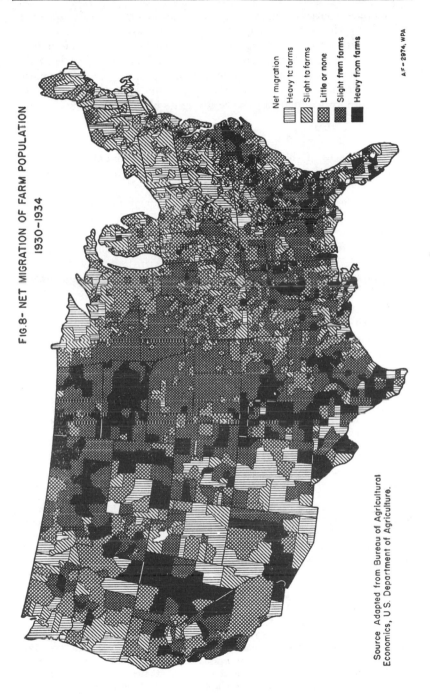

FIG. 8– NET MIGRATION OF FARM POPULATION
1930–1934

Net migration

Heavy to farms

Slight to farms

Little or none

Slight from farms

Heavy from farms

A F – 2974, WPA

Source Adapted from Bureau of Agricultural
Economics, U.S. Department of Agriculture.

The areas reporting net migration from farms are, broadly speaking, the major agricultural regions, the areas producing cotton and wheat together with a section of the Corn Belt. Relatively high birth rates in the past, the increasing use of agricultural machinery, agricultural readjustments as a result of governmental programs, and changing market conditions contributed to the migration from these areas. To such factors were added the severe droughts of 1934 and 1936 in large portions of these areas.

Effect of Drought

The estimates of the Bureau of Agricultural Economics as well as the data from the 1935 Census of Agriculture unfortunately deal only with gross movements of farm population and do not permit one to follow the individual migrant from point of origin to point of destination. Since they deal exclusively with farm population, they give only limited information about the migrations to and from the drought States.[7] Moreover, if agricultural laborers lived in tourist camps, migratory workers' camps, and nonfarm locations, they were not counted as farm population although their major employment was in agriculture.

Recent studies on a State basis, however, indicate the extent of the migrations both from the Great Plains drought area to the Pacific coast and eastward into Minnesota, Iowa, Missouri, Arkansas, and Louisiana.[8] The States which were most severely affected by the drought were States in which the population has for some time shown a high rate of turnover, and it appears that drought and economic depression accentuated previously existing trends without radically

---

[7] For a summary of the reports available late in 1936 see Taeuber, Conrad and Taylor, Carl C., *op. cit.*, pp. 45–47. See also Taeuber, Conrad and Hoffman, C. S., "Recent Migration From the Drought Areas," *Land Policy Circular*, U. S. Department of Agriculture, Farm Security Administration, Division of Land Utilization, Washington, D. C., September 1937, pp. 16–20.

[8] See Taylor, Paul S. and Vasey, Tom, "Drought Refugee and Labor Migration to California, June–December 1935," *Monthly Labor Review*, Vol. 42, No. 2, 1936, pp. 312–318; Rowell, Edward J., "Drought Refugee and Labor Migration to California in 1936," *Monthly Labor Review*, Vol. 43, No. 6, 1936, pp. 1355–1363; Landis, Paul H., *Rural Immigrants to Washington State, 1932–1936*, Rural Sociology Series in Population, No. 2, Washington Agricultural Experiment Station, Pullman, Wash., July 1936; Breithaupt, L. R. and Hoffman, C. S., *Preliminary Information Concerning Immigration into Rural Districts in Oregon, January 1933 to June 1936*, Circular of Information No. 157, Oregon Agricultural Experiment Station, Corvallis, Oreg., August 1936; Breithaupt, L. R., *Preliminary Data Concerning an Immigrant Family Survey in Oregon, January 1930 to November 1936*, Circular of Information No. 164, Oregon Agricultural Experiment Station, Corvallis, Oreg., January 1937; Hoffman, C. S., "Drought and Depression Migration into Oregon, 1930 to 1936," *Monthly Labor Review*, Vol. 46, No. 1, 1938, pp. 27–35; and Hill, George W., *Rural Migration and Farm Abandonment*, Research Bulletin Series II, No. 6, Division of Research, Statistics, and Finance, Federal Emergency Relief Administration, Washington, D. C., June 1935.

They Too Know Drought.

Leaving the Farm.

altering the direction of movement which had prevailed during the 1920's. The problems of the migrants and the manner in which the areas of settlement have absorbed the migrants, however, have been radically changed.

EXCHANGE OF POPULATION

Migration between two areas is normally a process of two streams moving in opposite directions. To speak of migration as proceeding in one direction ordinarily means that the stream of migrants in that direction is greater than the counter current. The statement that from 1930 through 1934 the net migration from farms amounted to nearly 600,000 persons is not to be interpreted as indicating that only 600,000 persons moved from farms to villages, towns, and cities. Actually nearly 6,600,000 persons moved to farms during the 5 years, while 7,200,000 persons left farms.[9]

According to the 1935 Census of Agriculture nearly 2,000,000 persons who were living on farms on January 1, 1935, had a nonfarm residence in 1930.[10] If figures both for the net migration from farms from 1930 through 1934 and for those who had a nonfarm residence in 1930 are correct, the number of persons who were on farms in 1930 and living elsewhere on January 1, 1935, must be nearly 2,600,000. Clearly not all of the people who moved from farms to villages, towns, and cities stayed there, nor did all of the people who moved to farms remain. Many persons made the shift from farm to town or from town to farm more than once during the 5 years.[11] However, at least 4,600,000 different individuals were included. On the other hand, the largest possible number of migrants would have been 13,756,000, the total moves to and from farms.

Thus, the net movement of nearly 600,000 persons from farms to villages, towns, and cities was the result of movements of approximately 8 times as many persons, and the total number of migrations

---

[9] Bureau of Agricultural Economics, *Farm Population Estimates, January 1, 1938, op. cit.*

[10] It is assumed that the change in farm population as reported by the census is correct and that the persons who were reported as "Persons on farms on January 1, 1935, who lived in a nonfarm residence 5 years earlier" actually moved from a nonfarm to a farm residence between 1930 and 1935. If it should be demonstrated that the farm population was relatively underenumerated in 1930 or that it was relatively overenumerated in 1935, it would be necessary to assume that migration from farms between 1930 and 1935 was greater than is indicated and that the net migration from farms during the period was actually greater than it is here stated to be.

[11] Each person would be counted each time he moved. Thus, if a person had moved once from town to farm and back again each year, he would appear 10 times. The figure of 1,995,000 persons who moved from a nonfarm to a farm residence between 1930 and January 1, 1935, as reported by the census, however, is an unduplicated figure, as is that of 2,593,000 migrants from farms, which is used here as its counterpart.

between farm and nonfarm territory was 23 times as great as the number of persons involved in the net change resulting from migration. This shifting of population to and from farms indicates a large amount of experimentation, for in terms of numbers the net result of these movements might have been achieved with approximately four out of every hundred migrations that actually occurred.

But even these figures do not give the full measure of the extent to which people on farms moved about during the 5-year period, for they do not include the movement from one farm to another, which is the largest single item in the mobility of the farm population. The interstate farm-to-farm movement was even larger in volume and extent than the movement between farms and nonfarm territory.[12] Yet the bulk of the farm-to-farm movement was a local milling about that did not carry the individual outside his community or his county or State. On the other hand, the migration between farm and nonfarm territory, though predominantly for short distances, more frequently carried the individual beyond the bounds of the immediate vicinity.

EFFECT OF DECREASED MIGRATION FROM FARMS

The net migration from farms for the period 1930–1934 was nearly 2,500,000 less than it would have been if migration had continued at the same level which it reached during the 1920's. When the migration from farms was reduced without a correspondingly sharp decline in the excess of births over deaths, a growth in farm population was inevitable, even if there had not been some movement to the land. Moreover, an increase under such circumstances is cumulative. The persons who would have moved if earlier conditions had continued to prevail were young people.[13] Remaining on the farms and marrying, they in turn added to the excess of births over deaths in the farm population. From 1930 through 1934 the farm population increased by 5.4 percent.[14] But if there had been no migration to or from farms, the increase would have been at least 6.7 percent or 2,023,000 persons, which is the computed excess of births over deaths.

Changes in the age composition of the farm population also resulted from the fact that fewer persons moved from farms during the depression years than formerly (table 8). The number of persons aged 15–39 years increased more than the number aged 40–64 years during the 5-year period. That is, there was a greater increase in the age group which normally would have contributed the largest proportion

---

[12] Data on file in the U. S. Department of Agriculture, Bureau of Agricultural Economics, Washington, D. C.

[13] Approximately one-half of the migrants from farms between 1920 and 1930 were 10–19 years of age in 1920.

[14] Bureau of Agricultural Economics, *Farm Population Estimates, January 1, 1938, op. cit.*

Table 8.—Age of the Farm Population, 1930 and 1935 (Estimated)

Age	January 1, 1930		January 1, 1935	
	Number	Percent	Number	Percent
Total	30,169,000	100.0	31,801,000	100.0
Under 5 years	3,343,000	11.1	3,329,000	10.5
5–14 years	7,530,000	25.0	6,913,000	21.7
15–39 years	11,139,000	36.9	12,614,000	39.7
40–64 years	6,604,000	21.9	7,118,000	22.4
65 years and over	1,553,000	5.1	1,827,000	5.7

Source: Bureau of Agricultural Economics, *Farm Population and Rural Life Activities*, U. S. Department of Agriculture, Washington, D. C., July 1, 1937, p. 26.

of the migrants from farms, while proportionately the age group which would be more directly affected by migration to farms increased less rapidly.

MIGRATION TO FARMS BY GEOGRAPHIC DIVISIONS AND STATES

Approximately 7 out of every 10 persons who had moved from villages, towns, and cities to farms from 1930 through 1934 had left the farms by 1935 (table 9). The largest proportion remaining on farms was reported from the East North Central States, particularly Michigan, Ohio, and Indiana. In the Middle Atlantic and New England States the proportion of these migrants who remained on their farms in 1935 was also somewhat above the average for the entire country. Together, these three geographic divisions reported 28 percent of the migrants to farms and 35 percent of those who remained on farms, although they had only 22 percent of the total farm population in the United States in 1930 and nearly the same proportion in 1935.[15] The percent of migrants remaining on farms was also above the

Table 9.—Migrants From Cities, Towns, and Villages to Farms, 1930–1934, and Migrants Remaining on Farms, January 1, 1935

Geographic division	Total migrants to farms [1]	Migrants remaining on farms, January 1, 1935 [2]	Percent of migrants remaining on farms
United States	6,578,000	1,995,000	30
New England	240,000	82,000	34
Middle Atlantic	529,000	196,000	37
East North Central	1,081,000	414,000	38
West North Central	1,104,000	279,000	25
South Atlantic	767,000	265,000	35
East South Central	693,000	214,000	31
West South Central	1,165,000	267,000	23
Mountain	421,000	114,000	27
Pacific	578,000	164,000	28

[1] Bureau of Agricultural Economics, *Farm Population Estimates, January 1, 1938*, U. S. Department of Agriculture, Washington, D. C., June 16, 1938.
[2] Persons on farms on January 1, 1935, who lived in a nonfarm residence 5 years earlier. Bureau of the Census, *United States Census of Agriculture: 1935*, Vol. II, U. S. Department of Commerce, Washington, D. C., 1936, table XIII.

[15] Bureau of the Census, *United States Census of Agriculture: 1935*, Vol. II, U. S. Department of Commerce, Washington, D. C., 1936.

average in the South Atlantic States, which, however, received less than a proportionate share of the migrants in terms of their farm population. The West North Central and West South Central Divisions received their share of the migrants to farms, but they retained only one-fourth of them. The severe drought experienced in those States undoubtedly was the largest factor in reducing the proportion which remained. In the Mountain States the more densely settled river valleys and irrigated districts apparently attracted and retained more migrants than did the more sparsely settled and more arid areas.

While farm residents on January 1, 1935, who had moved from a nonfarm residence since 1930 made up 6.3 percent of the farm population of the United States (appendix table 6), the proportion of the 1935 farm population composed of persons who were not on farms 5 years earlier was greatest in the Pacific Coast States, where approximately one out of every seven farm residents (13.7 percent) had moved from a city, town, or village after 1929. Oregon led all other States in this movement, 18 percent of its farm population having come from villages, towns, or cities during the 5 years preceding 1935. In that State the migrants to farms sought out chiefly the fertile Willamette Valley, where the major share of Oregon's agriculture is concentrated.

New England and the Middle Atlantic States also had secured relatively large proportions of their 1935 farm population through migrants who came from nonfarm areas, approximately 12 and 10 percent, respectively. In the Mountain and the East North Central States 10 and 9 percent of the farm residents, respectively, had moved to farms since April 1, 1930. Michigan was outstanding among the latter group of States with 13 percent of its farm population reported as recent arrivals on farms.

The five geographic divisions in which migrants to farms constituted more than 6 percent of the 1935 farm population were, except for the Mountain Division, much more urbanized than the remainder of the country. Only 30 percent of the farm population in 1935 was reported in those divisions. In the other four divisions—West North Central, South Atlantic, East South Central, and West South Central—which contained 70 percent of the farm population and the majority of those engaged in commercial agriculture, migrants formed less than 6 percent of the farm residents. The East South Central Division—Kentucky, Tennessee, Alabama, and Mississippi—reported the smallest proportion of migrants; only 4.0 percent of the persons on farms in 1935 had not been on farms in 1930.

The concentration of the migrants on farms in the northern and eastern industrial States also stood out clearly when the number of these migrants in each State was related to the area of the State. The States with the highest ratio of migrants per 100 square miles of territory were among the most highly urbanized States in the country:

Connecticut, Delaware, Indiana, Massachusetts, Michigan, New Jersey, New York, Ohio, Pennsylvania, and Rhode Island. Kentucky and West Virginia, which were also included in such a classification, had large rural-nonfarm populations.

MIGRATION TO FARMS IN RELATION TO URBAN CENTERS

The location of migrants to farms indicates to what a large extent the movement was to areas near the larger cities (fig. 9). The counties which included a city of 100,000 or more in 1930 reported 4.4 percent of the total farm population that year. During the 5 years, 1930–1934, their farm population increased by 16 percent, nearly four times as rapidly as that of the entire country. The 205,000 migrants to farms in these counties constituted slightly more than 10 percent of the total. In other words, these urban counties, with only 4.4 percent of the farm population in 1930, received more than 10 percent of the migrants to farms.

FIG. 9 – PERSONS LIVING ON FARMS, JANUARY I, 1935,*WHO
HAD A NONFARM RESIDENCE 5 YEARS EARLIER

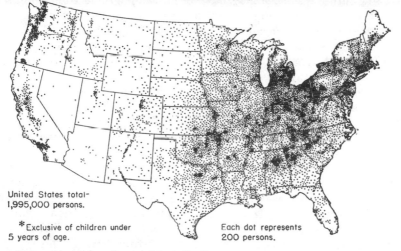

United States total–
1,995,000 persons.

*Exclusive of children under
5 years of age.

Each dot represents
200 persons.

Source: Adapted from Bureau of Agricultural
Economics, U.S. Department of Agriculture.

AF - 2975, WPA

A similar tabulation for the counties adjoining each county with a large city showed the same concentration of migrants to farms.[16]   The

---

[16] The counties which in 1930 had a density of 100 persons or more per square mile included 12.3 percent of the farm population. They received nearly twice as large a proportion of the migrants to farms, 22.1 percent of the total. The farm population of these counties increased by 12.6 percent, and migrants to farms were 10.5 percent of the farm population in 1935, the corresponding national percentages being 4.5 and 6.3, respectively. The increase in farm population was greater in these counties than the national average in every geographic division except the Pacific States. The greater proportion of migrants, however, was found in all divisions.

counties including cities with 250,000 population or more and the adjoining counties had 9 percent of the farm population in 1930, but they received 15 percent of the migrants to farms which were reported by the census. These results are in agreement with those which would have been expected on the basis of the principle that most migrations are for short distances—one phase of the Law of Limited Circulation.[17]

If the data were analyzed by minor civil divisions, the tendency to locate near cities would be shown even more clearly. Such a tabulation was made for South Dakota, a State which reported a net migration from farms between 1930 and 1935. Minor civil divisions were grouped into three classes: A—those including or adjoining a city of 5,000 or more; B—those including any incorporated place of less than 5,000 persons; and C—all others. Migrants to farms were proportionately more numerous in the minor civil divisions included under "A" than in those included under "B," and these in turn exceeded those included under "C." Whatever their intentions concerning future residence may have been, the migrants from nonfarm to farm territory to a large extent moved to areas near urban centers.

Much of the movement to farms from 1930 through 1934 was to places near which nonagricultural employment had previously been available. A large proportion of the nonagricultural population is concentrated within relatively few counties.[18] A list of 167 manufacturing, 167 mining, and 41 other urban counties is given in the Study of Population Redistribution. These counties included 13 percent of the farm population in 1930, but in 1935 they accounted for 24.5 percent of the "persons on farms January 1, 1935, who were not on farms 5 years earlier."

Increases in total farm population in these counties between 1930 and 1935 were considerably above the national average, and a large share of these increases was due to the migration from nonfarm to farm areas (table 10). In the mining counties the migration to farms did not account for all of the increase in farm population. The figures suggest that there was virtually no migration from farms in these counties and that some families changed their occupational classification from nonfarm to farm between 1930 and January 1, 1935, without moving.[19] In the manufacturing and other urban counties there appears to have been some migration from farms as well as to farms, although in both groups the movement to farms exceeded the national average.

[17] Lively, C. E., "Spatial Mobility of the Rural Population With Respect to Local Areas," *The American Journal of Sociology*, Vol. XLIII, 1937, pp. 89–102.

[18] Goodrich, Carter, Allin, Bushrod W., and Hayes, Marion, *Migration and Planes of Living, 1920–1934*, Bulletin No. 2, Study of Population Redistribution, Philadelphia: University of Pennsylvania Press, 1935.

[19] It is possible also that the farm population figures in these areas are not entirely comparable because of different interpretations of census instructions.

Table 10.—Farm Population, 1930, and Changes in Farm Population, 1930–1934, in 375 Selected Counties

Group	Percent of total farm population, 1930	Percent of migrants to farms, 1930–1934	Percent increase in farm population, 1930–1934	Percent increase in 1930 farm population because of migrants from nonfarm territory, 1930–1904	Percent change in farm population, exclusive of migrants from nonfarm territory, 1930–1934
United States_____	100.0	100.0	+4.5	+6.6	−2.1
Total counties (375) _____	13.0	24.6	+15.0	+12.4	+2.6
Manufacturing counties (167)_____	7.2	14.5	+14.3	+13.2	+1.1
Mining counties (167)_____	3.8	6.9	+20.5	+11.9	+8.6
Other urban counties (41) _____	2.0	3.2	+7.4	+10.3	−2.9

Sources: Bureau of the Census, *United States Census of Agriculture: 1935*, Vol. II, U. S. Department of Commerce, Washington, D. C., 1936, county table IV; and Goodrich, Carter, Allin, Bushrod W., and Hayes, Marion, *Migration and Planes of Living, 1920–1934*, Bulletin No. 2, Study of Population Redistribution, Philadelphia: University of Pennsylvania Press, 1935.

The clustering around large cities of persons who moved to farms between 1930 and January 1, 1935, and remained there indicates that the movement was not primarily to the areas from which migrants had come between 1920 and 1930. While some of these migrants from cities to farms returned to the areas from which they had come, many others obviously went to areas near the cities of their recent residence.

MIGRATION TO FARMS AND QUALITY OF LAND

The available evidence does not support the thesis that recent migrants went primarily to the poorest agricultural areas. For the United States as a whole the proportion of the 1930 farm population in problem areas, as delimited by the National Resources Board,[20] and the proportion of migrants in these areas were 24.8 percent and 26.6 percent, respectively (appendix table 7). Even when the problem areas were further subdivided according to the proportion of their land which should be withdrawn from agriculture, there was no clear evidence that the poorest agricultural areas attracted an unduly large proportion of the migrants. Those counties for which it was recommended that 60 percent or more of the agricultural land should be transferred to other uses included 640,000 farm residents in 1930, 2.1 percent of all farm residents in the United States. These counties reported almost exactly the same percent (2.3) in 1935 of those persons who had moved to farms since 1930 and remained there.

---

[20] In connection with studies of soil resources and their most effective utilization the National Resources Board has prepared a map showing areas of land-use problems. These are the areas in which some or all of the farm land should be transferred to grazing, forests, or other conservational uses. In 1930, 25 percent of the farm population was living in counties classified as being in these problem areas. In general they are areas in which income from agriculture is low and in which other economic and social problems are prevalent.

While 6.3 percent of the persons on all farms in the United States on January 1, 1935, had not lived on a farm 5 years previously, in the most severely affected problem area counties the comparable figure was 6.4 percent. For all problem area counties it rose to 6.5 percent, and for those counties not classified as problem areas, it was 6.2 percent.

When the data were classified by six geographic regions, the same results were obtained (appendix table 7). The proportion of migrants in the problem areas of four regions was slightly higher than would have been expected on the basis of the distribution of the farm population in 1930, but in two of the regions the proportion of migrants in the problem areas was less than would have been expected on that basis.

Except in the Northwestern States, where the influence of drought undoubtedly was the basis for the exception, there was less migration from farms in the problem areas than from farms in the nonproblem areas. Disregarding migrants from nonfarm territory there was a decrease of 2.1 percent in the total farm population from 1930 through 1934. In the nonproblem areas the comparable figure was 3.1, but in the problem areas there was actually an increase of 1.0 percent.[21] Birth rates in the problem areas are generally high; and if there were no migration, their population would increase at a rapid rate. In the instances in which the number of migrants from farms in problem areas within the six regions was greater than the excess of births over deaths, the differences were usually small. The major exception was the most severely affected problem areas of the Far West.

It is clear, therefore, that in relation to the distribution of the farm population in 1930 the problem areas attracted only slightly more than their share of the migrants from villages, towns, and cities. Rather, the generally high rates of reproduction in problem areas together with retention of a larger than average share of the natural increase were primarily responsible for the disproportionate increase in the farm population of such areas.[22]

---

[21] It is not likely that migration from farms in other areas could account for more than a small fraction of the increase. Therefore, the interpretation given here that this represents failure to migrate is probably correct.

[22] It has been asserted that the change in number of farms and in farm population as reported by the census for the years 1930–1934 is an overstatement of the true situation and that the census of 1930 underenumerated the farms and farm population. If such assertions are correct, the argument above needs to be modified somewhat, for it assumes the correctness of the census figures. The number of persons on farms on January 1, 1935, who were not on farms in 1930 may probably be accepted as essentially correct in indicating the migration to farms which had occurred. If the 1930 farm population as reported by the census is too small, the effect would be to reduce the amount of change shown. The correction would probably be greatest in the problem areas and in the areas near the larger cities, where part-time and self-sufficing farms occur in large numbers and make accurate classification of places as farm or nonfarm difficult. Any upward adjustment of the 1930 Census figures would not detract from the argument that

To test further the conclusion that the back-to-the-land movement was primarily a movement away from the larger industrial centers and not a movement to the more remote agricultural areas, the problem area counties were divided into two groups on the basis of whether more of the gainfully employed workers (excluding trade, commerce, and public and private service) were engaged in agriculture or in manufacturing, forestry, and mining in 1930. Those problem area counties classified as industrial on this basis failed to experience as much migration away from farms as the agricultural counties and, with the exception of the Far West, they also received a larger proportion of migrants from nonfarm territory (table 11). In only 2 States, Iowa and Indiana, was there a decrease in the farm population in industrial counties, but decreases in agricultural counties were reported for 14 of the States where the migration from farms was sufficiently great to match the migration to farms and, in addition, to match the additions to the population through the excess of births over deaths.

Table 11.—Farm Population, 1930, and Changes in Farm Population, 1930–1934, in Industrial and Agricultural Counties [1] in Agricultural Problem Areas

Region and type	Percent of total farm population, 1930	Percent change in farm population, 1930–1934	Percent increase in 1930 farm population because of migrants from nonfarm territory, 1930–1934	Percent change in farm population, exclusive of migrants from nonfarm territory, 1930–1934
United States	100.0	+8.1	+7.0	+1.1
Industrial	20.6	+17.7	+11.1	+6.6
Agricultural	79.4	+5.6	+6.0	−0.4
Northeast	100.0	+18.5	+12.2	+6.3
Industrial	58.9	+21.0	+13.6	+7.4
Agricultural	41.1	+14.9	+10.1	+4.8
Middle States	100.0	+11.4	+9.8	+1.6
Industrial	24.1	+17.1	+11.6	+5.5
Agricultural	75.9	+10.0	+9.2	+0.8
Northwest	100.0	−3.4	+4.1	−7.5
Industrial	0.9	+29.6	+19.4	+10.2
Agricultural	99.1	−3.7	+4.0	−7.7
Southeast	100.0	+6.3	+4.8	+1.5
Industrial	10.5	+22.3	+8.4	+13.9
Agricultural	89.5	+4.4	+4.3	+0.1
Southwest	100.0	+4.9	+6.4	−1.5
Industrial	—	—	—	—
Agricultural	100.0	+4.9	+6.4	−1.5
Far West	100.0	+4.2	+13.1	−8.9
Industrial	50.3	+12.4	+8.8	+3.6
Agricultural	49.7	−4.0	+17.4	−21.4

[1] The problem area counties were divided into 2 groups on the basis of whether more of the gainfully employed workers (excluding trade, commerce, and public and private service) were engaged in agriculture or in manufacturing, forestry, and mining in 1930.

Source: National Resources Committee, *The Problems of a Changing Population*, Washington, D. C., May 1938, table 6, p. 107.

migration from nonfarm territory was not disproportionately large in the problem areas and that it was not the major factor in the increases that did occur. It is assumed here that the figures for persons on farms in 1935 who were not on farms 5 years previously are reliable. For a discussion of this point see Thompson, Warren S., *Research Memorandum on Internal Migration in the Depression*, Bulletin 30, Social Science Research Council, New York, 1937.

In a number of States another development is discernible. In addition to receiving persons from nonfarm areas, and, in effect, retaining their natural increase, the industrial counties in these States appear to have gained some farm population through a shift from nonfarming occupations to farming without any change in residence.[23] Unemployed miners or forest workers living in the open country on a plot of land which could be utilized for agricultural production shifted to agriculture when they lost their industrial employment, and their holdings were classified as farms in 1935.[24]

MIGRATION TO FARMS AND THE INCIDENCE OF RELIEF AND LOW INCOMES

A somewhat different classification of problem areas has been made in the Federal Emergency Relief Administration.[25] In these six problem areas, based primarily upon the occurrence of high relief rates, farm population increased a total of 3.3 percent between 1930 and January 1, 1935, but in two of the areas, the Appalachian-Ozark and the Lake States Cut-Over, the increase was approximately 17 percent. These six areas with more than two-fifths of the farm population in 1930 received only one-third of the migrants to farms. The Lake States Cut-Over Area received more than twice as large a share of the migrants as it would have received if the migrants had been distributed according to the farm population of 1930. The Appalachian-Ozark Area received slightly more and the Winter Wheat Area slightly fewer migrants than would have been expected on that basis. In the other three areas there were fewer migrants to farms; in the Eastern Cotton Area the number of migrants was only about half that which would have been expected (table 12).

In the three areas which were most severely affected by the drought, there were decreases in the farm population; and in the Eastern Cotton counties the increase was only 0.8 percent. In these four areas of commercial agriculture the migration to farms was more than offset by migration from farms to other areas. In the Appalachian-Ozark Area the increase in farm population through the arrival of migrants to farms was 6.7 percent and an increase of 9.9 percent was due to other factors, including the high rate of natural increase. In the Lake States Cut-Over Area the rate of total increase as well as

---

[23] See also p. 36.

[24] The correctness of the census classification is not called into question here. It is possible, however, that the completeness of enumeration may have differed as between 1930 and 1935. This would have the same effect as the creation of farms by the process mentioned. The correction, if any, which would be made for this factor would probably not be sufficiently great to alter the conclusions stated above.

[25] Beck, P. G. and Forster, M. C., *Six Rural Problem Areas, Relief—Resources—Rehabilitation*; Research Monograph I, Division of Research, Statistics, and Finance, Federal Emergency Relief Administration, Washington, D. C., 1935.

Table 12.—Farm Population, 1930, and Changes in Farm Population, 1930–1934, in 6 Rural Problem Areas [1]

Area	Percent of total farm population, 1930	Percent of migrants to farms, 1930–1934	Percent change in farm population, 1930–1934	Percent increase in 1930 farm population because of migrants from nonfarm territory, 1930–1934	Percent change in farm population, exclusive of migrants from nonfarm territory, 1930–1934
6 rural problem areas_____ _____	45.2	33.0	+3.3	+4.8	−1.5
Appalachian-Ozark_____	8.6	8.8	+16.6	+6.7	+9.9
Lake States Cut-Over_____	1.4	3.2	+17.4	+14.5	+2.9
Spring Wheat_____	2.1	1.2	−5.5	+3.7	−9.2
Winter Wheat_____	2.8	2.7	−1.3	+6.3	−7.6
Eastern Cotton_____	22.6	12.0	+0.8	+3.5	−2.7
Western Cotton _____ _____	7.7	5.1	−2.4	+4.4	−6.8

[1] The areas are those used by Beck, P. G. and Forster, M. C. in *Six Rural Problem Areas, Relief—Resources—Rehabilitation*, Research Monograph I, Division of Research, Statistics, and Finance, Federal Emergency Relief Administration, Washington, D. C., 1935.

Source: Bureau of the Census, *Fifteenth Census of the United States: 1930*. Population Vol. III, table 13, and *United States Census of Agriculture: 1935*, Vol. II, county table IV, U. S. Department of Commerce, Washington, D. C.

the rate of increase from migration was larger than in the other areas. Migration to farms alone was sufficient to increase the farm population by 14.5 percent. The fact that, with so large an increase from migration to farms, the total increase was only 17.4 percent indicates that there was also some migration from farms, for the rate of natural increase in this area in 5 years probably would amount to more than 3 percent.

These facts have a significant bearing on the relation of migration to farms and relief. These problem areas were selected primarily on the basis of their high relief rates; in each of them there were counties in which 30 percent or more of the total population was on relief during at least 1 month between October 1933 and April 1934. In June 1934 when 15 percent of the families in the United States were on relief, the percent of rural families on relief ranged from 8 in the Eastern Cotton Belt to 25 in the Lake States Cut-Over Area and 33 in the Spring Wheat Area. The fact that only 5 percent of the farm population in these areas in 1935 (12 percent in the Lake States Cut-Over) consisted of persons who had not been on farms 5 years previously indicates clearly that recent migrants were not the primary reason for the high relief rates.[26]

Another approach to the problem may be made in terms of the returns received by farm operators. The 1930 Census of Agriculture

[26] *Ibid.*, p. 27; and Bureau of the Census, *United States Census of Agriculture: 1935*, Vol. II, *op. cit.*, county table IV. See also Asch, Berta and Mangus, A. R., *Farmers on Relief and Rehabilitation*, Research Monograph VIII, Division of Social Research, Works Progress Administration, Washington, D. C., 1937, p. 43. Similar findings are reported in unpublished data collected by the Research Section, Social and Economic Division, Tennessee Valley Authority, 1935.

secured information concerning the total value of all products sold, traded, or used by the operator's family. This is a gross income figure which makes no allowance for operating expenses, taxes, etc., and is generally considerably larger than the cash income or the net amount available for family living. For purposes of this comparison counties were classified according to the percent of farms which reported total products valued at less than $600. The larger the percent of these farms the poorer the area was from an agricultural standpoint (table 13).[27]

This comparison also shows a greater increase in farm population in the poorer agricultural areas, although they received less than their proportionate share of the migrants to farms. In the better areas, however, the larger migrations to farms were partly offset by larger migrations from farms and they, therefore, had smaller net increases of farm population after 1930.

Table 13.—Farm Population, 1930, and Changes in Farm Population, 1930–1934, by Counties Having Specified Percent of Farms With Products Valued at Less Than $600 [1] in 1929

Percent of farms with products valued at less than $600 in 1929	Percent of total farm population, 1930	Percent of migrants to farms, 1930-1934	Percent increase in farm population, 1930-1934	Percent increase in 1930 farm population because of migrants from non-farm territory, 1930-1934	Percent change in farm population, exclusive of migrants from non-farm territory, 1930-1934
Total _____	100.0	100.0	+4.5	+6.6	−2.1
Less than 10 _____	14.8	10.2	−1.7	+4.5	−6.2
10–19 _____	21.7	25.1	+1.5	+7.5	−6.0
20–29 _____	20.9	24.5	+5.0	+7.7	−2.7
30–39 _____	17.0	17.4	+5.2	+6.7	−1.5
40–49 _____	12.6	11.5	+7.4	+6.0	+1.4
50 or more _____	13.0	11.3	+11.6	+5.6	+6.0

[1] Total value of all products sold, traded, or used by the operator's family in 1929.

Sources: Bureau of the Census, *Fifteenth Census of the United States: 1930*, Agriculture Vol. III, county tables III and IV, and *United States Census of Agriculture: 1935*, Vol. II, U. S. Department of Commerce, Washington, D. C.

In a study of the population of the drought States [28] it was shown that recent migrants from villages, towns, and cities to farms in the drought area went to areas of greatest distress less frequently than to other areas. The most severely affected counties reported 10 percent of the farm population in 1930 and only 6 percent of the migrants during the following 5 years. For the least severely affected areas the comparable figures were 28 percent and 39 percent, respectively.

---

[27] For the relation of this measure of agricultural distress to others see Taylor, Carl C., Wheeler, Helen W., and Kirkpatrick, E. L., *Disadvantaged Classes in American Agriculture*, Social Research Report No. VIII, U. S. Department of Agriculture, Farm Security Administration and Bureau of Agricultural Economics cooperating, Washington, D. C., April 1938.

[28] Taeuber, Conrad and Taylor, Carl C., *op. cit.*, p. 52.

Thus, while some of the migrants to farms went to areas with high relief rates and low annual incomes, they were generally under-represented in such problem areas, taking the 1930 farm population as a base. In many instances a high rate of natural increase and a low rate of migration from farms have been more important factors in farm population increase than the so-called "back-to-the-land movement."

THE MIGRANTS

Migration from villages, towns, and cities to farms may involve primarily the return of young people to the farm home they had left for urban employment. It may, on the other hand, be a move-ment of families, with or without previous farm experience, which attempt to find on the farm a degree of economic security or an occu-pational outlet which they could not find in the city. Obviously there are other possibilities; not all of the single persons who moved to farms returned to their homes and in some instances urban families were divided, the members moving to more than one farm.

The census does not classify these migrants directly as to their relationship to other migrants or to the other residents of the farms upon which they are located. It does give the number of farms by counties reporting such migrants and classifies them further into farms reporting one such person, farms reporting two such persons, and farms reporting three or more such persons.[29] For the purposes of this analysis it was assumed that persons on "farms reporting one such person" were single individuals, most of whom were returning to the parental home, and that persons on "farms reporting three or more such persons" were members of family groups which had migrated as units. No similar assumption seemed valid for the persons included on "farms reporting two such persons," and they were not included. Without more detailed data it seemed impossible to allocate them properly among single persons and family groups.

Ten percent of all farms on January 1, 1935, reported persons who had been living in a nonfarm residence 5 years earlier.[30] The pro-portions were highest in the Pacific (17.7 percent) and New England (17.2 percent) States and lowest in the East South Central (6.1 per-cent), South Atlantic (7.1 percent), and West South Central (7.4 percent) States. Among individual States Oregon led with 23.8 percent of its farms reporting persons not on farms 5 years previously while Mississippi reported the smallest percent, 3.4.

These figures again bear out the assertion that the migration was largely a movement to the vicinity of cities and that it was not a

[29] For the States the last mentioned category is divided into farms reporting 3–9 such persons and farms reporting 10 or more such persons.

[30] Bureau of the Census, *United States Census of Agriculture: 1935*, Vol. II, *op. cit.*, table XIII.

movement to the agricultural areas which had sent the majority of migrants from farms to urban areas between 1920 and 1930. The States in which the proportion of farms reporting these migrants was greater than the national average of 10 percent were, almost without exception, Northern and Eastern or far Western States. Among the Southern States only Oklahoma reported more than 10 percent of its farms in that category, and in the West North Central Division only Missouri and Kansas had more than 10 percent, but the excesses were small.

Nearly 700,000 farms reported 1,995,000 persons [31] who were not on farms 5 years previously or an average of 3 persons per farm (table 14). Nearly one-half of the farms reporting the presence of migrants in 1935 reported three or more. The average number of persons on these farms was 4.8. Approximately 3 percent of these farms reported 10 or more migrants. It is likely, however, that these latter included some institutions and other places which should be classified as abnormal farms. Farms reporting one migrant were slightly more numerous than farms reporting two migrants.

Table 14.—Farms Reporting Persons on January 1, 1935, Who Had a Nonfarm Residence in 1930 and Number of Persons Reported

Number of migrants per farm	Farms reporting persons		Number of persons reported		Average number of persons per farm reporting
	Number	Percent	Number	Percent	
Total	671,316	100.0	1,995,253	100.0	3.0
1	192,864	28.7	192,864	9.7	1.0
2	172,619	25.7	345,238	17.3	2.0
3 or more	305,833	45.6	1,457,151	73.0	4.8

[1] Arithmetic mean.

Source: Bureau of the Census, *United States Census of Agriculture: 1935*, Vol. II, U. S. Department of Commerce, Washington, D. C., 1936, table VII.

The average number of migrants per farm reporting migrants was greatest in the Southern States.[32] Presumably the proportion of migrants who traveled in family groups was greater there than elsewhere. Mississippi was the only 1 of the 13 Southern States in which the average number of migrants per farm reporting was less than the national average of 3. Florida with an average of 3.8 had the largest number. On the other hand, family groups were less important among the migrants to farms in the Northern States, west of Ohio, where the average was generally less than 3.0 migrants per farm reporting migrants. In three States which suffered from severe

[31] Exclusive of children under 5 years of age.
[32] Bureau of the Census, *United States Census of Agriculture: 1935*, Vol. II, *op. cit.*, table XIII.

Farm Security Administration (Lange).

drought—North Dakota, South Dakota, and Nebraska—the average was particularly small, being only 2.3. Whether this indicates that relatively fewer families left a village, town, or city residence for farms in the drought area, or that a larger proportion of the families which moved to farms left those farms before 1935, cannot be ascertained from the data at hand. It seems likely, however, that migrants who were still on farms in the drought area in 1935 included a large proportion of unmarried persons who had returned to their former homes during the depression years.

Many of the migrants from nonfarm territory to farms came with little or no resources and, therefore, could hardly become owners of the farm to which they moved. The resources to purchase needed equipment to begin operating a farm even as a tenant were lacking in many instances. For this reason the migrants turned primarily to part-time and subsistence farming rather than to commercial farming. Furthermore, there were many persons among the migrants who had no intention of becoming farm operators but rather of living with farm operators as paid or unpaid laborers. Migrant families appear to have settled as tenants more frequently than as owners, whereas single persons moved to the homes of farm owners in larger proportions than to the homes of tenants.[33] Perhaps the most striking fact is that owners' farms reported as large a proportion of the migrants as they did.

Negroes and other colored persons were markedly underrepresented among the migrants to farms. The movement was largely one of white persons to farms near the larger industrial centers and was less important in those areas where Negroes normally comprise a large proportion of the population. In the Southern States the farms of colored operators received less than half as many of these migrants, proportionately, as the farms of white operators. On the latter the proportion of all farm residents who had not been on farms in 1930 was 5.0 percent; on the former it was only 2.3 percent. Moreover, although about one-fourth of the farm residents were on farms of colored operators, only one-eighth of the migrants who remained on farms were on farms of colored operators.[34] In view of the census practice of classifying croppers as well as owners under the heading "farm operator," it seems probable that the ratios for the total farm population in the South were similar to the ratios for farm operators and that the farmward migration of colored farm laborers to farms of white operators was not sufficiently great to introduce any significant change.

---

[33] *Ibid.*

[34] Bureau of the Census, *United States Census of Agriculture: 1935*, Vol. III, U. S. Department of Commerce, Washington, D. C., 1937, pp. 157–163.

Chapter III

MIGRATION AND RURAL REPRODUCTION

SHARP DIFFERENTIALS in the rate of rural reproduction occur among the subdivisions of the United States. Since pressure of population upon available resources is generally regarded as a fundamental factor affecting migration, the rate of reproduction of the rural population is important in any analysis of rural migration. Both factors serve to redistribute the population, the one by transferring persons from place to place and the other by varying from place to place the rate at which population is produced.

The measure of rural reproduction used throughout this analysis is the fertility ratio. This measure consists of the ratio of children under 5 years of age to women 20–44 years of age and is expressed as a given number of children per 1,000 women. Since the number of children under 5 years of age does not represent all of the children born but rather the number born less the weighted average number of deaths during the first 5 years, the fertility ratio is really a measure of effective fertility, i. e., fertility modified by child mortality.[1] As this ratio is based upon the total female population of childbearing age, it constitutes a fair measure of the rate at which a population is reproducing itself.

Although certain exceptions occur, in general the larger the community the lower is the rate of reproduction of the population. The principle holds for the rural-farm and rural-nonfarm populations [2] as well as for larger communities. In 1930 the rate of reproduction of the rural-nonfarm population was higher in all sections of the country than that of communities of 2,500 population or more. In turn the rate of reproduction of the rural farm population was higher than that of the rural-nonfarm population.

---

[1] Lorimer, Frank and Osborn, Frederick, *Dynamics of Population*, New York: The Macmillan Company, 1934, p. 397.

[2] Woofter, T. J., Jr., "The Natural Increase of the Rural Non-Farm Population," *The Milbank Memorial Fund Quarterly*, Vol. XIII, 1935, pp. 311–319.

RURAL REPRODUCTION BY GEOGRAPHIC DIVISIONS AND STATES

The rate of reproduction of both the rural-farm and rural-nonfarm populations varies significantly by divisions and States. In 1930 the ratio of children under 5 years of age to women 20–44 years of age was 736 for the rural-farm population as a whole but ranged from 478 in Connecticut to 915 in Utah (table 15).[3] In the rural-nonfarm population the corresponding ratio for the United States was 592, or nearly 20 percent less than the ratio for the rural-farm population. Again the ratio was lowest in Connecticut (454) and highest in Utah (848).

In the rural-farm population only four States (Maine, Vermont, Rhode Island, and New York) failed to show a lower ratio of children to women in 1930 than in 1920. In eight States the 1930 ratio was less than 85 percent of the 1920 ratio. Heaviest declines occurred in States in the West North Central, Mountain, and Pacific Divisions and in Connecticut.

In the rural-nonfarm population the trend was also downward, the decline being slightly greater than for the rural-farm population. The decrease was most marked in the Middle Atlantic Division, while nine States had dropped to less than 85 percent of the 1920 ratio.

The trend in rates of reproduction since 1930 cannot be determined precisely as yet, but it is known to be downward. The general decline in the number of births reported by State bureaus of vital statistics was sharp from 1930 to 1934 when a slight upward trend appeared. This upturn has failed to bring back the birth rates of 1930, however, and apparently the general trend is reflected in both the rural and the urban populations. Indeed, there is some reason to believe that in recent years the decline in the rate of reproduction of the rural population has been more pronounced than that of the urban population.

RURAL REPRODUCTION BY COUNTIES

Although sharp differences in the rates of reproduction of the rural-farm and rural-nonfarm populations are indicated by the fertility ratios of the various States, State averages conceal geographic variations of considerable significance. Not only are States large territorially but also their limits are determined by political boundaries which are frequently unrelated to the variations in those economic and social factors that influence the rate of reproduction of the population. Thus, a State like Missouri, which includes as varying areas as the Ozark Highlands and the prosperous farming communities

---

[3] In this and subsequent tables fertility ratios are based upon census figures not corrected for underenumeration. It is recognized that underenumeration occurs, but no reliable correction for variations by counties, by color, is available. For purposes of this monograph the variations in rural population fertility are more significant than the absolute ratios.

Table 15.— Children [1] Under 5 Years of Age per 1,000 Women 20 Through 44 Years of Age in the Rural Population, by Geographic Division, State, and Residence, 1920 and 1930

Geographic division and State	Rural-farm			Rural-nonfarm		
	Children under 5 per 1,000 women 20–44		1930 ratio as percent of 1920 ratio	Children under 5 per 1,000 women 20–44		1930 ratio as percent of 1920 ratio
	1920	1930		1920	1930	
United States	806	736	91.3	658	592	90.0
New England	623	609	97.8	590	521	88.3
Maine	657	686	104.4	616	619	100.5
New Hampshire	555	547	98.6	569	536	94.2
Vermont	663	694	104.7	598	594	99.3
Massachusetts	586	521	88.9	545	488	89.5
Rhode Island	562	587	104.4	508	503	99.0
Connecticut	612	478	78.1	593	454	76.6
Middle Atlantic	638	624	97.8	694	578	83.3
New York	576	580	100.7	521	472	90.6
New Jersey	592	505	85.3	574	467	81.4
Pennsylvania	700	679	97.0	814	680	83.5
East North Central	697	635	91.1	628	577	91.9
Ohio	660	610	92.4	657	600	91.3
Indiana	648	602	92.9	589	569	96.6
Illinois	670	593	88.5	599	512	85.5
Michigan	756	693	91.7	679	643	94.7
Wisconsin	780	700	89.7	619	564	91.1
West North Central	780	677	86.8	586	515	87.9
Minnesota	810	702	86.7	630	531	84.3
Iowa	732	639	87.3	533	477	89.5
Missouri	729	657	90.1	599	537	89.6
North Dakota	1,014	836	82.4	720	580	80.6
South Dakota	866	732	84.5	599	502	83.8
Nebraska	789	655	83.0	531	487	91.7
Kansas	735	637	86.7	570	507	88.9
South Atlantic	911	828	90.9	729	665	91.2
Delaware	690	592	85.8	519	484	93.3
Maryland	743	691	93.0	629	579	92.1
Virginia	862	799	92.7	752	690	91.8
West Virginia	900	857	95.2	921	826	89.7
North Carolina	987	889	90.1	779	695	89.2
South Carolina	932	838	89.9	673	646	96.0
Georgia	912	811	88.9	620	558	90.0
Florida	825	738	89.5	617	591	95.8
East South Central	847	802	94.7	680	656	96.5
Kentucky	872	834	95.6	747	745	99.7
Tennessee	842	769	91.3	607	662	95.0
Alabama	901	845	93.8	670	644	96.1
Mississippi	775	764	98.6	572	514	89.9
West South Central	855	775	90.6	646	598	92.6
Arkansas	859	782	91.0	641	580	90.5
Louisiana	861	800	92.9	647	627	96.9
Oklahoma	932	825	88.5	705	633	89.8
Texas	819	743	90.7	617	575	93.2
Mountain	891	789	88.6	720	669	92.9
Montana	873	746	85.5	676	540	79.9
Idaho	916	767	83.7	711	630	88.6
Wyoming	800	719	89.9	634	571	90.1
Colorado	834	743	89.1	686	615	89.7
New Mexico	902	871	96.6	776	818	105.4
Arizona	899	868	96.6	724	686	94.8
Utah	1,050	915	87.1	968	848	87.6
Nevada	742	626	84.4	502	565	112.5
Pacific	664	566	85.2	573	494	86.2
Washington	701	555	79.2	629	502	79.8
Oregon	666	541	81.2	599	505	84.3
California	644	580	90.1	536	488	91.0

[1] Number not corrected for underenumeration.

Sources: Thompson, Warren S., Ratio of Children to Women, 1920, Census Monograph XI, U. S. Department of Commerce, Bureau of the Census, Washington, D. C., 1931, p. 97; and Bureau of the Census, Fifteenth Census of the United States: 1930, Population Vol. II, U. S. Department of Commerce, Washington, D. C., 1933, ch. 10, table 31.

that border Iowa and Illinois, is scarcely well represented by an average fertility ratio of 657 for the rural-farm population. Certain counties in Missouri have fertility ratios that are double those of other counties. For example, Carter, Iron, and Reynolds Counties had fertility ratios in 1930 of 971, 977, and 1,048, respectively, for the white rural-farm population. At the other extreme, Lewis, Monroe, and Knox Counties had ratios of only 432, 434, and 497, respectively. Similar situations exist in other States with respect to both the rural-farm and the rural-nonfarm populations. It appears to be clear, therefore, that a more precise notion of the geographic distribution of differential fertility may be obtained by analyzing the data by counties.

Of the 3,052 counties in the United States having 100 women or more aged 20–44 years in 1930, more than one-half had rural fertility ratios ranging from 550 to 769 (table 16). Only 36 counties had ratios lower than 440,[4] while 45 counties had ratios of 990 or more.

Table 16.—Counties of the United States by Number of Children [1] Under 5 Years of Age per 1,000 Women 20 Through 44 Years of Age in the Rural Population, by Color and Residence, 1930

Children under 5 per 1,000 women 20–44	Total		White				Colored			
			Rural-farm		Rural-nonfarm		Rural-farm		Rural-nonfarm	
	Number	Percent	Number	Percent	Number	Percent	Number	Percent	Number	Percent
Classified counties	3,052	100.0	2,982	100.0	2,978	100.0	903	100.0	935	100.0
Fewer than 440	36	1.2	41	1.4	292	9.8	5	0.6	182	19.5
440–549	478	15.7	303	10.2	1,027	34.4	19	2.1	204	21.8
550–659	923	30.2	794	26.6	886	29.8	67	7.4	209	22.3
660–769	837	27.4	800	26.8	449	15.1	151	16.7	157	16.8
770–879	560	18.3	647	21.7	216	7.3	274	30.4	59	6.3
880–989	173	5.7	298	10.0	80	2.7	225	24.9	54	5.8
990–1,099	34	1.1	69	2.3	23	0.7	116	12.8	44	4.7
1,100 or more	11	0.4	30	1.0	5	0.2	46	5.1	26	2.8
Unclassified counties [2]	7	—	77	—	81	—	2,156	—	2,124	—

[1] Number not corrected for underenumeration.
[2] Counties with fewer than 100 women 20–44 years of age and of the specified color.

Source: Unpublished data from the Bureau of the Census, U. S. Department of Commerce, Washington, D. C.

For the white population living on farms, more than the average proportion of counties had fertility ratios of 990 or more. In the white rural-nonfarm population, on the other hand, a disproportionately large proportion of counties had ratios below 440. Among the colored rural population, which is located chiefly in the South, county fertility ratios for the farm population ran distinctly higher than among whites, but in the rural-nonfarm population the opposite tendency prevailed.

Within individual States important variations by counties were likewise found in the rural fertility ratios of 1930 (appendix table 8). For the white rural-farm population in the majority of the States the largest number of counties fell in the 660–879 group. In Utah, however, the largest number of counties had ratios of 880 or more

---

[4] For the significance of this ratio see p. 55.

and no county had a ratio of less than 660. In only one county in New England and in none in the Middle Atlantic or Pacific Divisions was the fertility ratio for the white rural-farm population as high as 880. The largest number of counties with a ratio of 1,100 or more was found in Kentucky.

In the colored rural-farm population most of the counties within each State were in the 660–879 and 880 or more classes (appendix table 9). Of the 46 counties with ratios above 1,100, 11 were in California in sections where Mexicans and other foreign-born are concentrated.

Data by counties emphasize the fact that fertility ratios in 1930 ran definitely lower in the rural-nonfarm than in the rural-farm population. For the white rural-nonfarm population in the great majority of the States the largest number of counties fell in the 440-659 class in comparison with the 660–879 class for the rural-farm population (appendix table 8). Nearly 10 percent of the counties had fertility ratios under 440 in the white rural-nonfarm population, and only 11 States had no county in this lowest group. At the other extreme, well over 10 percent of the counties had fertility ratios of 770 or more Eleven of the twenty-eight counties with ratios of 990 or more were located in Kentucky.

In the colored rural-nonfarm population also the largest group of counties in a majority of the States fell within the 440-659 group (appendix table 9). Nearly 20 percent of the classified counties had ratios under 440, while 13 percent had ratios of 880 or more. In the Southern States, where the colored population consists almost wholly of Negroes, all States except Delaware and Maryland listed one or more counties with fertility ratios under 440. Among the Western States, where the colored population consists largely of Mexicans, Indians, and orientals, only one California county had a ratio lower than 440. On the other hand, more than one-half of the counties having fertility ratios of 880 or more were located in the Mountain and Pacific Divisions.

The highest rural-farm fertility ratios in 1930 prevailed generally throughout the Southern States, except for Florida and portions of Texas; throughout the Western Plains area; in much of the Rocky Mountain section; and in northern Michigan, Minnesota, and Wisconsin (figs. 10 and 11). From the standpoint of the numbers of persons involved, as well as from the standpoint of high rates of reproduction, the most significant rural-farm fertility ratios were found in the Southern States. The lowest rural-farm fertility ratios occurred in the New England group of States; in the North Central States of Ohio, Indiana, Illinois, Missouri, and Iowa, and in the eastern half of Nebraska and Kansas; in portions of Texas and Florida; and on the Pacific coast. Thus, in the older, more urbanized New England Area, in the best farming region of the United States,

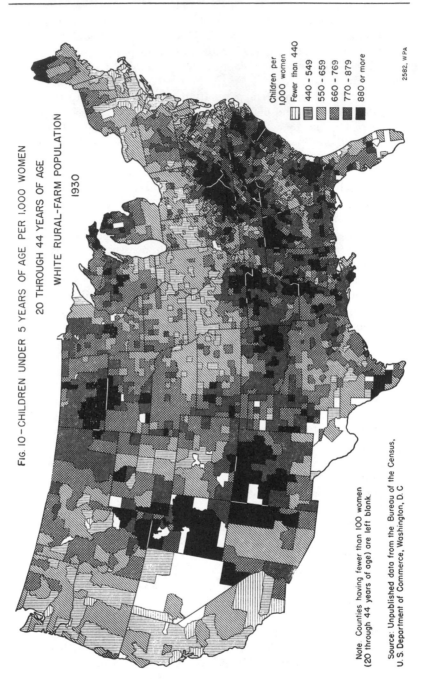

FIG. 10—CHILDREN UNDER 5 YEARS OF AGE PER 1,000 WOMEN
20 THROUGH 44 YEARS OF AGE
WHITE RURAL-FARM POPULATION
1930

Children per
1,000 women

Fewer than 440
440 - 549
550 - 659
660 - 769
770 - 879
880 or more

Note. Counties having fewer than 100 women
(20 through 44 years of age) are left blank.

Source: Unpublished data from the Bureau of the Census,
U. S. Department of Commerce, Washington, D. C

2582, WPA

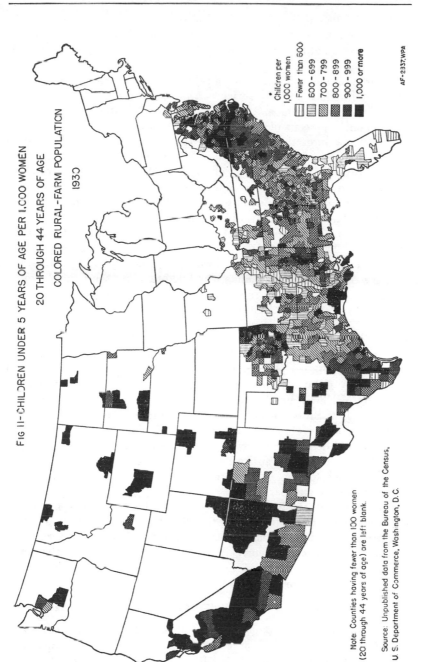

FIG II–CHILDREN UNDER 5 YEARS OF AGE PER 1,000 WOMEN
20 THROUGH 44 YEARS OF AGE
COLORED RURAL-FARM POPULATION
1930

Children per
1,000 women

Fewer than 500
600 - 699
700 - 799
800 - 899
900 - 999
1,000 or more

AF-2337,WPA

Note Counties having fewer than 100 women
(20 through 44 years of age) are left blank.

Source: Unpublished data from the Bureau of the Census,
U. S. Department of Commerce, Washington, D. C.

and on the Pacific coast the rural-farm birth rates were lowest. In the rural-nonfarm population the same general picture is indicated except that fertility ratios were distinctly below those of the rural-farm population (fig. 12).

Combining the rural-farm and rural-nonfarm populations gave somewhat intermediate fertility ratios. Almost equal numbers of counties fell into the two groups, 440–659 and 660–879 (appendix table 10). Only about 1 percent of the counties had rural fertility ratios of less than 440, and more than one-third of these were located in the Middle Atlantic Division. Approximately 7 percent of the counties had fertility ratios of 880 or more. The Pacific Division had none of these counties and only one each was to be found in the New England and Middle Atlantic Divisions. Nearly one-third of these counties were located in the South Atlantic Division.

The general picture of rural population fertility in the United States in 1930 (fig. 13) emphasized the following characteristics. Three clusters of counties with fertility ratios of 880 or more stood out: the Appalachian Highlands, the Dakotas, and the Utah-Arizona-New Mexico Area. The remainder of the counties with the highest ratios were scattered. Relatively high rural fertility ratios (660–879) prevailed throughout the counties of the Southern States (except in Delaware, Maryland, and Florida); in Arizona, New Mexico, Utah, the Dakotas, eastern Colorado and Montana, and Kansas and Nebraska west of the 100th meridian; and in northern Michigan, Minnesota, and Wisconsin. Relatively low rural fertility ratios (440–659) prevailed generally in New England, New York, New Jersey, and Delaware; in the Corn Belt States of Ohio, Indiana, Illinois, Missouri, and Iowa; in Kansas and Nebraska east of the 100th meridian; in southern Minnesota, Michigan, and Wisconsin; in Florida, Nevada, and western Idaho; and on the entire Pacific coast. Exceptionally low rural fertility ratios (under 440) occurred in the general neighborhood of New York City and San Francisco.

The fact that combining the figures for the rural-farm and rural-nonfarm populations did not materially change the rural population fertility map of the United States suggests that the fertility ratios of the two populations are correlated. While the fertility of the rural-farm population and that of the rural-nonfarm population do tend to vary together, the relationship is far from perfect.[5]

RURAL POPULATION FERTILITY AND REPLACEMENT NEEDS

What does the variation in the fertility of the rural population of the United States by local areas mean in relation to rural population growth? How do the actual fertility ratios compare with the ratio

---

[5] The coefficient of correlation for the counties of six States selected at random (Alabama, California, Iowa, New Jersey, Virginia, and Wyoming) was $+0.64 \pm 0.02$.

which would be necessary exactly to reproduce the rural population, i. e., to keep its total stationary, assuming no migration?

In order to determine the number of children needed to maintain a stationary population, it is necessary to have at hand the age distribution of the population by sex and a life table based upon the same population. Given these data, it is possible to estimate the number of children under 5 years of age per 1,000 women 20–44 years of age necessary under conditions of prevailing mortality to replace the population and keep it stationary. The number of children under 5 years of age required under conditions of 1930 has been calculated at 443 for the white population of the United States as a whole.[6] Because of the differences in mortality between rural and urban populations, the number of children under 5 years of age required to replace the white rural population is 440.[7] This means that in any area where the number of white rural children under 5 years of age is fewer than 440 per 1,000 white rural women 20–44 years of age, the white rural population will not permanently replace itself. In areas where the number of children under 5 years of age is as high as 550 per 1,000 women 20–44, a 25 percent surplus of children above actual replacement needs is being produced, and so on. Areas in which the ratio of children to women is as high as 880 are producing twice as many children as would be required permanently to maintain the rural population, assuming no migration.

In no State as a whole was the rural population failing to replace itself in 1930 (table 15, p. 49). This statement applies to both the rural-farm and rural-nonfarm populations, although in 8 States the rural-nonfarm excess was very small, the fertility rate being less than 500. The data for counties, however, indicate that in 41 counties the white rural-farm population and in 292 counties the white rural-nonfarm population had fertility ratios too low for permanent replacement and, at birth and death rates prevailing in 1930, would eventually begin to decrease in population, barring the effect of migration (appendix table 8). In the colored population only 5 counties showed evidence of a declining rural-farm population, but in 182 counties the rural-nonfarm population appeared not to be reproducing itself (appendix table 9). When the rural-farm and rural-nonfarm populations were considered together, they combined in such a way that the fertility ratio for the entire rural population was below 440 in only 36 counties (appendix table 10).

It should be remembered, however, that the numbers of children

---

[6] Lorimer, Frank and Osborn, Frederick, op. cit., p. 10.

[7] Based on unpublished information supplied by the Metropolitan Life Insurance Company. The figure is slightly higher for Negroes, but for purposes of this monograph 440 has been used throughout. It is recognized, however, that there are wide differences both among States and within States.

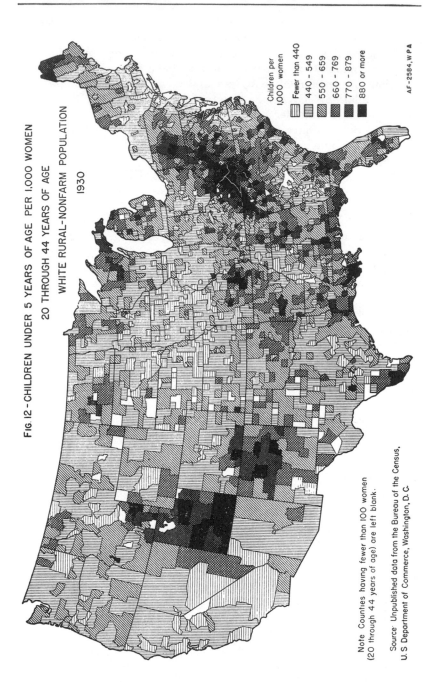

Fig. 12—CHILDREN UNDER 5 YEARS OF AGE PER 1,000 WOMEN
20 THROUGH 44 YEARS OF AGE
WHITE RURAL-NONFARM POPULATION
1930

Children per
1,000 women

Fewer than 440
440 - 549
550 - 659
660 - 769
770 - 879
880 or more

AF-2584, W P A

Note: Counties having fewer than 100 women
(20 through 44 years of age) are left blank.

Source: Unpublished data from the Bureau of the Census,
U. S Department of Commerce, Washington, D. C.

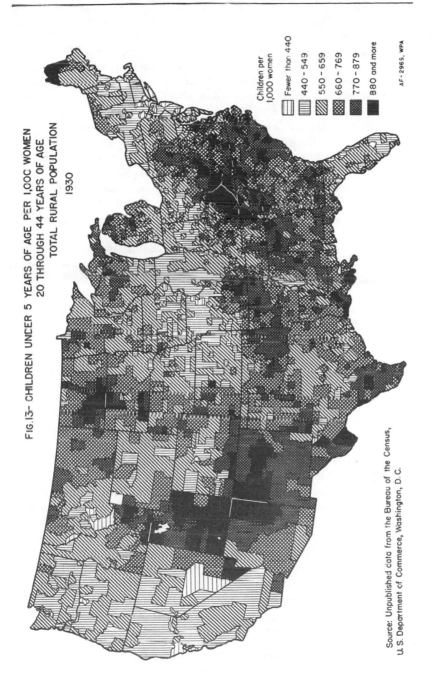

FIG. 13– CHILDREN UNDER 5 YEARS OF AGE PER 1,000 WOMEN 20 THROUGH 44 YEARS OF AGE
TOTAL RURAL POPULATION
1930

Children per
1,000 women

Fewer than 440
440 – 549
550 – 659
660 – 769
770 – 879
880 and more

AF - 2965, WPA

Source: Unpublished data from the Bureau of the Census,
U. S. Department of Commerce, Washington, D. C.

upon which these fertility ratios are based were not corrected for underenumeration by the census. Although there is at present no adequate basis for correcting the underenumeration of children under 5 years of age with the county as the unit, it may be assumed for purposes of this discussion that the corrections elsewhere applied to States and regions hold for counties also.[8] In applying these corrections to the 36 counties with rural fertility ratios below 440, it was found that in 22 counties the rural fertility ratio still remained below replacement requirements. For the white population the rural-farm fertility ratios of 24 counties remained below 440 after corrections for the underenumeration of children under 5 years of age had been made, and the rural-nonfarm fertility ratios of 177 counties remained similarly low. For the colored population the rural-farm fertility ratios of 2 counties and the rural-nonfarm fertility ratios of 101 counties remained below 440 after corrections were made.

At the other extreme, the rural-farm populations of the entire States of North Carolina and of Utah were producing more than 880 children per 1,000 women 20–44 years of age in 1930 or more than twice as many children as would be required to maintain a stationary farm population (table 15, p. 49). On a county basis there were 397 counties in the United States in which the white rural-farm population and 108 counties in which the white rural-nonfarm population were producing at least a 100-percent surplus of children above replacement needs (appendix table 8). The corresponding number of counties for the colored population was 387 for the rural-farm and 124 for the rural-nonfarm population (appendix table 9). In terms of the total rural population there were 218 counties in which the surplus of children above actual replacement needs was equal to 100 percent or more (appendix table 10).[9]

The location of these extreme counties is of interest. Of the 22 counties in which the rural population fertility ratio was below the requirements for maintaining a stationary population after corrections for underenumeration, 4 were located in California; 3 each were located in Montana, New Jersey, and New York. There were two each in Missouri and Nevada. The States of Massachusetts, Connecticut, Georgia, Colorado, and Oregon had one county each. Seven of the counties were entirely rural in 1930, while ten were largely urban or suburban in nature. Agriculture was the leading industry in few of the counties.

[8] To correct for underenumeration the number of white children under 5 years of age was increased by 5 percent and the number of colored children by 13 percent. See footnote 8, p. 13.

[9] Statements in this paragraph are conservative since corrections for the underenumeration of children would further raise these ratios. It was considered unnecessary for present purposes, however, to make this correction at the upper end of the scale.

The counties having rural fertility ratios of 880 or more were concentrated in relatively few States, most of which were in the southeastern portion of the United States. Kentucky had 37 of these counties; North Carolina, 23; and Virginia, 16. West Virginia and Tennessee had 14 each and Georgia claimed 11. North Dakota had 11 and Utah 15. No other State had as many as 10 such counties. Of the 10 counties having rural fertility ratios of 1,100 or more, 7 were located in eastern Kentucky, 2 in western Virginia, and 1 in Utah. In three of the Kentucky counties, Breathitt, Clay, and Leslie, and in Buchanan County, Va., agriculture is the chief occupation. All the others except the Utah county possess considerable coal mining. The highest ratio found among the counties was that of Leslie County, Ky., which had an uncorrected rural fertility ratio of 1,254.

NET RURAL MIGRATION AND RURAL REPRODUCTION

Rural reproduction as measured by the ratio of children to women was only slightly related to the rate of gain or loss of population through migration during the decade 1920–1930. This relationship was analyzed for a sample of 765 counties (table 17). Since these counties were chosen at random from the 3,059 counties of the United States, there is no reason to suppose that the entire list of counties would yield different results. There was a slight positive correlation between the two factors; [10] i. e., there was a slight tendency for counties losing rural population through migration to have higher fertility ratios than the counties which gained by migration. The counties losing 30 percent or more by migration had somewhat higher fertility ratios than those with smaller losses by migration. Nearly all of the counties with fertility ratios of 880 or more were in the group reporting a loss by migration, but two-fifths of them had a loss by migration equal to less than 20 percent of their 1920 population.

Substantially the same results were obtained when the rural fertility ratio was related to the total number of persons gained or lost as a result of migration. For the same sample of 765 counties there was a slight tendency for the net volume of migration to be proportional to the size of the fertility ratio, the gains being related to low fertility ratios and the losses to high fertility ratios.

If rural populations were similar and local conditions identical, the disposition to emigrate would probably be proportional to the increased pressure upon local resources resulting from natural increase. Local conditions vary greatly, however. Opportunity to rise in the economic and social scale varies enormously among the cotton plantations of Georgia, the coal plateaus of the Southern Appalachians, and

---

[10] The coefficient of correlation was $+0.20 \pm 0.03$.

Table 17.—Fertility Ratio,[1] 1930,[2] and Percent Gain or Loss Through Migration, 1920–1930,[3] of the Rural Population in 765 Sample Counties [4]

Children under 5 per 1,000 women 20–44, 1930	Number of counties														
	Gained rural population, 1920–1930								Lost rural population, 1920–1930						
	Total	Percent							Total	Percent					
		100 or more	50–99	40–49	30–39	20–29	10–19	Less than 10		Less than 10	10–19	20–29	30–39	40–49	50 or more
Total	136	8	13	7	12	12	33	51	629	132	283	163	41	7	3
Fewer than 440	5	—	1	—	1	1	2	—	2	1	—	—	1	—	—
440–494	14	2	—	—	2	4	3	3	17	9	6	1	—	—	1
495–549	21	1	2	2	2	3	5	6	66	22	36	7	1	—	—
550–604	23	1	2	1	4	1	5	9	111	27	55	24	5	—	—
605–659	18	1	2	1	1	—	3	10	90	19	48	18	4	—	1
660–714	18	1	1	1	1	—	6	8	81	14	42	19	5	—	1
715–769	13	—	—	2	1	1	3	6	90	12	41	25	11	1	—
770–824	17	2	2	—	—	2	3	8	79	15	25	30	8	1	—
825–879	1	—	—	—	—	—	1	—	48	10	14	17	5	2	—
880–934	4	—	3	—	—	—	1	—	27	3	10	12	—	2	—
935–989	1	—	—	—	—	—	—	1	12	—	5	5	1	1	—
990 or more	1	—	—	—	—	—	1	—	6	—	1	5	—	—	—

[1] Children under 5 years of age per 1,000 women 20–44 years of age.
[2] Unpublished data from the Bureau of the Census, U. S. Department of Commerce, Washington, D. C.
[3] For method of computation see appendix B.
[4] 25 percent random sample.

the Corn Belt farms of Illinois and Iowa.[11] In some sections, such as in the Appalachian-Ozark Highlands and in the Lake States Cut-Over Area, economic opportunity of an agricultural nature has always been very limited. Economic opportunity in these areas, in so far as it exceeds the possibilities of bare subsistence, consists of the shifting demand for man power in nonagricultural industries, such as coal mining and lumbering.

In other sections, such as the Old Cotton Belt and portions of the Western Plains area, economic opportunity had previously been exploited and during the decade 1920–1930 was definitely on the wane. On the other hand, it appears that the Pacific coast and portions of the Southwest possessed opportunity during that decade in excess of the capacity of the local population to exploit it. Finally, in the best agricultural areas of the Corn Belt the ample economic opportunity appeared to be so well within the grasp of the resident population that additional population could not gain a foothold.

TYPE OF NET RURAL MIGRATION AND RURAL REPRODUCTION

Counties may be classified into types according to the relation of net migration to natural increase. If a county retained, in effect, all of its natural increase during the decade 1920–1930 and in addition

[11] For an excellent discussion of the geography of economic opportunity see Goodrich, Carter and Others, *Migration and Economic Opportunity*, Philadelphia: University of Pennsylvania Press, 1936, chs. I–VIII.

to that received a number of migrants from outside the county, it may be designated as a county of *absorption*. If a county experienced a net loss from migration but did not suffer a decrease, i. e., did not have a smaller population at the end than at the beginning of the decade, it may be classified as a county of *dispersion*. Finally, if, in effect, a county lost all of its natural increase and in addition some of its base population as a result of migration, it may be called a county of *depopulation*. This classification is valuable since it shows at a glance where the rural population is thinning out and where it is tending to concentrate. Furthermore, it facilitates the study of the relation of population fertility to trends in migration.

Of the 3,059 counties of the United States [12] 17 percent were classed as counties of absorption during the decade 1920–1930, 32 percent as counties of dispersion, and 51 percent as counties of depopulation (appendix table 11). Among the divisions the Pacific led with more than one-half (55 percent) of its counties absorbing population in addition to their natural increase and with only one-fourth (25 percent) losing rural population in excess of their natural increase. The New England Division was second with 41 percent of the counties classed as areas of absorption and 28 percent as areas of depopulation. Much of this apparent absorption of population was the result of the changed definition of rural territory adopted for the 1930 Census. In the Middle Atlantic Division 26 percent of the counties were in the group growing by absorption and in the West South Central Division there were 29 percent. In each of these divisions more than two-fifths of all counties were areas of depopulation. The two North Central Divisions and the East South Central Division each had a small proportion of their counties in the group growing by absorption, the percentages ranging from 5 to 11. These were also divisions which had a high proportion of counties in the group losing in excess of natural increase. The percentages ranged from 46 in the East South Central Division to 66 in the East North Central Division. The Mountain Division also had a high proportion (53 percent) of counties in the group being depopulated by migration.

Among the States the proportion of counties that might be classed as areas of absorption varied greatly. Aside from Massachusetts, New Hampshire, and Rhode Island, where the classification was affected by definition, there were three States in which half or more of the counties were classed as areas of absorption—Arizona, California, and New Jersey. The States also varied greatly with respect to areas of dispersion. Only one division, the East South Central, had approximately half of the counties dispersing some of their natural increase, but seven States had more than half of their counties in that group. North Carolina led with 75 percent. With approximately

[12] With rural population. See footnote 18, p. 20.

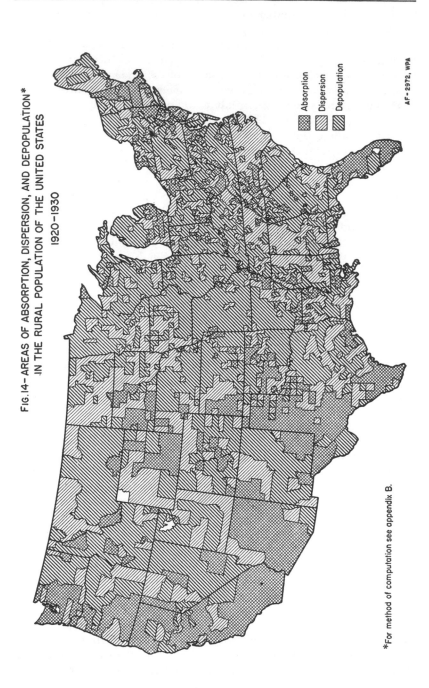

FIG. 14.– AREAS OF ABSORPTION, DISPERSION, AND DEPOPULATION*
IN THE RURAL POPULATION OF THE UNITED STATES
1920–1930

Absorption

Dispersion

Depopulation

AF - 2972, WPA

*For method of computation see appendix B.

half of all counties (51 percent) classed as areas of depopulation, only three States (California, Connecticut, and North Carolina), aside from Massachusetts and Rhode Island, had less than 15 percent of their counties in this class.

From this classification of counties by type of migration it may be seen that during the decade 1920–1930 the absorption of population by means of migration occurred chiefly on the Pacific coast; in the Western Plains, Florida, and local areas in the environs of large cities; and in rural-industrial areas (fig. 14). Areas in effect losing all of their natural increase and a certain percentage of their base populations were located in the Corn Belt and southwestern Cotton Belt where lies much of the best farm land of the United States; the Old Cotton Belt; the Lake States of Michigan, Minnesota, and Wisconsin; the mountain and semiarid regions of the West and Northwest; and the Appalachian foothills and highlands, especially in Kentucky, Pennsylvania, and Virginia.

The direct relation of rural reproduction to counties by type of net rural migration is slight (appendix table 11). For all counties the average fertility ratio was highest in counties of dispersion and lowest in counties of absorption. Among the divisions, however, the average fertility ratio was highest for counties of dispersion in four divisions, highest for counties of depopulation in four divisions, and highest for counties of absorption in one division. Among the States, exclusive of Massachusetts, Rhode Island, and Vermont, the average fertility ratio was lowest for counties of absorption in 25 States, highest in 10 States, and intermediate in 10 States. Excluding Massachusetts and Rhode Island, the average fertility ratio was lowest for counties of depopulation in 19 States, highest in 14 States, and intermediate in 13 States. In the Northeastern States the tendency for fertility to be lowest in areas of absorption was marked; but among West North Central States low fertility was associated with depopulation.

The assumption that the lowest fertility in the rural population is to be found in areas of absorption, intermediate fertility in areas of dispersion, and highest fertility in areas of depopulation is not substantiated by these data. In 12 States this sequence occurred, but in 8 States the reverse occurred.

The slight relation between rural population fertility and type of migration is further emphasized by the fact that as rural population fertility increases there is a slight decrease in the probability that a county will be classified as an area of absorption and a slight increase in the probability that it will be classified as a county of dispersion (table 18). Areas of absorption are likely to be located in the neighborhood of urban centers where population fertility is not high. Other areas of low fertility, and hence low natural increase, are likely to become areas of depopulation even though loss from migration is only

Table 18.—Counties of the United States by Rural Fertility Ratio, 1930,[1] and Type of Net Migration, 1920–1930 [2]

Type of net migration, 1920–1930	Number of counties	Children under 5 per 1,000 women 20–44, 1930								
		Fewer than 440	440–549	550–659	660–769	770–879	880–989	990–1,099	1,100 or more	Unclassified
Total	3,059	36	478	923	837	560	173	34	11	7
Absorption	517	19	128	145	126	67	25	4	1	2
Dispersion	994	1	102	265	268	245	90	13	8	2
Depopulation	1,548	16	248	513	443	248	58	17	2	3
		Percent								
Total	100.0	1.2	15.6	30.1	27.4	18.3	5.7	1.1	0.4	0.2
Absorption	100.0	3.7	24.7	28.0	24.4	13.0	4.8	0.8	0.2	0.4
Dispersion	100.0	0.1	10.3	26.7	26.9	24.6	9.1	1.3	0.8	0.2
Depopulation	100.0	1.0	16.0	33.2	28.7	16.0	3.7	1.1	0.1	0.2
		Percent								
Total	100.0	100.0	100.0	100.0	100.0	100.0	100.0	100.0	100.0	100.0
Absorption	16.9	52.8	26.8	15.7	15.1	12.0	14.5	11.8	9.1	28.5
Dispersion	32.5	2.8	21.3	28.7	32.0	43.7	52.0	38.2	72.7	28.6
Depopulation	50.6	44.4	51.9	55.6	52.9	44.3	33.5	50.0	18.2	42.9

[1] Unpublished data from the Bureau of the Census, U. S. Department of Commerce, Washington, D. C.
[2] For method of computation see appendix B.

moderate. Areas of high fertility seldom retain all of their natural increase because as fertility increases, economic opportunity is likely to decrease. Any net loss from migration classifies such counties as areas of dispersion. On the other hand, as fertility increases, the volume of loss through migration necessary to drain off all of the natural increase rises also and tends to decrease the probability that the area will become one of depopulation. Thus, only a slight relationship between rural reproduction and type of net rural migration can be claimed.

Chapter IV

MIGRATION AND SELECTED SOCIO-ECONOMIC FACTORS

CAREFUL CONSIDERATION of the factors which supposedly are related to migration reveals that not only is there no one-way relationship of cause and effect but also that it is not profitable to assign to one factor the responsibility for certain variations in the other. Even if close relationships were found, the question of which factor was dependent on the other would still be far from solved.

MECHANIZATION OF AGRICULTURE

The increased use of machinery and the greater productivity per worker in agriculture have frequently been stressed as important factors in the migration from rural areas and in the maintenance of a nearly stationary farm population for a third of a century in spite of an increasing national population. Grave concern is now being voiced over the prospective results of increased mechanization in the production of cotton. If mechanization is rapid, those effects may be severe. The mechanization of much of our commercial farming in the past, however, may have been a result of the migration from farms and other rural areas as well as a cause of such movements.

The period since the World War has seen rapid gains in the mechanization of agriculture, and the same period has been one of heavy migration from rural areas. The need for man power during the war, coupled with the need for increased production, sharply stimulated a process which, in turn, has given rise to further migration from rural areas. Moreover, mechanization proceeds most rapidly during periods of prosperity, which are also the periods when industry is competing most directly with agriculture for workers. There is ample evidence that in some agricultural areas, such as parts of the Corn Belt and large sections of the Cotton Belt, where mechanization is entirely feasible, it has been delayed because of the ready availability of cheap labor. Should this supply of labor be depleted through migration or any other development, mechanization would probably proceed rapidly.

An attempt to relate migration to increased use of machinery by means of the statistical measures available showed very little relationship (appendix tables 12, 13, and 14). It was not pronounced within the Corn Belt, and migration from rural areas was also heavy in those sections in which mechanization has made very little progress and especially in those where hoe culture is still practiced, such as the Appalachian-Ozark Area and the Cotton Belt.

While the increased use of farm machinery may have been an important element in rural population migration in recent years and may continue to become more important if commercial agriculture continues to be predominant, one important effect of the rapid introduction of machinery to do those tasks which are now largely done by hand will be to leave many workers unemployed and stranded,[1] either directly at or near the place where last employed. Only as alternative opportunities, real or apparent, come to their attention is the process likely to be accompanied by a large-scale migration. As has been amply shown in recent years, stranded communities—industrial and agricultural—are testimony to the unwillingness of people to move unless there is some prospect of improving their condition as a result.

QUALITY OF LAND

The attempt to find a relationship between the rate of rural migration and quality of land meets with many obstacles. Recent studies have supplied rough estimates of the quality of much of the land actually or potentially available for agriculture. Needless to say, the technical judgments upon which these estimates are based do not always correspond with the local judgments concerning the value of the land for certain purposes. But it may be assumed that over a period of time experience will bear out these technical judgments and that there will be some tendency for people to migrate from poor land to better land. Few people have migrated to the deserts of the West for agricultural purposes, and even the most densely inhabited portions of the Appalachians have hillsides that have not been cleared or have been allowed to revert to natural vegetation. Severely eroded soil, which has become unfit for agricultural purposes, is likely to give rise to migration. The droughts in the Great Plains in recent years have stimulated many families to move out of that area. The history of agricultural settlement in northern New England shows much abandonment of land too steep or too poor for the traditional agriculture.[2] On the other hand, rumors of openings of good lands have always brought numerous prospective settlers, and the development of a

[1] Taylor, Paul S., *Power Farming and Labor Displacement in the Cotton Belt, 1937*, Parts 1 and 2, Serial No. R. 737, U. S. Department of Labor, Bureau of Labor Statistics, Washington, D. C., 1938.

[2] Wilson, Harold Fisher, *The Hill Country of Northern New England, Its Social and Economic History, 1790–1930*, New York: Columbia University Press, 1936.

Farm Security Administration (Mydans).

A Potential Migrant From Poor Land.

reclamation project attracts many more applicants than can possibly be accommodated. With a change in other circumstances, such as the introduction of new types of land utilization and the development of markets for the products of a new type of agriculture as well as growing use of lands for recreational and residential purposes, there have been movements in many areas offsetting earlier evacuations.

Intensity of agricultural use and density of rural population are related not only to the available resources in the form of soil fertility, forests, minerals, water, etc., but also to the socio-economic organization for the utilization or exploitation of those resources. The fertile soils of the Corn Belt are supporting a far less dense population than the less hospitable slopes of the Southern Appalachians. Slow changes in the quality of land for agriculture through erosion and depletion are not likely to produce widespread migration. The gradual impoverishment which follows in their wake may ultimately lead to some migration or simply to the development of another stranded community. Only when efforts at adaptation are proved to be completely futile can any direct and large-scale migration be expected.

Disregarding such extremes, the relationships are somewhat less clear. It may be assumed that the land classification presented by the National Resources Board in 1934 represents not only conditions of that time but that lands for which withdrawal from agriculture was recommended then were generally poor during the entire decade before 1930. For the country as a whole the relation of rural migration to the quality of land as shown by this classification indicates that those counties classified as problem counties were somewhat more likely to have experienced net losses as a result of migration of the rural population between 1920 and 1930 than were those counties which were classified as nonproblem. The corresponding percentages were 87 and 82, respectively (table 19). Similar relationships were observed in most regions. The Far West was the only region in which as many as half of the counties reported gains by migration. If the counties losing population by migration are classified by the degree of loss, however, no clear relationship is found In some cases problem counties reported relatively large losses by migration, while in others their losses were slight.

In general, changes in the farm population between 1920 and 1930 were not related directly to land quality as measured by this method. Attention has been called, however, to the results of an analysis of the movement of farm population between 1930 and 1935 in relation to the quality of land.[3] During the depression years there was some tendency for farm population to increase on the poorest lands, but the most impressive aspect of the movement was the relative decline in the migration from farms in such areas. In contrast to the nonproblem

---

[3] See ch. II, p. 37.

Table 19.—Counties of the United States Gaining or Losing Rural Population by Migration, 1920–1930,[1] by Region [2] and Area

Region and area	Total counties		Counties gaining by migration		Counties losing by migration	
	Number	Percent	Number	Percent	Number	Percent
United States	3,059	100.0	517	16.9	2,542	83.1
Problem [3]	821	100.0	105	12.8	716	87.2
Nonproblem	2,238	100.0	412	18.4	1,826	81.6
Northeast	288	100.0	81	28.1	207	71.9
Problem	103	100.0	22	21.4	81	78.6
Nonproblem	185	100.0	59	31.9	126	68.1
Middle States	736	100.0	55	7.5	681	92.5
Problem	172	100.0	7	4.1	165	95.9
Nonproblem	564	100.0	48	8.5	516	91.5
Northwest	534	100.0	75	14.0	459	86.0
Problem	85	100.0	18	21.2	67	78.8
Nonproblem	449	100.0	57	12.7	392	87.3
Southeast	976	100.0	101	10.3	875	89.7
Problem	397	100.0	34	8.6	363	91.4
Nonproblem	579	100.0	67	11.6	512	88.4
Southwest	376	100.0	129	34.3	247	65.7
Problem	20	†	1	†	19	†
Nonproblem	356	100.0	128	36.0	228	64.0
Far West	149	100.0	76	51.0	73	49.0
Problem	44	†	23	†	21	†
Nonproblem	105	100.0	53	50.5	52	49.5

† Percent not computed on a base of fewer than 50 cases.

[1] For method of computation see appendix B.
[2] Regions are those used by Odum, Howard W., *Southern Regions of the United States*, Chapel Hill: University of North Carolina Press, 1936.
[3] Problem areas are those in which some or all of the farm land should be transferred to grazing, forests, or other conservational uses, according to the National Resources Board.

areas and to some of the best commercial agricultural lands, the natural increase and the failure to migrate were important factors in the growth in number of people on farms in the problem areas generally. The back-to-the-land movement was insufficient to account for the increases reported by the census, whereas in the nonproblem areas the reported increases were less than they would have been had the movement to farms been the only factor. The fact that migration from areas of poor land resources and of little economic and cultural opportunity has been relatively heavy should not obscure the fact that some of the better land areas have also contributed a large proportion of their rural population as migrants.

PROPORTION OF WORKERS IN AGRICULTURE

Despite the fact that the rural-farm population had a rate of natural increase larger than that of any other population group, it had a net loss of approximately 1,200,000 persons during the decade 1920–1930,[4] resulting from the net loss by migration of approximately 6,000,000 persons. Since this result was so largely due to the shrinking of the population base of agriculture, it is of interest to note that the most

[4] Bureau of the Census, *Fifteenth Census of the United States: 1930*, Population Vol. III, Part 1, U. S. Department of Commerce, Washington, D. C., 1932, p. 6.

agricultural counties contributed relatively more to this movement than did the counties with a smaller proportion of their population engaged in agriculture.

The greater the proportion of agricultural workers (table 20, fig.15, and appendix table 15) the more likely was the county to have had so large a net migration from its rural territory that it had fewer persons at the end than at the beginning of the decade. The proportion of the counties which gained rural population through migration was smallest in the most agricultural counties and greatest in the least agricultural counties. The proportion classified as counties of dispersion remained approximately the same except in the least agricultural group where it was less than in the other groups of counties. Thus, the more completely a county was devoted to agriculture the more likely it was to have experienced a heavy migration from its rural areas. The chief exceptions to the fact that those counties which had only a small proportion of their total population engaged in agriculture, especially in urban or manufacturing areas, were most likely to have gained rural population by migration were to be found in those agricultural areas in the Great Plains in which settlement was still going on during the 1920's. These were the areas in which the last phase of the homesteading of the West was being completed, but they accounted for only a small number of persons in comparison with the totals involved.

Table 20.—Counties of the United States by Percent of Gainful Workers 10 Years of Age and Over Engaged in Agriculture, 1930, and Type of Net Migration,[1] 1920–1930

Percent of gainful workers engaged in agriculture, 1930	Total counties		Type of net migration, 1920–1930		
	Number	Percent	Absorption	Dispersion	Depopulation
Total	3,059	100.0	16.9	32.5	50.6
Less than 10	188	100.0	54.8	22.3	22.9
10–24.9	401	100.0	34.7	31.9	33.4
25–49.9	899	100.0	15.7	33.8	50.5
50 or more	1,571	100.0	8.5	33.1	58.4

[1] For basis of classification of counties see ch. III, pp. 60–61.

Sources: Bureau of the Census, *Fifteenth Census of the United States: 1930*, Population Vol. II, ch. 10, table 16, and Vol. III, table 20, U. S. Department of Commerce, Washington, D. C.

Since the poor agricultural areas lost population by migration at a more rapid rate during the 1920's than did the better agricultural areas, it might be inferred that rural-urban migration during that period was part of the process of adjustment of numbers to natural resources. Those areas where depletion of natural resources or rapid population growth had produced maladjustments were the same ones in which rapid emigration was working toward the establishment of a more tolerable balance. It may be open to some question, however,

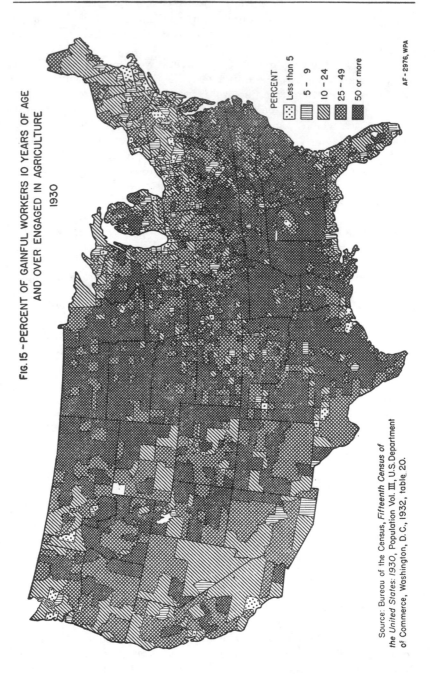

FIG. 15 — PERCENT OF GAINFUL WORKERS 10 YEARS OF AGE AND OVER ENGAGED IN AGRICULTURE

1930

PERCENT

Less than 5

5 – 9

10 – 24

25 – 49

50 or more

AF-2976, WPA

Source: Bureau of the Census, *Fifteenth Census of the United States: 1930*, Population Vol. III, U.S. Department of Commerce, Washington, D.C., 1932, table 20.

whether such migration is ever sufficient to correct maladjustments. The existence of numerous stranded communities is evidence of the difficulty of achieving a balance by this method.

AGRICULTURAL INCOME

In order to test further the relationship between migration and socio-economic factors, per capita agricultural income was used. For each county the total value of farm products sold, traded, or used by the operators' families in 1929 was divided by the total number of persons, male and female, who were gainful workers engaged in agriculture as reported by the 1930 Census (fig. 16 and appendix table 16). The direct relationship between agricultural income and migration while not close is statistically significant.[5]

EDUCATIONAL FACILITIES

The proportionate migration from rural areas does not appear to vary directly with the educational facilities which the various communities provide. Correlation of the proportion of 16- and 17-year olds attending school in 1930 with the rate of migration from rural areas was attempted, but no relationship, either positive or negative, could be established (appendix tables 12, 13, and 14). The map showing net migration from rural areas (fig. 6, p. 22) also suggests that educational facilities are not of primary importance in determining the rate of migration.

In Ohio, where areas of depopulation during the 1920's were to be found in both the western Corn Belt counties and the hill counties of the southeastern part of the State, only a slight relationship was found between the migration of the rural population and an index of educational facilities based on expenditures per rural pupil.[6] The northwestern part of the State had a combination of better land, higher income, superior schools, and more opportunities in agriculture than the southeastern section. The comparatively high rate of migration from the former was partly a result of the circumstance that the superior educational facilities gave the young people of that area familiarity with alternative opportunities and thus aided migration from rural areas. In the southeastern part of the State the rate of natural increase was considerably higher and, therefore, opportunities

---

[5] The coefficient of correlation is $+0.23 \pm 0.03$.

[6] Lively, C. E. and Almack, R. B., *A Method of Determining Rural Social Sub-Areas With Application to Ohio*, Bulletin No. 106, Parts I and II, Ohio Agricultural Experiment Station and Social Research Section, Farm Security Administration, Region III, Columbus, Ohio, January 1938, p. 9.

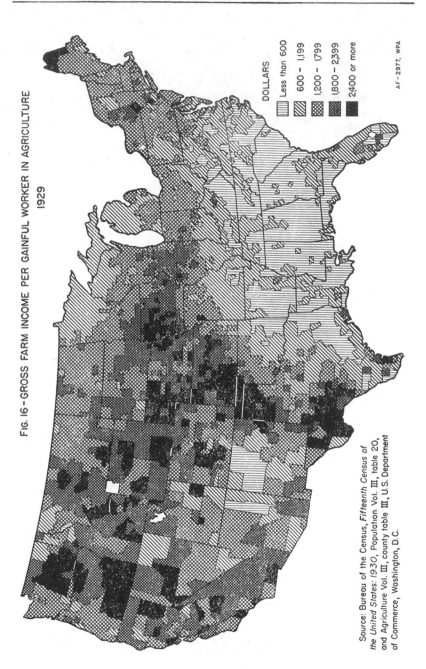

FIG. 16 – GROSS FARM INCOME PER GAINFUL WORKER IN AGRICULTURE
1929

DOLLARS

Less than 600
600 – 1,199
1,200 – 1,799
1,800 – 2,399
2400 or more

AF-2977, WPA

Source: Bureau of the Census, *Fifteenth Census of
the United States: 1930*, Population Vol. III, table 20,
and Agriculture Vol. III, county table III, U.S. Department
of Commerce, Washington, D.C.

in agriculture were more restricted.   Apparently this is also a situation that is favorable to heavy migration from rural areas.[7]

That educational opportunities may be closely related to the adjustments which the rural-urban migrants make at their destinations and that they may have a considerable influence on the contributions to society which they ultimately make is not called into question.   It may be that the migrants enter occupational and social strata in accordance with their training in the cities to which they go, the better trained entering business and professional groups in the larger proportions and the others becoming primarily unskilled laborers.[8]

PLANE OF LIVING INDEX

Measures of the economic well-being of the population suggest further that there is no simple relationship between the rate of migration and the presence or absence of a given level of income.   Persons living in areas which provide only limited incomes may be willing to migrate because a small income at the point of destination offers enough of a differential to make the move attractive.   On the other hand, young people who have grown up on farms providing a relatively high level of living may have frequent occasion to compare their lot with that of urban residents and desire certain advantages which cities seem to afford.

In order to secure a measure of economic well-being, a plane of living index was constructed to take into account the extent to which rural families in all counties possessed certain facilities generally considered desirable.   It is assumed that most families live in the best house they can afford and provide themselves with modern conveniences to the extent which their incomes over a period of years will permit.   If this is correct, it is fair to assume that a plane of living index is a measure of economic well-being, albeit not a perfect one. For both rural-farm and nonfarm families it was possible to secure the estimated value of dwellings and the proportion of homes having a radio.   For rural farm families, in addition, information was available concerning the proportions having a telephone, electric lights, an

---

[7] The loss by migration, expressed as a percent of the total population in 1920, may underemphasize the loss in certain age groups.   For the United States as a whole 41 percent of the total persons in the rural-farm population aged 15–19 in 1920 migrated during the following decade.   A rate of migration based on all age groups in the population will have a somewhat different significance in a population in which this most mobile age group is 10 percent of the total and one in which it is 15 percent of the total.

[8] Leybourne, Grace G., "Urban Adjustments of Migrants From the Southern Appalachian Plateaus," *Social Forces*, Vol. 16, 1937, pp. 238–246.

automobile, and running water in the house.[9]   The several parts of the country can be differentiated by means of such an index into areas of varying degrees of economic well-being (figs. 17 and 18).

When the counties were grouped according to the rural plane of living index (table 21 and appendix tables 17 and 18), it was found that as the rural plane of living index decreased, with one exception, the net rate of migration from rural areas increased.[10]   This would indicate that there was more migration from the poorer rural areas than from the more prosperous ones, although apparently numerous counties are exceptions to the indicated relationship.   Nevertheless, the general contention that migration during 1920–1930 was disproportionately greater from the poorer areas is supported by the data.

Table 21.—Rural Plane of Living Index,[1] 1930,[2] and Net Rural Migration, 1920–1930 [3]

Rural plane of living index, 1930	Rural population, 1920	Percent net rural migration, 1920–1930
Total	[4] 51,368,088	−11.0
Less than 30	5,815,647	−17.4
30–59	12,445,516	−16.1
60–89	6,066,293	−13.6
90–119	6,449,531	−15.0
120–149	6,696,914	−11.0
150–179	6,849,759	−8.0
180–209	3,551,029	−0.8
210 or more	3,493,399	+13.8

[1] Computed on a county basis.
[2] Bureau of the Census, *Fifteenth Census of the United States: 1930*, Population Vol. VI and Agriculture Vol. II, U. S. Department of Commerce, Washington, D. C.
[3] For method of computation see appendix B.
[4] Excluding Hudson County, N. J., and Yellowstone National Park.

DISTANCE TO CITIES AND SUBURBAN DEVELOPMENT

Opportunity for contact with urban areas appears to bear some relationship to the rate of migration to or from rural areas.   In order to examine this relationship further all counties were classified with reference to the distance of the major part of their area from the nearest city with a population of 100,000 or more.   Three classifications were set up—less than 50 miles, 50–99 miles, and 100 miles or more (table 22).   It is admitted that such a measure is not an adequate one if it is intended to show the effective distance from a large city, for air-line distance is not a good measure of the channels of communication.   If migration from rural to urban areas depends on opportunities, the frequency and intimacy of contacts with the prospective residence may be more important than distance.   Proximity to cities

[9] For a description of the development of the index see appendix B.   Two of these items, telephone and electric lights, are more readily available where population density is greater.   The index is especially high in areas near cities, which are also the areas most likely to gain by migration.
[10] The coefficient of correlation is $+0.25 \pm 0.03$.

is related to migration also by virtue of the fact that during the twenties there was a marked suburban development, and some of the counties reporting increases by migration were essentially suburban areas. The nearby counties (less than 50 miles from cities) less frequently experienced losses by migration and those which did report losses were more likely to report a relatively smaller loss than the more distant counties.

Table 22.—Counties of the United States Gaining or Losing Rural Population by Migration, 1920–1930,[1] by Distance From a City

Distance from a city	Total counties		Counties gaining by migration		Counties losing by migration	
	Number	Percent	Number	Percent	Number	Percent
Total	3,059	100.0	517	16.9	2,542	83.1
Less than 50 miles from a large city [2]	795	100.0	181	22.8	614	77.2
50–99 miles from a large city	945	100.0	100	10.6	845	89.4
100 miles or more from a large city	1,319	100.0	236	17.9	1,083	82.1
Less than 50 miles from a small city [2]	379	100.0	60	15.8	319	84.2
50–99 miles from a small city	466	100.0	59	12.7	407	87.3
100 miles or more from a small city	474	100.0	117	24.7	357	75.3

[1] For method of computation see appendix B.
[2] Large city—100,000 or more; small city—25,000–99,999.

The relationships found by this analysis suggest that in most cases the larger cities have little effect upon the rate of rural migration beyond a distance of 100 miles. The counties within the 50–99 mile zone showed net losses from rural migration more frequently than those nearby, but beyond that distance no clear relationship could be established. In order to test further the relationship between rate of migration and distance, the counties which were 100 miles or more from a large city were subdivided with reference to their distance from a smaller city, 1 having between 25,000 and 100,000 inhabitants. The same distance categories were used, but in this case no clear and consistent relationship could be established. Those counties nearest the smaller cities appeared to show a slight tendency to gain through rural migration, but the differences found could not be regarded as statistically significant.

Another way in which the volume of rural migration may be related to proximity to large cities is through the attraction of people to the rural areas adjacent to large cities. The 1930 Census outlined 96 metropolitan areas, including 1 or more central cities of 50,000 or more, as well as adjacent or contiguous minor civil divisions with a density of 150 or more per square mile.[11] The number of people living in these areas in 1930 was equal to nearly half of the total population. One-seventh of the population of these areas was classi-

[11] Bureau of the Census, *Fifteenth Census of the United States: 1930*, Population Vol. II, U. S. Department of Commerce, Washington, D. C., 1933, pp. 16–19.

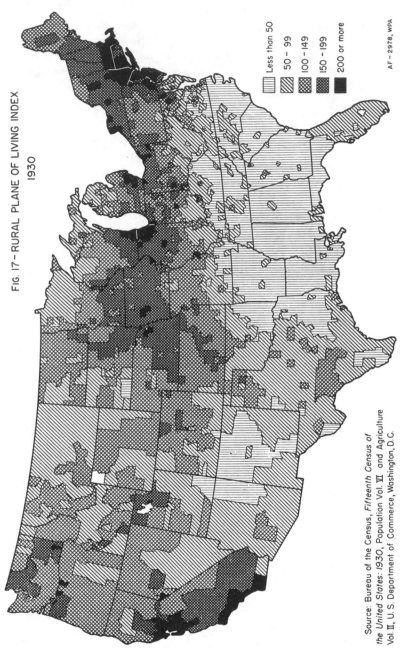

FIG. 17—RURAL PLANE OF LIVING INDEX
1930

Less than 50
50 – 99
100 – 149
150 – 199
200 or more

AF – 2978, WPA

Source: Bureau of the Census, *Fifteenth Census of the United States: 1930*, Population Vol. VI and Agriculture Vol. II, U. S. Department of Commerce, Washington, D.C.

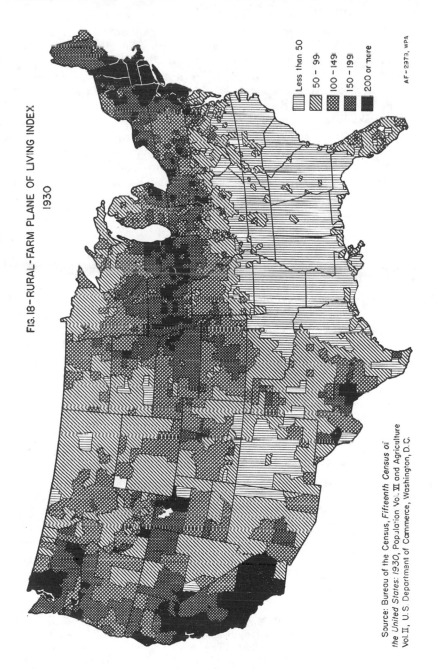

FIG. 18 – RURAL-FARM PLANE OF LIVING INDEX
1930

Less than 50
50 – 99
100 – 149
150 – 199
200 or more

AF – 2373, WPA

Source: Bureau of the Census, *Fifteenth Census of
the United States: 1930*, Population Vol. II and Agriculture
Vol. II, U.S. Department of Commerce, Washington, D.C.

fied as rural. The rural population in these metropolitan districts reported a remarkable increase between 1920 and 1930, having grown by 54.8 percent or more rapidly than any other part of the metropolitan population except small cities.[12] Part of this gain by migration was probably at the expense of the remainder of the counties in which these areas are located. The increase for the entire rural population during the decade was only 4.7 percent.[13]

The very high rate of migration into suburban areas is the result of two types of movement. The one consists of former rural residents who are coming to the vicinity of the city. The other represents former city residents who have changed their domicile from the city to its periphery.[14] This suburban trend, which has been an important element in the growth of cities, promises to continue to be of major importance.

RELIEF RATES

Further evidence concerning factors associated with rural migration is found in the relation of relief rates after 1930 to rural migration during the 10 years preceding that date (table 23). Relief rates for the total population from July 1934 through June 1935 can only partially reflect chronic situations in the rural parts of those areas, however, as financial and administrative factors affect relief rates from area to area as well as relative intensity of need. Moreover, relief rates are subject to fluctuations resulting from acute conditions whose onset may be sudden, such as the drought during 1934. Since droughts exert their major influence upon agricultural areas and these, as shown above, are likely to have experienced a heavy loss by migration, a relationship might be expected.

About 6 percent of the rural population, more than 3,000,000 persons, lived in counties in which the average relief load amounted to 30 percent or more during the year July 1934–June 1935. Many of these counties are very poor, as measured by other criteria, and it is safe to say that the unusually high relief rates reflected an especially difficult economic situation which in many instances was chronic.

This same group of counties experienced a greater net migration from rural areas than any group in which the relief rates were less, the net rural migration being equal to 21 percent of the 1920 population. For the groups of counties in which relief rates were less than 30 percent, the net rural migration rates were approximately 10 percent.

[12] All areas classified as rural in 1920 included as rural in 1930. Thompson, Warren S. and Whelpton, P. K., *Population Trends in the United States*, New York: McGraw-Hill Book Company, Inc., 1933, p. 30.

[13] Corrected for underenumeration. The census figure is also 4.7 percent.

[14] For a description of the suburbanization movement see Whetten, N. L. and Devereux, E. C., Jr., *Studies of Suburbanization in Connecticut, 1. Windsor,* Bulletin 212, Storrs Agricultural Experiment Station, Storrs, Conn., October 1936.

Table 23.—Relief Rates,[1] July 1934–June 1935,[2] and Net Rural Migration, 1920–1930[3]

Percent on relief (monthly average—July 1934–June 1935)	Rural population, 1920	Percent net rural migration, 1920–1930
Total_____	51,406,017	−11.0
Less than 7.5_____	9,932,904	−10.9
7.5–14.9_____	21,578,081	−10.3
15.0–29.9_____	10,555,999	0.0
30.0 or more_____	3,339,033	−20.9

[1] Average monthly number of resident persons receiving aid under the general relief program (direct relief and emergency work relief) computed on a county basis. Rates based on the 1930 general population.
[2] Bureau of Foreign and Domestic Commerce, *Consumer Market Data Handbook: 1936*, U. S. Department of Commerce, Washington, D. C., table B.
[3] For method of computation see appendix B.

In so far as this comparison is valid, that is, in so far as these relief rates measure chronic maladjustments, they suggest the difficulty of achieving adjustments through unplanned migration from rural areas. The areas with high rates of migration, equivalent to more than one-fifth of the 1920 rural population moving away, were most in need of Federal aid after 1930. No estimate can be made of what would have happened had migration not taken place. It does appear clear from this comparison that the relatively heavy migration was not sufficient to effect basic readjustments of numbers to natural resources.

SUBJECTIVE FACTORS INFLUENCING MIGRATION

It is ordinarily assumed that the conditions of living influence migration and that when problems are sufficiently acute in any area people will move to some place where conditions of living are considered more nearly adequate. That a certain amount of migration occurs because people leave their former residences when conditions become intolerable cannot be denied. But such cases are relatively rare, and there are few rural areas so poor that there are not some people at some time who are willing to live there. The evaluation of relative opportunities is essentially a subjective matter, and no arbitrary evaluation of opportunities or desirable levels of living is likely to meet with widespread acceptance. To meet the difficulty which this fact imposes, it has been urged that the public in some cases is justified in taking measures for the evacuation of certain areas as a matter of policy.[15] Even if agreement upon a program of evacuation could be secured, past experience indicates that the general characteristics of the areas selected for settlement because of better economic opportunities should be as nearly like the characteristics of the areas of original residence as possible.

A statement of the complicated motives which are in operation when people move would probably have to deal primarily with differentials.

[15] See, for example, Wehrwein, George S. and Baker, J. A., "The Cost of Isolated Settlement in Northern Wisconsin," *Rural Sociology*, Vol. 2, 1937, pp. 253–265.

People do not move primarily because the level of living in the area where they are is low but rather because they have become aware of a different level of living which appears more attractive. The realization that another area offers better opportunities may come about through a marked difference between conditions at one time and another, as through a major catastrophe like the recent droughts. In the affected areas there is such a marked decline in income within a short period of time that there is active dissatisfaction and a search for something better. Migration from the area may take place even though the level of living is not lower than that prevailing in some other areas where the lower level has been maintained for some time. The controlling element in the decision whether or not to move may not be the objective reality; rather it may be the individual's subjective evaluation of the various alternatives which he is considering.

As a result migration occurs not only from rural areas of relatively little opportunity; the areas which appear to offer better opportunities, such as the Corn Belt, have also experienced considerable out-migration. Here the prospective migrant compares what appears to be a rather desirable situation with the level of living prevailing elsewhere, frequently in an urban area. Thus, rural areas which provide many of the opportunities and facilities that are ordinarily associated with urban areas appear to lose migrants in as great volume, relative to their natural increase, as those areas which have few or none of these advantages. The former apparently enable their residents constantly to compare their condition with that prevailing elsewhere and thus to develop and maintain an awareness of the differentials which do exist. In the latter there is a much more limited range of opportunity for the study of comparative advantages. Although the desire to secure a larger income for the energy expended, to secure greater security, etc., are important, the comparisons obviously are not cast entirely in economic terms. Leisure time, gregariousness, prestige, freedom from primary group restraints, the glamour of the city, and more extensive community facilities are some of the factors which have always motivated rural-urban migrations as well as migrations from one rural area to another. Decreased employment opportunities at the present place of residence, as through the increased use of farm machinery, changes in the customs of retirement and transmission of property to the next generation, or changed ownership or tenure relations may exert a powerful influence in the weighing of opportunities. But the choice preceding migration is not always a rational one, involving a careful balancing of alternative opportunities. Frequently it consists of a comparison of poorly defined alternatives, and chance may play a large part in the final outcome. Hence, important crosscurrents of migration constantly occur.

The distinction between the relative importance of elements that "push" people out of certain areas and of those which "pull" them to other areas has some significance for any program that involves the movement of people from one area to another. Local pride and identification with the local community act as powerful reinforcements to the desire to remain in a particular locality, and it may be futile to wait until conditions become so bad that "people will just have to move." On the other hand, the presentation of alternative opportunities which offer a better living in those terms which are currently accepted in the area would probably have a much greater chance of success. In areas in which there is a tradition of stability of residence, there has also been developed an adaptation to resources or absence of resources. Since a large segment of the farm and rural-nonfarm population has made this adjustment, it may be necessary to modify quick judgments concerning the need for migration and to examine further the possibilities of better utilization of available economic resources as well as improved training and educational facilities. Unless improvement of the status of the persons encouraged to migrate can be assured, it would perhaps be better to consider other means of alleviation of unsatisfactory local conditions.

While it may be assumed that many rural migrants leave the country to escape from what they regard as unsatisfactory conditions at home, it may also be assumed that many leave because they are drawn toward what appear to be more desirable conditions elsewhere. Traditionally, the American people have believed that one should not merely accept his station in life but should attempt to improve it. Hence, it is probable that the relatively high rate of mobility of the population is related to this social philosophy as well as to the ready access to easy means of communication and transportation. Farm families have been eager to send one or more sons into the professions; captains of industry have been national heroes; and the schools have suggested to pupils the possibility of achieving the presidency of the republic. Fiction and biography have told the stories of poor boys who rose to wealth and power, usually in the city. It is small wonder, therefore, that the quest has resulted in unprecedented internal migration in the direction of urban areas.

The "pull" of cities for rural youth may fairly be expressed in terms of the fact that the city is a place of jobs, of wealth and power, of adventure, and of restless activity and endless variety. It draws most heavily upon nearby territory regardless of the condition of agriculture within that territory though the range of its "pull" has been greatly extended with modern communication facilities. Historically, in times of depressed agricultural conditions the volume of rural-urban migration has tended to increase, giving rise to the theory that agricultural depression always accentuates migration away from the farms. Recent experience, however, has demonstrated that urban depression coincident with agricultural depression may result in a definite decrease in the volume of rural-urban migration, even to the extent of reversing the net rural-urban trend if rural areas seem to offer greater opportunities than depressed urban areas. Even so, the movement toward the city does not cease. The stream flows on, although the net movement may dwindle to relatively small proportions.

The movement in the direction of apparent opportunity does not proceed with any high degree of precision. Only at certain times and in certain places is the location of opportunity fairly obvious to any considerable number of people. Furthermore, as a result of movement and experience the standards of the individual with respect to what constitutes opportunity tend to change. There is scarcely an employment opportunity which someone is not ready to take. Many people accept what appears to be opportunity, and, upon finding that it is not what it appeared to be, they search elsewhere. Secondary migration may be the result of finding another opportunity that appears to be superior to the first. Hence, we have people migrating westward while others are migrating eastward, and people migrating from country to city while others are migrating from city to country. Thus, a large amount of internal movement may occur with relatively little net change in the distribution of population.

BACKGROUND FACTORS PART OF LARGER COMPLEX

The absence of simple and clear relationships between volume of rural migration and selected socio-economic factors does not prove the absence of such relationships. It indicates rather that the background factors which are frequently considered to be of major importance are only part of a larger complex and that the influence of any one of them may be modified or offset by the effect of others. The major conclusion that can be drawn is that simple generalizations, alleging uniform relationships between rural migration and conditions in the rural areas affected, are not possible. Nor is the correlation between volume of migration and general business conditions a perfect one. Urban prosperity while agriculture is relatively depressed undoubtedly is a condition favoring large-scale rural-urban migrations. What urban and rural areas will be affected most and why the effects vary as they do, however, depend on the interaction of numerous subtle factors whose influence is purely individual or local.[16]

---

[16] Heberle, Rudolf and Meyer, Fritz, *Die Groszstädte im Strome der Binnenwanderung*, Leipzig: S. Hirzel, 1937.

Some Move East While Some Move West.

The poverty of an area may serve to encourage migration by impelling comparisons with other areas having superior opportunities. On the other hand, its very poverty means that the younger generation is less well equipped to enter the competition of modern industry and thus it may serve as a barrier to migration. Not only does lack of knowledge of opportunities interfere with ready adjustments but there is also an unwillingness or an inability to accept certain current notions of desirable status or achievements. Some of the poorest areas are also those in which there is a tradition of stable residence, of family solidarity, of an unwillingness to move, and of an extremely low regard for the traditional canons of material success.[17]

---

[17] Zimmerman, Carle C. and Frampton, M. E., *Family and Society*, New York: D. Van Nostrand Company, Inc., 1935, pp. 185–188.

Chapter V

RURAL MIGRATION IN SELECTED AREAS

DATA ON the volume and direction of migration, such as have been presented in preceding chapters, are usefully supplemented by more intensive studies which focus attention upon the migrants themselves and their successive migrations. From such studies it is possible to gain a more complete account of certain aspects of mobility than can be gained from a comparison of conditions at the beginning and at the end of a given period. Because considerable interest is attached to the migrations of the rural population since the 1930 Census, comparable studies of rural population movements were carried on in eight States [1] during 1935 and 1936. In each State the selection of sample areas and the size of the sample were determined by local needs, interests, and resources.[2] The scattered studies have shown considerable uniformity in their results, and it is believed to be of some value to indicate the similarities and differences

---

[1] All of these surveys, whether conducted under the Works Progress Administration, Farm Security Administration, or Bureau of Agricultural Economics, used the schedule and instructions prepared by the authors of this monograph when they were members of the research staff of the Federal Emergency Relief Administration. Reports have been published by Lively, C. E. and Foott, Frances, *Population Mobility in Selected Areas of Rural Ohio, 1928-1935*, Bulletin 582, Ohio Agricultural Experiment Station, Wooster, Ohio, June 1937; Kumlien, W. F., McNamara, Robert L., and Bankert, Zetta E., *Rural Population Mobility in South Dakota*, Bulletin 315, South Dakota Agricultural Experiment Station, Brookings, S. Dak., January 1938; and Dodson, L. S., *Living Conditions and Population Migration in Four Appalachian Counties*, Social Research Report No. III, U. S. Department of Agriculture, Farm Security Administration and Bureau of Agricultural Economics, Washington, D. C., October 1937. Reports are in preparation for Arizona, Iowa, Maryland, and North Dakota by members of the staffs of the respective experiment stations. The data for the Arizona sample were not available in time to be used in this report.

[2] See appendix B for areas sampled.

in the findings. The totals for the eight samples obviously give too much weight to some areas. Nevertheless, they possess the justification that they are convenient ways of stating the tendencies revealed by the data for individual areas.

The field surveys of rural population mobility secured information concerning the residence history of each family head over a period of years.[3] In selecting the aspects of residential mobility which were to be included in the surveys, an attempt was made to include only changes in residence of a relatively permanent nature. It seemed desirable to limit the moves to be included still further in order to eliminate short distance movements which were probably unimportant from the standpoint of the person's integration with the social organization of the community in which he lived. Since no method was available for measuring directly the degree to which social bonds are affected, it was necessary to assume that the distance covered by a move could be used as an index of the probability that the move was of some significance. As a practical approximation to a measure of distance the arbitrary limits of minor civil divisions were used,[4] and only those migrations which involved a change of residence from one minor civil division [5] to another were recorded.[6] Obviously family heads who had moved out of the areas surveyed could not be included.

In using the limited definition it was found that there was relatively little mobility in rural sample areas. Nearly three-fourths (73 percent) of the heads of families had not moved at all during the survey period (table 24). In the sample areas in Maryland and North Dakota 80 percent of the family heads had not moved during the 10 years preceding January 1, 1936. Areas in Iowa yielded the smallest proportion of family heads reporting no movement, 71 percent not having moved within the 7 years preceding January 1, 1935.

There were relatively slight differences between village and open country family heads in regard to the proportions which had moved, and the differences were not consistent. Apparently, among the families residing in the sample areas at the time of the surveys, village residents had moved almost as infrequently as open country residents.

---

[3] January 1, 1928, to January 1, 1935, in Iowa, Ohio, and South Dakota; January 1, 1926, to January 1, 1936, in Kentucky, Maryland, North Carolina, and North Dakota.

[4] Lively, C. E., "Spatial Mobility of the Rural Population With Respect to Local Areas," *The American Journal of Sociology*, Vol. XLIII, 1937, pp. 89–102.

[5] This term is used here to include incorporated as well as unincorporated villages and open country townships.

[6] If a person moved into or out of any village, town, or city, the move was counted. Similarly, if he moved from one township to another in the open country, the move was counted. Changes of residence from one open country place to another within the same township or from one place to another within the same village, town, or city, however, were omitted.

Table 24.—Heads of Families Reporting Continuous Residence During the Period of Survey,[1] by Area and Residence

Area	All heads of families		Residence			
			Open country		Village	
	Total	Percent with continuous residence	Total	Percent with continuous residence	Total	Percent with continuous residence
Total	20,033	73	12,280	75	7,753	70
Iowa [2]	1,902	71	1,319	68	583	77
Kentucky	632	72	526	78	106	67
Maryland	1,813	80	711	80	1,102	79
North Carolina	495	76	408	78	87	63
North Dakota	443	80	339	83	104	72
Ohio [3]	2,364	74	1,676	73	688	75
South Dakota	12,384	72	7,301	75	5,083	67

[1] January 1, 1928, to January 1, 1935, in Iowa, Ohio, and South Dakota; January 1, 1926, to January 1, 1930, in Kentucky, Maryland, North Carolina, and North Dakota.
[2] 4 counties only.
[3] Families established throughout period only.

Similar results were obtained by comparing county of residence with county where reared.[7] Of all persons in the sample areas who were 16 years of age and over, approximately one-half were living in the same county in which they had been reared.[8] There was considerable variation among the sample counties in this respect, however. In Custer, Haakon, and Tripp Counties in western South Dakota only one-third of the persons interviewed had been reared in the county in which they were then living. In the older parts of South Dakota, such as Turner County, two-thirds of the youth and adults had been reared in the county in which they were living at the time of the survey. In the older communities in the Appalachian Mountains the proportions which had been reared in the county of residence varied between 71 and 89 percent. In nearly every instance the proportions were higher for persons living in the open country than for those living in villages. Thus, it seems certain that the oldest and most isolated areas have had the greatest degree of population stability.

FREQUENCY OF RESIDENCE CHANGES BY HEADS OF FAMILIES

The frequency of residence changes may be more significant in relation to population mobility than distance of migration. As cultural differences become less distinct throughout the country, radical changes in environment following long-distance migrations

[7] Data on file in the U. S. Department of Agriculture, Bureau of Agricultural Economics, Washington, D. C.
[8] Place reared was defined as the place where the individual lived longest between the ages of 8 and 16. For a discussion of the extent to which the county in which an individual was born was also the county in which he was reared, see Lively, C. E., "Note on Relation of Place-of-Birth to Place-Where-Reared," *Rural Sociology*, Vol. 2, 1937, pp. 332–333.

are less frequent. The new location may be similar in many respects to the last residence. A household moving from the open country to a nearby village may experience a greater change in its economic and social environment than would occur as a result of migration to a distant open country place. Hence, mobility should be studied with reference to the number or frequency of moves as well as with reference to the distance migrated.

Of the heads of households who had changed residence at some time during the period of survey, the great majority (71 percent) had moved only once (table 28, p. 91). One-fourth (25 percent) had moved two or three times while very few had moved as many as four times.

On the average, the male heads of families who had changed residence during the period of survey had moved only 1.4 times (table 25). Changes were most numerous in the Kentucky counties where family heads who had moved reported an average of 1.8 changes in residence. In most areas open country heads of families who had changed residence had moved at least as frequently if not more frequently than village heads.

Table 25.—Average Number of Changes in Residence by Male Heads of Families [1] During the Period of Survey,[2] by Area and Residence in 1935–1936

Area	Total	Residence	
		Open country	Village
Total [3]	1.4	1.5	1.4
Iowa	1.4	1.4	1.3
Kentucky	1.8	1.9	1.7
Maryland	1.6	1.5	1.7
North Carolina	1.7	1.8	1.6
North Dakota	1.5	1.4	1.5
Ohio	1.4	1.4	1.4
South Dakota	1.4	1.5	1.4

[1] Exclusive of male heads of families not changing residence and unknowns.
[2] January 1, 1928, to January 1, 1935, in Iowa, Ohio, and South Dakota; January 1, 1926, to January 1, 1936, in Kentucky, Maryland, North Carolina, and North Dakota.
[3] In the Ohio counties, Tripp County, S. Dak., and all but 4 Iowa counties families established after 1928 are excluded.

Residence changes are affected by such factors as occupation and type of residence. For example, although there were some exceptions, in general farm operators had changed their residence less frequently than heads of families employed at nonfarm work.[9] Male heads of families living in villages had changed their occupation slightly more often than their residence, and those living in the open country had changed residence more frequently than occupation (tables 25 and 26). In the Maryland sample, however, the heads of families in the open country had changed residence less frequently than occupation. This reflects the fact that living in the open

[9] See pp. 112–116.

Table 26.—Average Number of Changes in Occupation by Male Heads of Families[1] During the Period of Survey,[2] by Area and Residence in 1935–1936

Area	Total	Residence	
		Open country	Village
Total [3]	1.5	1.4	1.5
Iowa	1.2	1.2	1.3
Kentucky	1.8	1.8	2.1
Maryland	1.7	1.7	1.7
North Carolina	1.5	1.5	1.5
North Dakota	1.4	1.3	1.5
Ohio	1.7	1.4	2.0
South Dakota	1.4	1.4	1.5

[1] Exclusive of male heads of families not changing occupation and unknowns.
[2] January 1, 1928, to January 1, 1935, in Iowa, Ohio, and South Dakota; January 1, 1926, to January 1, 1936, in Kentucky, Maryland, North Carolina, and North Dakota.
[3] In the Ohio counties, Tripp County, S. Dak., and all but 4 Iowa counties families established after 1928 are excluded.

country is not synonymous with employment in agriculture. In North Carolina, on the other hand, changes in residence of family heads living in villages at the time of the survey had been more frequent than occupational changes.

RANGE OF MIGRATION OF HEADS OF FAMILIES

Physical distance of itself is not the primary factor in migration. The emphasis upon its importance ordinarily rests on the assumption that the intensity of social ties is in inverse ratio to physical distance. It cannot be concluded, however, that a 50- or 100-mile migration involves less change in the environment than a 1,000-mile migration or that intrastate migrations involve less important changes than do interstate migrations. A short-distance migration may involve as definite a break in the social ties of a neighborhood, school, church, or occupational group as a long-distance move. On the other hand, long-distance migration may involve more largely a physical transfer of residence than a major severance of social ties. When a person moves as part of a larger group, the major shift may be that of the location of the group's activities. Many individuals, though physically remote from an area of previous residence, are much more a part of the social groups of the earlier than of the later residence.

Among the heads of families in the survey areas who had moved at some time during the period of study, short-distance migrations predominated. Twelve percent of all family heads, or almost one-half of those who had moved, had come from another residence within the same county, six percent had come from adjoining counties, and smaller proportions had migrated from greater distances (table 27).

The method of determining distance moved corresponds roughly to actual measurement in terms of miles from the survey area as a center, although the correspondence is necessarily affected by accidents of location of survey areas.[10]   These location factors may actually make an adjoining State nearer than nonadjoining counties in the same State.   Such discrepancies affect the results, and some variation from the general pattern of decreasing migration with increasing distance does occur.   In the Maryland and North Carolina sample areas, for example, the proportions coming from nonadjoining counties in the same State were less than the proportions coming from adjoining States (table 27).   Also, the fact that county or State boundaries often do not determine lines of contact or transportation is well known.   In Kentucky, for example, more migrants came from distant areas within the State than from counties adjoining the survey areas.   In addition, factors, such as the location of relatives or friends and the reported existence of employment opportunities, may cause variations in the general pattern.

Table 27.—Range of Migration of Heads of Households [1] During the Period of Survey,[2] by Area

Range of migration	Total	Area						
		Iowa	Kentucky	Maryland	North Carolina	North Dakota	Ohio	South Dakota
Total: [3]								
Number_____	20,988	3,844	581	1,694	474	429	2,292	11,674
Percent_____	100	100	100	100	100	100	100	100
Continuous residence_____	74	74	73	80	76	81	74	73
Lived in county of survey and in:								
No other county_____	12	15	6	6	9	7	11	12
Adjoining counties only_____	6	5	3	8	4	4	8	6
Other counties in State_____	4	3	8	*	3	3	4	5
Adjoining States only_____	3	2	8	4	4	3	2	3
Other States_____	1	1	2	2	4	2	1	1

*Less than 0.5 percent.

[1] The slight differences by States between tables 24 and 27 are due to the fact that one is based on families and the other on households.   The complete Iowa sample is included in this table.
[2] January 1, 1928, to January 1, 1935, in Iowa, Ohio, and South Dakota; January 1, 1926, to January 1, 1936, in Kentucky, Maryland, North Carolina, and North Dakota.
[3] Exclusive of migrants from foreign countries, households established after 1928, and unknowns.

Range of migration is also related to the frequency with which changes of residence are made.   As the frequency of change of residence increased, the proportion which had moved from places within the survey area or from adjoining counties generally decreased.   Thus, the previous location of families with one change of residence was somewhere within the county of survey in approximately one-half of the cases (table 28).   Among families moving five times or more, however, nearly two-fifths came from adjoining States.   Factors which limited or reduced the number of changes of residence apparently operated to limit the range of movement also.

[10] Lively, C. E., "Spatial Mobility of the Rural Population With Respect to Local Areas," *op. cit.*, pp. 96–98.

Table 28.—Number of Changes in Residence of Heads of Families During the Period of Survey,[1] by Range of Migration

Number of changes in residence	Total		Lived in county of survey and in—					
	Number	Percent	No other county	Adjoining counties only	Other counties in State	Adjoining States only	Other States	Other[2]
Total [3]_____	17, 196	100. 0	85. 2	5. 8	4. 0	3. 3	1. 6	0. 1
None_____	12, 682	100. 0	100. 0	—	—	—	—	—
1_____	3, 203	100. 0	49. 5	22. 3	13. 4	9. 9	4. 6	0. 3
2_____	882	100. 0	32. 1	21. 3	19. 8	17. 6	8. 5	0. 7
3_____	267	100. 0	25. 5	27. 7	19. 8	16. 8	9. 4	0. 8
4_____	108	100. 0	21. 3	17. 6	22. 2	22. 2	16. 7	—
5 or more_____	54	100. 0	7. 1	13. 0	16. 7	38. 9	22. 2	1. 8

[1] January 1, 1926, to January 1, 1935, in Iowa and South Dakota; January 1, 1926, to January 1, 1936, in Kentucky, Maryland, North Carolina, and North Dakota.
[2] Includes migrants from foreign countries and unknowns.
[3] Exclusive of the Ohio counties and all but 4 Iowa counties.

Possibly there is a tendency for families moving frequently to move farther at each move. The fact that several moves have already broken through former social ties weakens the influence of the community and facilitates the movement over greater distances. The family has either learned to adjust rapidly to the social environments in the new locations or to become less dependent upon social relationships outside the household. The influence of social relationships often is a strong factor in reducing the frequency and the distance of migration by forming a bond that families hesitate to break. The economic advantages to be gained from more remunerative employment in another locality are weighed against the advantages of existing social relationships. The effectiveness of such relationships undoubtedly is directly influenced by length of residence, inasmuch as brief tenure in a community is not conducive to the building of numerous or strong social ties.[11]

TYPES OF RESIDENCE CHANGES BY HEADS OF FAMILIES AND ALL PERSONS 16 YEARS OF AGE AND OVER

Among the male heads of families surveyed who had made residence changes, there was wide variation in the types of changes reported.[12] The most frequent movements consisted of the migration from one open country residence to another, movements of this type comprising 40 percent of all changes in residence which were noted (fig. 19). This shifting consisted primarily of farm families moving from one open country residence to another, with tenants somewhat more

[11] Eugenics Survey of Vermont, *Selective Migration From Three Rural Vermont Towns and Its Significance,* Fifth Annual Report, University of Vermont, Burlington, Vt., September 1931, p. 31.
[12] In surveys, such as these, it is possible to include only persons living in the areas at the time of the surveys. Persons who have moved out of the areas obviously cannot be included.

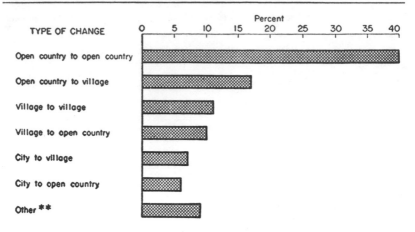

FIG. 19 – MALE HEADS OF FAMILIES REPORTING A CHANGE IN
RESIDENCE* DURING THE PERIOD OF SURVEY
BY TYPE OF CHANGE

*Exclusive of those reporting continuous residence.

**Includes those moving more than once, migrants
from foreign countries, and unknowns.

AF - 2981, WPA

numerous than owners. The second largest movement was from the
open country to villages. This movement was particularly marked
in the survey areas of South Dakota,[13] where a series of poor crops in
recent years had forced many families from their farms. Most of the
families which moved within the State went to nearby villages.

There was slightly more frequent moving between villages than from
villages to open country areas. This was much more pronounced in
South Dakota than in the other States, while in Kentucky a strong
counter movement from villages to the open country was found. The
movement in South Dakota was affected by the poor crop seasons
mentioned above, while the situation in Kentucky no doubt resulted
from decreasing nonfarm employment in villages.

The movements from city to open country and from city to village
were numerically the least important types of migration. One factor
in reducing the number of these shifts in residence was the fact that
they frequently involved long distances as well as the change from
urban to rural environments. In Ohio it was found that the villages
were areas of concentration, receiving population from both the open
country and urban centers.[14] The proportion of the population living
in the villages in the sample areas in 1929 was greater than the pro-

---

[13] Data on file in the U. S. Department of Agriculture, Bureau of Agricultural
Economics, Washington, D. C.

[14] Lively. C. E. and Foott, Frances, *op. cit.*, p. 12.

portion reared there and was greater in 1935 than in 1929. The movement from city to open country was marked only in Kentucky and North Carolina.

Another indication of the type of movements is found in a comparison of place of residence at the time of the surveys and on January 1, 1929, by place reared [15] for all persons 16 years of age and over. A total of 1,037 persons who had moved from city to open country was reported (table 29). One-third of these had been reared in the open country in the county of survey. There were, however, wide fluctuations in the proportions reported from the various areas.

Table 29.—Type of Movement of Persons 16 Years of Age and Over at Date of Survey Between January 1, 1929, and 1935–1936,[1] by Place Reared and Area

Type of movement and place reared	Total	Area					
		Iowa	Kentucky	Maryland	North Carolina	North Dakota	South Dakota
Persons who had moved from city to open country since January 1, 1929	1,037	450	56	72	69	6	384
Reared in open country in county of survey	353	185	38	27	34	1	68
Reared in open country elsewhere	292	98	9	5	17	3	160
Other	392	167	9	40	18	2	156
Persons who had moved from city to village since January 1, 1929	850	149	21	116	31	11	522
Reared in village in county of survey	113	27	6	45	5	1	29
Reared in village elsewhere	153	17	—	22	1	2	111
Other	584	105	15	49	25	8	382
Persons who had moved from village to open country since January 1, 1929	1,778	390	102	230	35	22	999
Reared in open country in county of survey	604	160	52	57	19	6	310
Reared in open country elsewhere	482	94	34	19	6	10	319
Other	692	136	16	154	10	6	370

[1] January 1, 1935, in Iowa and South Dakota; January 1, 1936, in Kentucky, Maryland, North Carolina, and North Dakota.

The movement back to the areas from which these persons had originally gone to cities was not the only one. Although one-third of the persons who had moved from a city to the open country had been reared in the open country in the county where they were living at the time of the surveys, the proportion of those who had been reared in an open country residence elsewhere was somewhat smaller. Conversely, almost two-fifths of the migrants from cities to the open country had not been reared in the open country, the proportions ranging from about one-sixth to more than one-half in the various areas surveyed.

Migration from villages to the open country was somewhat more frequent than migration from cities to the open country. The proportions of migrants from villages who were reared in the open country were, however, similar to those for migrants from cities. Approximately one-third had been reared in the open country in the

[15] See footnote 8, p. 87.

county of residence at the time of the surveys, and a somewhat smaller proportion had been reared in the open country elsewhere. The ratios were by no means uniform throughout the sample areas, however.

The proportion of migrants from cities to villages who had been reared in a village in the county of survey or in any village was only one-half as great as the corresponding proportion among the city migrants to the open country. Whether this was due to less migration from villages to cities or to a lesser attraction of villages as places to which to return from cities cannot be determined from these data. However, if migration from an urban to an open country residence is primarily to escape the effects of urban unemployment by resort to a type of activity which promises subsistence, migration to villages would seem to offer only slight advantages.

The proportion of all persons 16 years of age and over in villages who had come from cities was somewhat greater than the corresponding proportion in the open country (table 30). Moreover, the proportion of village residents who had come from the open country was somewhat greater than the proportion of open country residents who had migrated from villages. Nearly 4 percent of the persons living in the open country at the time of the surveys had been city residents in 1929, but almost 6 percent of the village residents had come from a city. Similarly, 5 percent of the open country residents had come from a village, but nearly 13 percent of the village residents had come from the open country.

Table 30.—Residence, 1935–1936, of Persons 16 Years of Age and Over in Survey Areas,[1] by Residence and Area of Residence, January 1, 1929

Residence, 1935–1936, and January 1, 1929	Total		Area of residence, January 1, 1929									
			County of survey		Adjoining counties only		Other counties in State		Adjoining States only		Other States	
	Number	Percent	Number	Percent	Number	Percent	Number	Percent	Number	Percent	Number	Percent
OPEN COUNTRY, 1935–1936												
Total	40,203	100.0	35,332	100.0	2,310	100.0	1,212	100.0	892	100.0	457	100.0
Open country	36,539	90.9	33,645	95.2	1,617	70.0	679	56.0	491	55.0	107	23.4
Village	2,038	5.1	1,267	3.6	316	13.7	231	19.1	157	17.6	67	14.7
City	1,565	3.9	420	1.2	377	16.3	302	24.9	244	27.4	222	48.6
Other	61	0.1	—	—	—	—	—	—	—	—	61	13.3
VILLAGE, 1935–1936												
Total	18,714	100.0	15,884	100.0	1,167	100.0	762	100.0	631	100.0	270	100.0
Open country	2,374	12.7	1,677	10.5	394	33.8	173	22.7	97	15.4	33	12.2
Village	15,277	81.6	14,115	88.9	542	46.4	341	44.8	236	37.4	43	15.9
City	1,040	5.6	92	0.6	231	19.8	248	32.5	298	47.2	171	63.4
Other	23	0.1	—	—	—	—	—	—	—	—	23	8.5

[1] Of Iowa, Kentucky, Maryland, North Carolina, North Dakota, Ohio, and South Dakota.

DECLINE IN MIGRATION OF CHILDREN FROM PARENTAL HOMES

The migrations of children who have left parental homes as well as the migrations of heads of families reveal trends in population movements in rural areas. The slowing down of migration or failure to migrate[16] was determined by comparing the proportion of youth 16–24 years of age in the survey areas who were living at home in 1929 with the comparable proportion in 1935–1936. Specifically, the households surveyed reported that 68 percent of the young men 16–24 years of age on January 1, 1929, were then living at home (table 31). At the time of the surveys the proportion of young men 16–24 years old and still living at home had risen to 80 percent. For young women the comparable proportions were 51 and 63 percent, respectively.[17]

Table 31.—Percent of Children 16 Years of Age and Over Living at Home, by Age and Sex, January 1, 1929, and 1935–1936

Age	Percent of males living at home		$\frac{\text{Column(2)}}{\text{Column(1)}} \times 100$	Percent of females living at home		$\frac{\text{Column(5)}}{\text{Column(4)}} \times 100$
	January 1, 1929	1935–1936		January 1, 1929	1935–1936	
	(1)	(2)	(3)	(4)	(5)	(6)
Total, 16–24 years	68	80	118	51	63	124
16–17 years	91	98	108	81	92	114
18–19 years	81	92	114	61	75	123
20–21 years	64	79	123	36	54	150
22–24 years	41	60	146	24	30	150
25 years and over	15	20	133	10	11	110

[16] It has been estimated that approximately 1,000,000 youth are on farms at present who would have migrated if the depression of the early thirties had not intervened. See Melvin, Bruce L., *Rural Youth on Relief*, Research Monograph XI, Division of Social Research, Works Progress Administration, Washington, D. C., 1937, p. 61.

[17] The method of computation minimizes the effect of the small number of persons who returned to the parental home after 1930. Persons who had left home before 1929 and returned during the depression years would, in the main, be classified as more than 25 years of age at the later date and, therefore, would not be included in the group considered. If a large number of persons had left their homes after January 1, 1929, but returned prior to January 1, 1935, they would appear as living at home in 1929 and 1935 and the conclusion that there had been no migration might be incorrect. Similarly, a person not living at home in 1929 may have returned to his home some time after 1929 and left again before the beginning of 1935. Such a migration would also be missed by the techniques used, and there would be an understatement of migration away from the sample households. It is not likely that either of these movements was large enough, however, seriously to affect the conclusions relative to a slowing down of migration.

Similar results were found in nearly every instance when the sample areas were analyzed separately.[18]

The migration from the parental homes in the sample areas began somewhat before the migrants had passed their sixteenth birthdays, and most of the children had left by the time they were 25 years of age. This was true in 1929 as well as at the time of the surveys. Thus, the peak of mobility appeared to be reached in the early twenties followed by a gradual tapering off with advancing age.

For every age group within the 16–24 year span the proportion of children living at home was greater when the surveys were made than it had been in 1929 (table 31). Of the young men 16 and 17 years of age, for example, 91 percent were living at home in 1929 in comparison with 98 percent in 1935–1936. Among young women of the same age 81 percent were at home in 1929 but 92 percent were still living at home at the later dates. As is usual in rural households the proportion of young women who were living at home was smaller than the proportion of young men for each age group.

Relatively few men and women 25 years of age and over were living in their parental homes in either 1929 or 1935–1936, but there were some increases in this age group as well. The proportion of persons in this age group living in their parents' homes was also greater among men than among women. Since the increase during the period of survey was greater for men than for women, the sex differences had become more pronounced by the end of the period.

Open country households retained their sons to a greater degree than did village households (table 32). During the depression years there were increases in the proportions of young men retained in each residence group, but village households increased their proportions more than open country households without altering their relative positions. Village and open country households were similar with respect to the proportions of daughters aged 16–24 years that were living at home at each period. From the standpoint of the persons involved, the effects of retention of young people in the parental household may be quite different in village and open country. In the sample areas almost every open country household was an agricultural household and failure to migrate often involved prolonging the period of apprenticeship in agriculture for those who expected to engage in agriculture as a vocation. For those young people who would not enter agriculture, it meant either an opportunity for further educational training or a period of inefficient employment or unemployment. The village youth who normally would have entered a nonagricultural labor market found himself restrained to a larger extent than his country cousin who was less likely to seek nonagricultural employment. The fact that many of the young women who

---

[18] Data on file in the U. S. Department of Agriculture, Bureau of Agricultural Economics, Washington, D. C.

Table 32.—Percent of Children 16 Through 24 Years of Age Living at Home, by Relief Status of Parental Household, Residence, and Sex, January 1, 1929, and 1935–1936

Relief status and residence	Percent of males living at home		Column (2)/Column (1)×100	Percent of females living at home		Column (5)/Column (4)×100
	January 1, 1929	1935–1936		January 1, 1929	1935–1936	
	(1)	(2)	(3)	(4)	(5)	(6)
RELIEF STATUS						
Relief	68	80	118	47	59	126
Nonrelief..........	68	80	118	54	65	120
RESIDENCE						
Open country.......	73	82	112	52	63	121
Village.............	60	78	130	49	61	124

leave the parental households do so to marry and hence do not become directly dependent upon the nonagricultural labor market was probably the major reason for the differences between young men and women with regard to the proportions which remained at home.

Age at migration and extent of migration from the parental home might be expected to be related to the economic status of the household, particularly as that affects the possibility of providing partial or total support for the young adult. Studies of rural relief households have shown not only that such households were economically at a disadvantage when compared with their nonrelief neighbors but also that these differences dated back to the period preceding the depression.[19] The families classified as relief families in the 1935–1936 surveys reported a smaller proportion of young women at home than their nonrelief neighbors both in 1929 and at the time of the surveys (table 32).[20] With employment possibilities reduced, there was a slightly greater increase in the proportion of young women remaining at home in relief than in nonrelief households. On the survey dates nonrelief households reported that 65 percent of their young women 16–24 years old were still living at home. In relief households the comparable figure was only 59 percent.

The factors which may have operated to create differences in the percentages of young women in relief and nonrelief households remaining at home appear not to have been operative for the young men in the same households. Sixty-eight percent of the young men aged 16–24 years were living at home in 1929, and eighty percent of the group were at home at the date of survey. Percentages for relief and nonrelief households were identical in each case.

[19] McCormick, T. C., Comparative Study of Rural Relief and Non-Relief Households, Research Monograph II, Division of Social Research, Works Progress Administration, Washington, D. C., 1935.

[20] A household was classified as "relief" if it had received public assistance at any time between January 1, 1933, and the date of the survey.

DISTANCE MIGRATED BY CHILDREN LEAVING PARENTAL HOMES

The migration of children from their parental homes during the period studied indicated that the movement of population is not governed primarily by distance, although as in other migrant groups studied, the bulk of the movement of the total group was limited to short-distance migrations. If there is a progressive adaptation to the urban environment through migration to increasingly larger centers of population,[21] as is widely held, there should be significant differences in the proportions of those adult children who had left their parental homes by January 1, 1929, and who were living in the several residence groups in 1929 and at the time of the surveys, 6 or 7 years later.[22] But no significant differences in the proportions living in open country, village, or city were found (table 33). Only in the North Dakota and South Dakota areas was there a noticeable decrease in persons living in the open country. The explanation is probably to be found in the effects of the drought upon persons chiefly dependent upon agriculture. These individuals apparently went directly to large and small cities as well as to villages. The data suggest that direct migration from open country to city occurs frequently and that established "channels" of migration may be more important in directing the stream of migration than distance itself.

If it were assumed that migration generally occurs by stages, that is, in a succession of shifts to nearby areas, it would be expected that adult children leaving home before 1929 would be living farther away from their parental homes than would children who had left more recently. Moreover, the greatest proportion of children who moved would be found in the areas nearest the point of departure with the more distant regions having fewer migrants. This principle of an orderly succession of moves to adjoining areas was not supported, however, by data for the areas surveyed. Almost one-half of the children who had left home before January 1, 1929, had remained in the county of survey. Excluding movement confined to the survey areas [23] and movement outside the United States, it was found that in 1935 the largest proportion of the migrant children consisted of residents in counties adjoining the survey area (30 percent) with the second largest group in adjoining States (25 percent). Approximately the same proportions were in nonadjoining States and in nonadjoining counties in the State of survey, 22 percent and 23 percent, respectively (tables 34 and 35, p. 101).

---

[21] Bücher, Carl, *Industrial Evolution*, New York: Henry Holt and Company, 1901, p. 377.

[22] Neither return migration nor mortality would seriously affect this group.

[23] Movement within the county of survey is excluded in this particular discussion of migration in relation to distance for purposes of clearness. This does not change the nature of the phenomenon, although it does aid in the presentation of supporting data. The few moves to foreign countries are also excluded as they have little effect on the pattern of movements.

Table 33.—Children 16 Years of Age and Over in 1935–1936 Who Had Left Home by January 1, 1929, by Area and Residence on January 1, 1929, and in 1935–1936[1]

Area	Total	Open country January 1, 1929	Open country 1935–1936	Village January 1, 1929	Village 1935–1936	Small city January 1, 1929	Small city 1935–1936	Large city January 1, 1929	Large city 1935–1936	Other[2] January 1, 1929	Other[2] 1935–1936
Total:											
Number	13,708	5,778	5,456	3,602	3,783	1,517	1,546	2,567	2,586	244	337
Percent	100	42	40	26	28	11	11	19	19	2	2
IOWA											
Number	2,476	879	841	645	622	452	477	473	479	27	57
Percent	100	36	34	26	25	18	19	19	20	1	2
KENTUCKY											
Number	549	312	304	123	137	24	18	81	74	9	16
Percent	100	57	55	22	25	4	3	15	14	2	2
MARYLAND											
Number	1,185	168	171	515	508	55	65	418	408	29	33
Percent	100	14	14	44	43	5	6	35	34	2	3
NORTH CAROLINA											
Number	424	222	218	78	92	42	42	63	60	19	12
Percent	100	52	51	18	22	10	10	15	14	5	3
NORTH DAKOTA											
Number	91	41	35	22	23	6	8	21	22	1	3
Percent	100	45	39	24	25	7	9	23	24	1	3
OHIO											
Number	2,027	678	720	428	480	485	442	402	358	34	27
Percent	100	33	35	21	24	24	22	20	18	2	1
SOUTH DAKOTA											
Number	6,956	3,478	3,167	1,791	1,921	453	494	1,109	1,185	125	189
Percent	100	49	45	26	28	7	7	16	17	2	3

[1] January 1, 1935, in Iowa, Ohio, and South Dakota; January 1, 1936, in Kentucky, Maryland, North Carolina, and North Dakota.
[2] Includes migrants to foreign countries and unknowns.

Some of the individual States had more contrasting distributions. For example, the majority of the migrant children leaving the survey areas in North Dakota had moved to nonadjoining States, while the smallest group had moved to counties adjoining the survey areas. In the Kentucky areas more moved to adjoining States than to counties adjoining the survey areas. Other marked variations were shown in the survey areas of Maryland and Iowa.[24] The dispersions cannot be fully explained as being the continuing movement of a closed group which left prior to January 1, 1929. If it was a migrant group whose source was suddenly stopped, i. e., a "closed" group, the peak or bulk of the migrants leaving the area would have been shifted farther from the point of departure, while the areas nearest the point of departure would gradually have been drained of temporary resi-

[24] Data on file in the U. S. Department of Agriculture, Bureau of Agricultural Economics, Washington, D. C.

dents.   Actually selective forces, such as the location of relatives and friends and employment opportunities, were active in determining the distribution of the migrant children.

The findings of the field studies reported here that distance is not the major factor in the spatial distribution of migrants bear out those of earlier works in a number of States.[25]   The inclusion of counties which were on the border of the sample States did not affect the pattern of movement among areas.   No relationship existed between the number of border counties and the order or range of dispersion in any State.   If a relationship had existed, the movement of North Carolina and Maryland migrants and of Iowa and Kentucky migrants would have been similar.   Instead wide variations existed in these States as far as the dispersion of adult children migrating prior to January 1, 1929, was concerned, indicating that the geographical location of the sample counties within each State did not alter the character or direction of migration shown in the samples.

Type of Areas Receiving Migrant Children

The distance covered by migration is ordinarily related to the type of area to which the migrants are going.   In comparing the migrations of adult children who left their parental homes prior to and after January 1, 1929, it was found that children migrating after January 1, 1929, were located within the county of survey more often than those who left their homes before that date (tables 34 and 35).   Forty-six percent of the group leaving their parental homes before 1929 were residing in the county of survey in 1935–1936, whereas fifty-three

[25] See Eugenics Survey of Vermont, *Selective Migration From Three Rural Vermont Towns and Its Significance, op. cit.*, p. 31; Thornthwaite, C. Warren, *Internal Migration in the United States*, Philadelphia: University of Pennsylvania Press, 1934, p. 15; Taeuber, Conrad and Taylor, Carl C., *The People of the Drought States*, Research Bulletin Series V, No. 2, Division of Social Research, Works Progress Administration, Washington, D. C., March 1937, p. 14; Gee, Wilson and Corson, John J., *Rural Depopulation in Certain Tidewater and Piedmont Areas of Virginia*, Institute Monograph No. 3, Institute for Research in the Social Sciences, University of Virginia, Charlottesville, Va., 1929, p. 34; Anderson, W. A., *Movement of Population to and From New York State*, Bulletin 591, Cornell University Agricultural Experiment Station, Ithaca, N. Y., April 1934, pp. 18–24; Hoag, Emily F., *The National Influence of a Single Farm Community*, Bulletin No. 984, U. S. Department of Agriculture, Washington, D. C., December 1, 1921; Anderson, W. A. and Loomis, C. P., *Migration of Sons and Daughters of White Farmers in Wake County*, Bulletin No. 275, North Carolina Agricultural Experiment Station, Raleigh, N. C., June 1930, pp. 13–14; Anderson, W. A., *Mobility of Rural Families. II*, Bulletin 623, Cornell University Agricultural Experiment Station, Ithaca, N. Y., March 1935, pp. 16–17; Beck, P. G. and Lively, C. E., *Movement of Open Country Population in Ohio, II. The Individual Aspect*, Bulletin 489, Ohio Agricultural Experiment Station, Wooster, Ohio, September 1931, p. 11; and Young, E. C., *The Movement of Farm Population*, Bulletin 426, Cornell University Agricultural Experiment Station, Ithaca, N. Y., March 1924, pp. 25–27.

Fresh From the Country.

percent of the group who left their homes after January 1, 1929, were still in the same county by the later date.

Table 34.—Residence in 1935–1936 of Children 16 Years of Age and Over Who Had Migrated From Open Country Homes,[1] by Period of Migration

Residence, 1935–1936	Left before January 1, 1929		Left after January 1, 1929	
	Number	Percent	Number	Percent
Total	8,052	100.0	4,709	100.0
In parental home [2]	111	1.4	119	2.5
Not in parental home	7,941	98.6	4,500	97.5
County of survey:				
Open country	2,867	35.5	1,842	39.1
Village	806	10.0	599	12.7
City	331	4.1	206	4.4
Adjoining counties only:				
Open country	473	5.9	261	5.6
Village	270	3.4	147	3.1
City	410	5.1	244	5.2
Other counties in State:				
Open country	242	3.0	95	2.0
Village	228	2.8	136	2.9
City	454	5.6	269	5.7
Adjoining States only:				
Open country	282	3.5	122	2.6
Village	196	2.4	102	2.2
City	504	6.3	211	4.5
Other States:				
Open country	117	1.5	36	0.8
Village	127	1.6	63	1.3
City	541	6.7	217	4.6
Other [3]	93	1.2	40	0.8

[1] The parents were living in the open country at the time of the survey.
[2] Children who had migrated but had returned to their parental homes by 1935–1936.
[3] Includes migrants to foreign countries and unknowns.

Table 35.—Residence in 1935–1936 of Children 16 Years of Age and Over Who Had Migrated From Village Homes,[1] by Period of Migration

Residence, 1935–1936	Left before January 1, 1929		Left after January 1, 1929	
	Number	Percent	Number	Percent
Total	5,656	100.0	2,014	100.0
In parental home [2]	92	1.6	63	3.1
Not in parental home	5,564	98.4	1,951	96.9
County of survey:				
Open country	766	13.5	206	10.2
Village	1,371	24.3	669	33.2
City	115	2.0	42	2.1
Adjoining counties only:				
Open country	368	6.5	47	2.3
Village	250	4.4	94	4.7
City	312	5.5	131	6.5
Other counties in State:				
Open country	127	2.2	23	1.2
Village	204	3.6	101	5.0
City	377	6.7	176	8.7
Adjoining States only:				
Open country	118	2.1	19	1.0
Village	186	3.3	69	3.4
City	301	8.0	165	8.2
Other States:				
Open country	65	1.1	10	0.5
Village	129	2.3	33	1.6
City	587	10.4	144	7.2
Other [3]	88	1.6	22	1.1

[1] The parents were living in villages at the time of the survey.
[2] Children who had migrated but had returned to their parental homes by 1935–1936.
[3] Includes migrants to foreign countries and unknowns.

Among both groups of migrating children from the open country, those who left before January 1, 1929, and those who left after that date, long-distance migrations were directed toward towns and cities while short-distance migrations were toward rural areas (table 34). The children who left home but remained within the survey area settled primarily in the open country. Among more recent open country migrants the proportion which settled in the open country areas of the county of survey was greater than among those children who had left home before 1929. Conversely, the proportion of children migrating to the more distant open country areas showed a slight decrease after January 1, 1929.

Among children who migrated from villages, migrations within the county of survey were usually to other villages while those who moved greater distances tended to go to cities (table 35). Migrations to other villages were more pronounced among the children who left home after January 1, 1929, than prior to that date, with the exception of those moving the greatest distances.

A definite relationship exists between the distance adult children migrate, the types of areas in which they settle, and their occupations. The tendency for sons to enter the occupations common to the open country or villages resulted in a large proportion of short-distance migrations. The daughters sought professional and clerical positions and were drawn toward the larger cities, and, therefore, not only predominated among urban migrants but also traveled comparatively greater distances than the sons.[26]

The most distant migrations of adult children from both open country and village homes were principally to cities. There was some evidence of a slight reduction in the long-distance migration to cities among children leaving home after January 1, 1929, and a slight increase in the proportion moving to nearby cities. The persons going to intermediate areas tended to select villages more frequently than those migrating greater distances. The fact that adult children exhibited a greater range and wider differences in types of areas selected than did the heads of families who came into the survey areas illustrates the fact that dispersion of migrants from a particular rural area tends to be more scattered than the areas from which incoming migrants move.

[26] For comparable findings see Anderson, W. A., *Mobility of Rural Families. II, op. cit.,* pp. 20–22; and Gee, Wilson and Runk, Dewees, "Qualitative Selection in Cityward Migration," *The American Journal of Sociology,* Vol. XXXVII, 1931, pp. 254–265.

Chapter VI

CHARACTERISTICS OF MIGRANTS IN SELECTED AREAS

BOTH THE extent and the direction of the migration of rural families are related to a variety of factors. Age, sex, family composition, employability of family, occupation, and relief status all significantly affected the mobility of the population within the areas surveyed.

AGE OF MALE HEADS OF FAMILIES

A close relationship was found between the age of male heads of families and the distance which they had migrated. Almost without exception, the older the heads of families, the more their movements during the period of survey had been restricted to short-distance migrations (table 36). Not only had more of the younger household heads migrated, but they had also moved greater distances.

The only exceptions to the successive decrease in the mobility of each older age group occurred in the Kentucky and North Dakota

Table 36.—Age of Male Heads of Families, 1935–1936, by Range of Migration During the Period of Survey

Age, 1935–1936	Total		Contin- uous resi- dence	Lived in county of survey and—					
	Num- ber	Per- cent		No other county	Ad- joining coun- ties only	Other coun- ties in State	Ad- joining States only	Other States	Other[1]
Total	20,930	100.0	68.8	11.4	5.8	3.9	3.0	1.4	5.7
Under 35 years	4,811	100.0	45.3	15.4	8.5	5.7	4.0	2.0	19.1
35–44 years	5,212	100.0	66.5	13.6	7.1	4.2	4.0	1.7	2.9
45–54 years	4,924	100.0	76.0	10.1	5.0	3.7	2.6	1.3	1.3
55–64 years	3,563	100.0	82.2	7.6	3.9	2.6	1.8	0.9	1.0
65 years and over	2,420	100.0	86.5	7.4	2.3	1.4	1.1	0.6	0.7

[1] Includes migrants from foreign countries and families established after 1928.

samples, in which the heads of families aged 65 and over were more mobile than heads in the age group 55–64 years.[1] The mobility in the older age groups did not vary from one State to another to as great an extent, however, as the mobility of younger heads of families. In the Ohio sample more than three-fourths of the family heads under 35 years of age had moved at least once during the period for which records were taken, but in North Carolina less than one-third of the family heads in this age group reported moves.

The younger heads of families were more mobile than older heads in both the open country and villages. The older heads of families in the open country areas had migrated greater distances on the average than the family heads in the older age groups in villages, while in the younger age groups the reverse was true.

Table 37.—Age of Male Heads of Families, 1935–1936, Who Moved Into the Survey Area[1] During the Period of Survey,[2] by Area

Age, 1935–1936	Total	Area						
		Iowa	Ken-tucky	Mary-land	North Caro-lina	North Dakota	Ohio	South Dakota
Total:								
Number	2,966	454	133	238	72	55	341	1,673
Percent	100	100	100	100	100	100	100	100
Under 35 years	33	28	35	40	29	39	16	37
35–44 years	30	32	30	28	39	36	34	28
45–54 years	21	22	23	18	20	16	28	20
55–64 years	11	12	7	11	6	9	15	11
65 years and over	5	6	5	3	6	—	7	4

[1] Exclusive of male heads of families reporting continuous residence or residence in county of survey only.
[2] January 1, 1928, to January 1, 1935, in Iowa, Ohio, and South Dakota; January 1, 1926, to January 1, 1936, in Kentucky, Maryland, North Carolina, and North Dakota.

When the age distribution of the male heads of families who moved into the survey areas during the period studied was considered, it was found that almost two-thirds òf the heads were under 45 years of age. Only 1 in 20 was 65 years of age and over (table 37). In general, there was little variation from area to area. North Dakota had the youngest migrants, however, with 75 percent under 45 years of age and none 65 years of age and over.

AGE OF MIGRANT CHILDREN

Modern migration is primarily a phenomenon of youth. The beginning of an occupational career ordinarily involves the breaking of home ties and frequently a migration from the place in which the parents reside. The young adult with fewer firmly established ties is usually less reluctant to move than an older, more firmly established person.

[1] Detailed data to support this and subsequent analyses in this chapter are on file in the U. S. Department of Agriculture, Bureau of Agricultural Economics, Washington, D. C.

Marriage and the founding of a new household are also closely related to leaving the parental home. Naturally this would affect girls somewhat more than boys, particularly in the case of farm families. In most cases the establishment of a family is a restraining factor, and young unmarried adults constitute a much larger proportion of all migrants than of the total population.

Table 38.—Children 16 Years of Age and Over Who Had Left Home by 1935–1936, by Residence on January 1, 1929

Age, 1935–1936	Total		Residence, January 1, 1929					
	Number	Percent	County of survey	Adjoining counties only	Other counties in State	Adjoining States only	Other States	Other [1]
Total	20,070	100.0	61.8	12.0	8.8	9.2	7.2	1.0
16–17 years	177	100.0	76.3	6.2	5.6	6.2	5.1	0.6
18–20 years	1,073	100.0	83.2	7.3	4.2	3.4	1.8	0.1
21–24 years	3,165	100.0	82.4	7.2	4.1	4.0	1.8	0.5
25–34 years	8,793	100.0	60.6	12.2	10.0	9.2	7.1	0.9
35–44 years	5,003	100.0	51.4	15.1	10.2	11.7	10.6	1.0
45–54 years	1,569	100.0	47.2	14.8	10.6	14.6	11.2	1.6
55 years and over	255	100.0	46.3	10.6	11.4	14.5	14.9	2.3
Unknown	35	†	†	†	†	†	†	—

†Percent not computed on a base of fewer than 50 cases.
[1] Includes migrants to foreign countries and unknowns.

Table 39.—Children 16 Years of Age and Over Who Had Left Home by 1935–1936, by Residence at Time of Survey

Age, 1935–1936	Total		Residence at time of survey					
	Number	Percent	County of survey	Adjoining counties only	Other counties in State	Adjoining States only	Other States	Other [1]
Total	20,070	100.0	48.9	15.0	12.2	12.4	10.6	0.9
16–17 years	177	100.0	52.5	10.7	16.4	8.5	11.9	—
18–20 years	1,073	100.0	50.2	15.7	14.6	11.4	7.2	0.9
21–24 years	3,165	100.0	52.0	15.6	11.2	11.8	8.4	1.0
25–34 years	8,793	100.0	48.3	15.1	13.0	12.1	10.6	0.9
35–44 years	5,003	100.0	48.8	15.0	11.1	12.5	11.7	0.9
45–54 years	1,569	100.0	46.5	14.9	10.9	14.7	11.9	1.1
55 years and over	255	100.0	44.6	9.8	11.4	16.1	16.9	1.2
Unknown	35	†	†	†	†	†	†	—

†Percent not computed on a base of fewer than 50 cases.
[1] Includes migrants to foreign countries and unknowns.

Two-thirds of the children who had migrated were under 35 years of age at the time of the surveys, and most of them had probably migrated before marriage. In any case the data serve to emphasize that the years ordinarily associated with the beginning of an occupational career are the years of greatest mobility. Before the individual is ready to start his active occupational career there is little occasion for moving except as a member of the family group. The proportion of children living outside the county of survey increased with increasing age.   The greatest decreases in the proportion living in the county of survey occurred in the groups under 25 years of age.   Children who were 35 years of age and over showed very little movement away from the county of survey during the period between January 1, 1929, and 1935–1936 (tables 38 and 39).

The older children were more widely dispersed than the younger ones both in 1929 and at the time of the surveys.   The longer the period available for migration from the parental home, the farther away the children had moved.[2]   In other words, many of them did not become permanently settled after the first move but continued to shift from one residence to another.

These movements were evidently continued during the depression years, for at the time of the surveys the children were more widely dispersed than they had been 6 or 7 years earlier.   Although most of the moves were made by young persons who had passed their eighteenth birthdays during the period under discussion, every age group showed a decrease in the proportion living in the county of survey and conversely an increase in the proportion living in more distant areas.

SEX OF HEADS OF FAMILIES

Over 90 percent of the heads of families surveyed were males, and two-thirds of them had made no residence change during the period of survey.   Of those changing residence, two out of three had moved within the State of survey.   The families with female heads reported slightly greater stability, more than three-fourths making no change during the period covered, but of those who moved more had crossed the boundaries of the State of survey.

Families located in open country areas were somewhat less mobile than village families, regardless of the sex of the head of the household.   Among the female heads of households who had changed location, those in the open country had moved greater distances than those in villages.

SEX AND RESIDENCE OF MIGRANT CHILDREN

Of the total persons in the rural households included in the field studies who had passed their sixteenth birthdays,[3] nearly 53 percent were males, or, in other words, there were 111 men for every 100 women (table 40).   Among the children 16 years of age and over who were not living at home at the time of the surveys, however, there were more women than men, the ratio being only 84 men per 100 women. The preponderance of women among the migrants was most marked

---

[2] Also, the older the children the more opportunity the parents had had to move away from them.

[3] Including all children of the head of the household, living at home.

Table 40.—Sex Ratio Among Persons in Households Surveyed and Among Children Who Had Migrated, by Age, 1935–1936

Age	Sex ratio	
	Persons in household	Children who had migrated
Total	111	84
16–19 years	109	36
20–24 years	108	59
25–34 years	104	87
35–44 years	106	102
45–54 years	111	117
55–64 years	128	139
65 years and over	129	(¹)

¹ Includes only 8 men and 5 women. Obviously there would be few children in either this or the preceding age group.

at the youngest ages, the result of the earlier migration of women. In the age groups 35–44 years and over, men predominated among those who were not living in the parental household. Thus, although young women appeared to leave the parental home earlier to enter an occupation or to be married, women 35 years of age and over were more likely to live with their parents than were their brothers of the same age. In part the persons 35 years of age and over who were living in the parental home were persons who had returned after an occupation or marriage had ceased to provide adequate support; in part they were persons who had never migrated; and in part they were children who had returned to provide care or companionship for the parents. Local conditions, such as employment opportunities, nearness to cities, the existence of previously established channels of migration, and local family attitudes and practices, served to introduce modifications from area to area, but the general pattern as outlined seemed to apply.

Both young men and young women whose parental homes were in the open country were more likely to migrate to other open country residences than to villages. A much greater proportion of males than of females moved from one open country residence to another, however, as sons from open country households were likely to enter farming in nearby localities. An exception to this general trend occurred in the Maryland sample where more children of both sexes migrated from the open country to villages than to other open country residences.

A greater amount of movement was reported for both young men and young women from rural areas to large than to small cities[4] and women exceeded men in the migration to both types of cities. Although in general large cities received more migrants than small cities, the reverse was true among children in the North Carolina and Ohio samples. In the case of the migrants from the North Carolina areas

[4] Small city—2,500 to 9,999; large city—10,000 or more.

the employment of many women and girls in the textile mills and other factories in the small cities of the State was probably the major factor in producing the exception. Whether small or large cities prove more attractive to any group of migrants probably depends upon a set of local conditions among which proximity and employment opportunities play a large role.

FAMILY COMPOSITION

Mobility was found to be directly related to family type. Families consisting of husband and wife with or without children not only were more numerous than other family types but also were more mobile. Families composed of man and wife without children were more mobile than those with children. Among broken families those composed of a man and children were more mobile than those consisting of a woman and children. Also, among one-person families men were more mobile than women.

The effect of additional persons in the household upon the migrations of a family varied greatly. The mobility of normal families was decreased by the addition of nonfamily persons while that of broken families appeared to be increased. The presence of nonfamily persons reduced the mobility of the family group to a lesser degree than the presence of children.

Nonfamily persons who migrated with the normal family were of two major types, unemployable persons relying upon the normal family unit for economic support and employable persons looking for more favorable opportunities at the new location. There were, of course, some persons with separate incomes who lived with the family unit and who, although not employed, were self-maintaining. The effect of such additional persons upon the mobility of the family group varied with the nature and circumstances of the nonfamily individual, but in general unemployable persons, whether they were economically dependent or not, tended to decrease the mobility of the family unit. On the other hand, employable persons seeking employment tended to increase the mobility of the unit.

GAINFUL WORKERS

In each area surveyed the average number of male workers per household was less in the households which had moved than in those maintaining continuous residence (table 41). The presence in a household of more than one gainful worker both retarded the need or desire for changes of residence to secure employment and increased the ties which would be broken by migration.

The increased residential stability arising from the presence of gainful workers in the household was greater in the open country than in

Modern Migrants.

One Poor Farm Supports Two Families.

villages. The predominance of nonfarm employment among gainful workers in villages partly explains this difference. Shifts of employment within the nonfarm group are usually more easily managed than are shifts from one farm to another. This obviously does not apply to farm laborers to the same extent as to farm operators. Likewise, in the nonfarm group it applies more directly to laborers and skilled workers than it does to many individuals in the professional group.

Table 41.—Average Number of Male Gainful Workers in Households With Male Heads, 1935–1936, by Area and Type of Residence Change During the Period of Survey [1]

Area	Households with no residence change	Households making residence change	Households moving only within State	Households moving from other States
Total	1.6	1.4	1.4	1.4
Iowa	1.5	1.4	1.4	1.4
Kentucky	1.7	1.5	1.6	1.3
Maryland	1.7	1.5	1.6	1.5
North Carolina	2.1	1.9	1.8	2.2
North Dakota	2.4	1.8	1.7	1.9
Ohio	1.5	1.4	1.5	1.4
South Dakota	1.5	1.4	1.4	1.3

[1] January 1, 1928, to January 1, 1935, in Iowa, Ohio, and South Dakota; January 1, 1926, to January 1, 1936, in Kentucky, Maryland, North Carolina, and North Dakota.

Open country households having no gainful worker were more mobile than such households in villages and than households with workers in either residence. The lack of a gainful worker through death or desertion made migration from a farm virtually a necessity, whether to the home of friends or relatives within the open country area or to villages or towns where employment might be obtained by the members of the household who were not previously considered employable. There may also have been some movement toward villages through the attraction of relief benefits, which would apply particularly to the households without gainful workers. Contrary to the situation in the open country, village households having no gainful worker were the least mobile of any households studied. The absence of gainful workers undoubtedly reduced the economic resources of the households so affected and hindered migration, while the absence of immediately employable workers apparently left nothing to be gained by migration as far as employment opportunities were concerned. In addition, the prospect of meeting residence requirements of relief administrations frequently retarded residence changes.

OCCUPATIONS OF MALE HEADS OF FAMILIES

The occupation of the head of the family is a significant factor in determining the extent of residential movement. The nonfarm group as a whole was considerably more mobile than the farm group, and the variations in mobility were greater among the nonfarm than the farm group. The head of a village family who is working in a factory or business firm can easily change his location by merely transporting his furniture and other personal goods to another residence. If a farmer wishes to change his residence, it almost invariably involves a change of farms under operation. He frequently has also invested a good deal of labor in the development or repair of ditches, fencing, building, etc., that will bring no return to him except through long-term operation. The benefits of these and other improvements will be received by the new operator. Such investments may raise the selling price, but in recent years it has been difficult for many farm owners to secure a price at which they were willing to sell. Hence, the greater part of the residence changes shown to exist in the open country group is contributed by farm tenants and laborers.

Nearly two-thirds of the heads of families surveyed were classified as rural-farm and less than one-third as rural-nonfarm; but among the heads of families who had moved during the period of survey, 53 percent were classed as farm and 30 percent as nonfarm, with 17 percent either of unknown occupation or not gainfully employed (table 42).

Table 42.—Range of Migration of Male Heads of Families During the Period of Survey, by Occupation and Employment Status in 1935–1936

Range of migration	Total	Occupation			Not gainfully employed [1]
		Farm	Nonfarm	Unknown	
Total:					
Number	20, 939	12, 886	5, 738	338	1, 977
Percent	100. 0	100. 0	100. 0	100. 0	100. 0
Continuous residence	68. 8	73. 1	65. 8	3. 0	61. 1
Lived in county of survey and in:					
No other county	11. 4	11. 1	10. 6	0. 9	17. 7
Adjoining counties only	5. 8	5. 3	6. 9	0. 3	7. 1
Other counties in State	3. 9	2. 8	6. 0	—	5. 1
Adjoining States only	3. 0	2. 1	4. 6	—	3. 8
Other States	1. 4	1. 0	2. 4	—	1. 7
Other [2]	5. 7	4. 6	3. 7	95. 8	3. 5

[1] Includes 1 case with employment status unknown.
[2] Includes migrants from foreign countries and heads of families established after 1928.

Maryland was the single State in which more than one-half of both the migrant group and the group having continuous residence were classified as nonfarm. At the other extreme was the Iowa sample where the proportions of farm family heads among those moving into and within the survey areas were greater than in any of the other sample areas.

Within the farm group the proportion changing residence varied from 13 percent of the farm owners and managers to 42 percent of the farm tenants and 44 percent of the farm laborers (table 43). Within the nonfarm group the range was from 25 percent among proprietors, managers, and officials to 50 percent among professional persons (table 44).

The migrants entering the survey areas represented the various occupational groups in approximately the same proportions as the nonmigrants. There was a slight tendency toward overrepresentation of professional persons and underrepresentation of proprietors, managers, and officials, but the differences were not statistically significant.

Range of Migration

Almost two-fifths of all male heads of farm families who had moved came from another location within the county of survey. One-fifth came from adjoining counties, while the proportion coming from the more remote areas decreased with increasing distance (table 42). Within the farm group laborers not only moved about most frequently but also averaged the greatest distances (table 43).

Although rural-nonfarm families were more mobile and had entered the survey areas from greater distances, on the average, than rural-farm families, there were some exceptions among the several occupational groups (table 44). Although the county of survey was least

Table 43.—Range of Migration of Male Heads of Farm Families During the Period of Survey, by Tenure in 1935–1936

Range of migration	Total	Owners and managers	Tenants	Laborers
Total:				
Number	12,886	6,814	5,441	631
Percent	100.0	100.0	100.0	100.0
Continuous residence	73.1	86.7	58.0	56.1
Lived in county of survey and in:				
No other county	11.1	5.3	18.3	12.4
Adjoining counties only	5.3	2.7	8.1	9.5
Other counties in State	2.8	1.6	4.0	5.2
Adjoining States only	2.1	1.3	3.0	3.8
Other States	1.0	0.7	1.1	2.9
Other [1]	4.6	1.7	7.5	10.1

[1] Includes migrants from foreign countries and heads of families established after 1928.

Table 44.—Range of Migration of Male Heads of Nonfarm Families During the Period of Survey, by Occupation in 1935–1936

Range of migration	Total	Professional persons	Proprietors, managers, and officials	Clerks and kindred workers	Skilled workers	Semi-skilled workers	Un-skilled workers
Total:							
Number	5,738	443	1,546	709	749	1,127	1,164
Percent	100.0	100.0	100.0	100.0	100.0	100.0	100.0
Continuous residence	65.8	49.7	74.5	65.5	64.8	64.1	62.9
Lived in county of survey and in:							
No other county	10.6	6.3	7.4	9.9	13.0	11.3	14.4
Adjoining counties only	6.9	7.2	5.2	5.6	6.6	10.8	6.1
Other counties in State	6.0	17.2	4.6	5.5	4.9	4.5	6.1
Adjoining States only	4.6	7.4	3.7	6.2	4.1	4.2	4.5
Other States	2.4	7.2	1.6	1.8	3.1	1.6	2.7
Other [1]	3.7	5.0	3.0	5.5	2.9	3.5	3.3

[1] Includes migrants from foreign countries and heads of families established after 1928.

important as a source of migrants for the professional group, it was the most important source for all other nonfarm groups. Professional workers were drawn from widely scattered localities and from considerable distances as a result of the need of a wider area for recruiting workers with special skills and training.

The movement within the county of survey was proportionately greatest among skilled and unskilled laborers. In the movement from adjoining counties semiskilled workers reported the largest proportion. Professional persons had the largest proportions from other counties in the State of survey and from more distant regions.

The proportion of farm to nonfarm migrants varied sharply when considered separately for each county, suggesting the need for further studies of internal population movements in rural areas with emphasis upon homogeneous groupings. There is need also for rating migration among areas on the basis of special factors, such as accessibility, employment, farm lands available, and living costs in proportion to income. The distance of migration is related to the knowledge of the migrant concerning other regions. The cost and difficulty of travel are becoming less dominant in affecting migration, while the other factors mentioned are increasing in importance. The analysis of population movements cannot be confined to the truism that a migrant is more apt to travel 10 miles than 1,000. The greatest possible distance he can migrate will be limited somewhere by physical, economic, and even social barriers. Within these limitations he can make his choice, and for different occupational groups the range within which he can choose varies widely. Needless to say, many of those who desire new locations could be greatly benefited by proper advice and financial aid, especially among those moving during periods of severe depression or moving from areas of intense distress.

Occupational Changes

One of the important occupational shifts in recent years has been the change from nonagricultural to agricultural occupations with or without a change of residence. The field surveys conducted in the Appalachian Mountains show this movement clearly, for one of the criteria used in selecting the sample counties in that area was a relatively large increase in the farm population between 1930 and 1935.

In the Kentucky and North Carolina counties surveyed, approximately one-fourth of the farm operators had begun farming since January 1, 1930 (table 45). In Garrett County in western Maryland one-sixth of those who were operating farms at the time of the survey had begun farming in recent years.

These figures are particularly significant because only a small proportion of the new farm operators were young persons without previous occupational experience, i. e., individuals who were beginning their occupational careers. Between one-half and three-fourths of the new farm operators reported that their last previous occupation was at unskilled labor, including farm labor. In Avery and Haywood Counties, N. C., farm laborers accounted for two-fifths and two-thirds, respectively, of the new farm operators. In Morgan and Magoffin Counties, Ky., where coal mining is an important industry, farm laborers and coal miners each contributed approximately one-third of the new farm operators.

Table 45.—Male Heads of Families in 5 Appalachian Counties Engaged in Agriculture 1936, by Time of Beginning Farm Operations

County	Percent of farm operators who began farming—	
	Before January 1, 1930	January 1, 1930, or later
Garrett, Md.	84	16
Magoffin, Ky.	75	25
Morgan, Ky.	71	29
Avery, N. C.	75	25
Haywood, N. C.	78	22

Next to unskilled laborers semiskilled and skilled workers were most important among the individuals who began to farm after January 1, 1930. The other occupational classifications, including professional persons, were also represented but in considerably smaller numbers.

In these counties in the Appalachian Mountains occupational shifts from agriculture to other occupations were relatively infrequent.[5] Although only seven-tenths of the persons in Morgan County, Ky., who were operating farms in 1936 had been operating farms in 1929, 92 percent of the persons who were operating farms in 1929 and were in the survey areas in 1936 were still on farms at the later date. The newcomers to farming in most cases were net additions to the number of farm operators, and few of them replaced persons who had left farming.

The new farmers appeared to find it easier to begin as tenants than as owners, as many of them undoubtedly lacked even the small amount of capital necessary to establish themselves as owners.[6] In Morgan County, Ky., where the average farm contained only 65 acres in 1935, the number of new farmers was about equally divided

[5] Obviously this is related to the fact that the surveys were made in rural areas.

[6] The tenure status is given as of the time of survey and therefore the persons who are given as having begun farming as owners may actually have started as tenants and vice versa. Undoubtedly there were a few shifts in tenure status between the time when the individual shifted his occupation and the time of the survey. In the case of the data for Morgan County this probably would tend to increase the proportion that had begun farming since 1930 as tenants.

between owners and tenants. Yet in 1935 only one-third of the farms in the county were operated by tenants, and in 1930 the proportion had been somewhat lower. Unskilled workers who changed their occupation to farming were more likely to begin as tenants, while semiskilled workers were more likely to begin as owners.

In addition to the occupational shifts which occurred, there were also some variations in the maintenance of tenure status by farm operators. Nine out of every ten persons who were farm owners in 1929, and for whom a report was secured in the field surveys, were still farm owners at the later date. The stability was greatest in the Appalachian Mountain counties, Avery and Magoffin, where 98 percent of the owners in 1929 reported farm ownership in 1936. The lowest rate of stability among owners was reported from Union County in south central Iowa, one of the less prosperous counties of that State. There, only 80 percent of the farm owners in 1929 were still owners in 1935.

Farm tenants maintained their tenure status to a less extent than did farm owners. Only 8 out of every 10 persons who were farm tenants in 1929 and still living in the sample areas at the time of the surveys were still tenants in 1935–1936. Custer County, S. Dak., with 56 percent represented the least and Somerset County on the Eastern Shore of Maryland with 93 percent represented the greatest persistence of tenure status reported.

The variations in the percentages reporting the same tenure status at the earlier and the later dates were due primarily to differences in the proportions that changed from farming to other occupations. Without exception every sample area reported that a larger proportion of tenants than of owners left farming for a nonfarm occupation. Five percent of the persons who were farm owners in 1929 and were still living in the survey area in 1935 had given up the operation of their farms, but more than twice as many tenants (12 percent) had gone into nonagricultural activities. This result is in accord with the observation that ownership of real estate imposes limitations upon the geographical and occupational mobility of the individual.

Among the farm operators who did not maintain their tenure status, some tenants succeeded in achieving the generally desired status of owner and at the same time some owners lost their ownership status and continued farming as tenants, often on the same farm. The relative shifting between the two tenure groups varied widely among the sample areas. Approximately 5 percent of the farm operators in the sample areas who had been owners in 1929 were tenants in 1935–1936, and this was matched by a similar proportion of the tenants achieving ownership status during the period. Every county except Somerset County, Md., where tenancy amounted to only 21 percent in 1935, reported some movement from tenancy to ownership. On the other hand, Magoffin County, Ky., where less than one-third of the farm operators in 1935 were tenants, stood alone in reporting no shifting from farm ownership to tenancy.

The frequency with which shifts in tenure status occurred and the direction which they took were dependent apparently upon conditions peculiar to each of the sample areas. In the Appalachian Mountain counties, where farm ownership does not ordinarily imply a large capital investment, there was uniformly more shifting from tenancy to ownership than vice versa. In Iowa, however, where farm ownership requires a much larger capital investment and where farming is predominantly commercial and more susceptible to the effects of a business depression, the changes in tenure status were more frequently shifts from ownership to tenancy than vice versa. In Black Hawk County, Iowa, which normally is ranked as one of the more prosperous counties in that State, one-seventh of the persons who had been farm owners in 1929 and were still in the county at the time of survey had become tenants, and one-tenth of the former tenants had become owners.

Table 46.—Shifts to and From Agriculture of Male Heads of Families [1] From January 1, 1929, to 1935–1936, by Area

Area [2]	Percent of farm operators in 1935–1936 [3] who were not operating farms on January 1, 1929	Percent of farm operators on January 1, 1929, who were not operating farms in 1935–1936 [3]
Total	14	8
Iowa	17	5
Appanoose	23	9
Black Hawk	16	4
O'Brien	12	3
Union	20	8
Kentucky	29	7
Magoffin	21	7
Morgan	34	8
Maryland	14	7
Garrett	17	7
Somerset	8	7
North Carolina	24	6
Avery	26	3
Haywood	21	9
North Dakota [4]	11	5
South Dakota	12	8
Custer	16	17
Edmunds	14	8
Haakon	12	5
Kingsbury	12	9
Turner	9	7

[1] Based only on persons residing in the survey area when schedules were taken. Data for persons who had left the survey area since January 1, 1929, are not included.
[2] For complete list of areas surveyed, see appendix B.
[3] January 1, 1935, in Iowa and South Dakota; January 1, 1936, in Kentucky, Maryland, North Carolina, and North Dakota.
[4] 12 townships.

At the same time that some persons were taking up farming or were shifting their tenure status, some were leaving farming to enter other occupations and others were retiring. In the predominantly rural and agricultural areas in which the field surveys were made, a change from farming to a nonfarming occupation often involved a movement out of the area, and hence the family head involved might not have been in the sample areas at the time of the surveys. Among the persons remaining in the sample areas who had been operating farms in 1929, 8 percent were no longer farming 6 or 7 years later (table 46).

RELIEF STATUS

The relationship between relief status [7] and mobility fluctuated from area to area, although on the average families on relief had moved more frequently than those not on relief. The mobility of farm families on relief was greater than that of nonrelief farm families, while the reverse was true for nonfarm families.

The migrations of nonrelief families were more likely to be for longer distances with the migrations of families on relief more frequently confined to the immediate vicinity of the survey areas. In both the relief and the nonrelief families the mobility and range of migration tended to decrease progressively from the younger to the older age groups (tables 47 and 48).

What the basis of the relationship between relief and mobility may be is not clearly revealed by the current figures. It may be that the instability revealed by the relief households is itself an indication of the need for relief. These figures do not distinguish the migrations before receiving relief from those which took place after the relief status was attained. Both the relief status and the greater mobility may be simply two different manifestations of the same basic condition, lack of economic security.

The changes from one type of area to another between 1929 and 1935–1936 were more varied among the nonrelief than the relief families, although for both types of families the most frequent movement was from one open country area to another (table 49). Among the relief families more than one-half of the changes of residence were confined to open country areas, while this was true of less than three-tenths of the nonrelief families. Next in numerical importance among relief families were movements from the open country to villages and among nonrelief families, movements from one village to another.

---

[7] All families included in the surveys which had received any public relief at any time between January 1, 1933, and the period of survey were included in the group defined as having a relief status. For purposes of the surveys, a relief family was defined as one which had received aid from public funds—Federal. State, or local. Both work and direct relief were included. Advances of money, materials, real estate, or chattels in connection with the rural rehabilitation program were not considered as relief, although work relief in order to work out rehabilitation advances was so considered. Employment on Public Works Administration projects was considered as employment, not relief, except where relief labor was used. The length of time during which such relief was received was not taken into account. For children the classification as relief or nonrelief was based upon the relief status of the parental household.

Table 47.—Age of Male Heads of Relief Families, 1935–1936, by Range of Migration During the Period of Survey

Age	Total		Con-tinuous resi-dence	Lived in county of survey and—					
	Num-ber	Percent		No other county	Adjoin-ing coun-ties only	Other counties in State	Adjoin-ing States only	Other States	Other [1]
Total [2]	7,490	100.0	66.0	14.8	6.5	3.7	3.1	1.3	4.6
Under 35 years	1,979	100.0	46.9	18.9	9.8	4.7	3.6	1.3	14.8
35–44 years	1,951	100.0	63.9	17.3	7.6	3.7	4.0	1.4	2.1
45–54 years	1,776	100.0	74.0	12.5	5.0	3.8	2.8	1.3	0.6
55–64 years	1,144	100.0	80.1	9.5	4.1	2.7	2.3	1.0	0.3
65 years and over	635	100.0	84.0	9.8	1.7	1.6	1.3	0.6	0.1
Unknown	5	†	†	—	—	—	—	—	—

†Percent not computed on a base of fewer than 50 cases.

[1] Includes migrants from foreign countries and heads of families established after 1928.
[2] Exclusive of data for Ohio.

Table 48.—Age of Male Heads of Nonrelief Families, 1935–1936, by Range of Migration During the Period of Survey

Age	Total		Con-tinuous resi-dence	Lived in county of survey and—					
	Num-ber	Percent		No other county	Adjoin-ing coun-ties only	Other counties in State	Adjoin-ing States only	Other States	Other [1]
Total [2]	11,019	100.0	72.1	9.5	5.1	3.9	3.0	1.7	4.7
Under 35 years	2,328	100.0	48.6	13.4	8.2	7.0	4.8	3.0	15.0
35–44 years	2,727	100.0	69.7	11.0	6.0	4.3	4.2	1.8	3.0
45–54 years	2,624	100.0	78.7	8.2	4.2	3.6	2.1	1.4	1.8
55–64 years	1,953	100.0	83.7	6.8	3.7	2.3	1.5	0.8	1.2
65 years and over	1,383	100.0	87.2	6.6	2.2	1.2	1.3	0.6	0.9
Unknown	4	†	†	—	†	—	—	—	—

†Percent not computed on a base of fewer than 50 cases.

[1] Includes migrants from foreign countries and heads of families established after 1928.
[2] Exclusive of data for Ohio.

Among the relief families the shifts from city to village and among nonrelief families the shifts from city to the open country were least important. The relative infrequency of movement from urban areas to the rural areas included in this survey suggests that, as far as these areas are concerned, the back-to-the-land movement during the depression years was a relatively unimportant factor.

The presence of dependents under 16 or over 64 years of age apparently was associated with decreased mobility and a reduced range of migration among the nonrelief households but seemed not to have retarded the rate of mobility of relief households. In the latter case the presence of dependents no doubt increased the need for adjustments through migration. For both relief and nonrelief households the range of migration was greater among the households having no dependents.

The relationships between frequency of change in occupation and frequency of change in residence appear to have been affected but little

Table 49.—Male Heads of Families Reporting a Change in Residence During the Period of Survey,[1] by Type of Change and Relief Status

Type of residence change	Total	Relief status	
		Relief	Nonrelief
Total:			
Number	2,189	1,050	1,139
Percent	100.0	100.0	100.0
Open country to village	16.7	17.6	15.8
Village to open country	10.0	9.7	10.4
City to village	6.8	2.5	10.7
City to open country	5.7	4.3	7.0
Open country to open country	39.6	51.1	29.0
Village to village	10.8	4.2	16.8
Other [2]	10.4	10.6	10.3

[1] January 1, 1928, to January 1, 1935, in South Dakota; January 1, 1926, to January 1, 1936, in Kentucky North Carolina, and North Dakota.
[2] Includes those moving more than once, migrants from foreign countries, and unknowns.

by relief status (table 50). Moreover, the proportions of any one occupational group which reported continuous residence appeared to differ only slightly between the relief and nonrelief groups. The small differences that were found were overshadowed by the differences among the several occupational groups. Since certain occupational groups are economically more vulnerable than others, and therefore persons in these occupational groups are more likely to need public assistance, this result would be expected.

Table 50.—Number of Changes in Residence and Occupation of Male Heads of Families During the Period of Survey,[1] by Relief Status

Number of changes	Relief		Nonrelief	
	Changes in residence	Changes in occupation	Changes in residence	Changes in occupation
Total: [2]				
Number	7,449	7,449	12,322	12,322
Percent	100.0	100.0	100.0	100.0
None	69.5	63.7	75.2	71.3
1	20.5	25.1	18.3	21.6
2	6.7	7.1	4.5	4.6
3	2.0	2.2	1.3	1.5
4	0.9	0.9	0.4	0.5
5	0.2	0.4	0.1	0.2
6	0.1	0.2	0.1	0.1
7	0.1	0.4	0.1	0.2

[1] January 1, 1928, to January 1, 1935, in Iowa, Ohio, and South Dakota; January 1, 1926, to January 1, 1936, in Kentucky, Maryland, North Carolina, and North Dakota.
[2] Excludes heads of families established after 1928.

Chapter VII

THE SOCIAL SIGNIFICANCE OF RURAL MIGRATION

MIGRATION AS a social process is stimulated by the operation of numerous economic, psychological, and sociological factors and may in turn serve as a stimulus which sets in motion other important processes. At certain times and in certain places population movements constitute a social problem. They may also aggravate existing social problems or give rise to social problems which have been nonexistent hitherto. Furthermore, the occurrence of population movements may serve in some cases as an index of other processes. Thus, the constant interchange of rural-urban population is coming to be regarded as a crude index of comparative rural-urban prosperity.

EFFECTS OF RURAL-URBAN MIGRATION UPON RURAL LIFE

The effects of net migration from country to city have generally been regarded as beneficial to both. For the country it has meant a slower actual increase in population, which has postponed the day of extreme overcrowding in agriculture. Although in some sections the volume of emigration has been insufficient to prevent overpopulation, the situation might have been far worse had no migration occurred. In many areas already overpopulated, migration has been more extensive than the natural increase, thereby reducing the total number of persons. But while migration may be regarded as a factor of relief for the poorer areas, it has served in the better farming areas to enable the farm population further to improve their status. Whether mechanization of agricultural processes precedes or follows the emigration of farm population, the fact is that by means of these two developments the farm population of the superior areas has been able to increase its income per gainful worker and hence to raise the plane of living.

The effects of rural-urban migration upon the age and sex composition of the rural population are well known. Since the migrants from the country are not drawn proportionally by sex and from the various age groups, their loss tends to upset the balance of the population that remains. The surplus of males in the farm population and the general scarcity of young adults between the ages of 15 and 35 years are effects accruing from migration. A further effect of this situation is the surplus of dependents (children and aged persons) relative to the number of gainful workers.

Whether the net effect of rural-urban migrations has been a lowering of the quality of the residual rural population remains a moot question. The selection of persons who migrate is determined by an indefinitely large number of factors operating in varying proportions in different localities and among the various social groups within the same locality.[1] The situation seems to have been fairly stated by a recent writer who said, "As for selective migration, it seems * * * that the use of such a blanket term to cover migration everywhere and at all times is entirely unwarranted. * * * The problem of selection undoubtedly varies with different communities; factors which operate in one region or in one race may be entirely absent in another; there is no formula which applies to them all." [2]

Rural-urban migration depletes the wealth of the rural communities from which the migrants come. This depletion occurs in several ways. In the first place, the rural population produces and rears children to adult age only to have them migrate to urban communities. The cost of bearing and rearing these children reaches a considerable amount, however estimated. Even though the food costs on the farm are low, the cost of clothing, schooling, and medical care for the first 15 to 20 years of life cannot be ignored. An average of $150 per year per child has been suggested, making each rural migrant represent an investment of between $2,000 and $3,000. This is possibly above the money cost, but even at the rate of $100 per year per child the loss to the farm population between 1920 and 1930 as a result of this gift to American cities amounted to more than 9 billion dollars, or about $150 per farm annually.

The cost of rearing children for the cities does not represent the only financial loss to the farmer that may be attributed to migration. In a social system, such as ours, in which the parental property descends to the children in equal proportions, the only way in which all of the wealth of one generation can remain in the rural districts is for all of the descendants of that generation to remain there also. However, one of the heirs has customarily purchased the rights of the others and

---

[1] This probably accounts in part for the varying results obtained in different localities by different investigators of this subject.

[2] Klineberg, Otto, *Negro Intelligence and Selective Migration*, New York: Columbia University Press, 1935, pp. 61–62.

in so doing some of the wealth produced annually by a large number of American farmers has migrated to cities to satisfy the claims of rural-urban migrants.

It must not be supposed though that the movement of wealth incident to migration is entirely in one direction. Some migrants, after a sojourn in the city, return to the country with some accumulation of wealth which they invest in farming. Others, failing to return to the country, nevertheless assist in supporting the home farm during periods of distress. On the whole, however, past trends suggest that the major current has been from country to city rather than in the reverse direction.

The effect of rural-urban migration upon rural organizations and institutions is not thoroughly understood. Obviously, the effects are greatest where rural depopulation is most severe and where it occurs most rapidly. Rural institutions, like all institutions, are not sufficiently flexible to adjust readily to rapid population movements. Where heavy depopulation occurs, institutions are disrupted, services must be discontinued for lack of support, and taxes become intolerable. Such maladjustments are inevitable, however, until a greater degree of stabilization of the rural population occurs.

EFFECTS OF RURAL-URBAN MIGRATION UPON CITIES

The most obvious effect of rural-urban migration upon cities has been the contribution to urban growth. The urban population structure has been built largely with rural materials drawn either from at home or from abroad. Furthermore, it may be that the urban birth rate has been bolstered by this heavy migration from the rural districts. While available data do not permit any generalization regarding the birth rate of rural migrants [3] living in cities, it seems probable that for some groups at least it is higher than that of the native urban population.

That the future growth of cities is dependent largely upon the volume of rural-urban migration can hardly be doubted. Even in 1930 only 3 cities of 100,000 inhabitants or more were producing enough children permanently to reproduce the population. In two others the number of deaths among whites already exceeded the number of births in certain years.[4] As a class cities of 10,000 inhabitants or more were failing permanently to reproduce their population. Since 1930 the birth rate has declined still further. If urban growth depended entirely upon natural increase, it would shortly cease. It is estimated that without the aid of migration the urban population

---

[3] See Woofter, T. J., Jr., "The Natural Increase of the Rural Non-Farm Population," *The Milbank Memorial Fund Quarterly*, Vol. XIII, No. 4, 1935, pp. 311–319.

[4] National Resources Committee, *Population Statistics, 3. Urban Data*, Washington, D. C., October 1937, pp. 3 and 25.

in 1960 would be about the same size as in 1930.[5] It seems clear, therefore, that the future expansion of cities must be based largely upon the extent of rural-urban migration.

A second effect of rural migration has been its influence upon the sex and age composition of the urban population. Since females leave the country in larger proportion than males, they tend to predominate in the cities. This is particularly true of those cities in which the surplus of women in the rural-urban migration is not offset by a surplus of men through foreign immigration and in which the clerical occupations and lighter industries predominate. In cities devoted chiefly to the heavy industries a surplus of men tends to persist.

With respect to age composition the urban population exhibits a surplus of persons in the economically productive ages. The proportion of persons aged 20–49 years in the urban population in 1930 was equal to 48 percent. In the farm population it was only 36 percent. Moreover, the ratio of dependents to gainful workers is relatively low in urban areas. Because of migration the cities have been at no expense for rearing or educating a large proportion of their man power,[6] and often the supply is such that many workers may be employed at near subsistence wages. This abundance of man power has contributed to an elaboration of all occupations and to an unprecedented development of service occupations.

Probably a third effect of rural migration upon the city has been the maintenance of a degree of continuity between country and city. With such a high percentage of the urban population originating on the farms and in the villages, the degree of understanding of rural life and its problems that occurs is bound to be greater than would be the case if all of the urban population originated in the city. In addition, the large number of temporary migrants from city to country annually and the number of urban dwellers with previous farm experience who purchase farms are evidence that rural life is highly valued by a large proportion of the urban population.

MOBILITY WITHIN AGRICULTURE

Much of the difference of opinion regarding the desirability of population movements within the field of agriculture itself could be resolved if the volume and types of mobility essential for the promotion of the normal economic and social processes of agriculture and rural life could be ascertained. The social significance of population mobility within agriculture attaches chiefly to three types of movement: (1) parent-child succession in the occupation; (2) move-

---

[5] National Resources Committee, *The Problems of a Changing Population*, Washington, D. C., May 1938, p. 112.

[6] This situation is changing in those States where education is now largely supported by State funds, thereby reducing the proportion of local rural support.

ment of families from farm to farm; and (3) movement of farm operators and their families up and down the socio-economic scale.

One of the most common types of population mobility in agriculture is associated with the fact that agriculture is chiefly an individual or family occupation. A certain proportion of all farm-reared youth becomes established upon the parental farm and incurs no mobility except that of change of occupational status. Those who do not begin operations on the parental farm do not migrate far as a rule from the parental home. This tendency is significant in view of the marked differentials in the rate of natural increase of the farm population in various sections of the United States. Children reared in poor agricultural areas are not likely to leave merely because their economic and social status is low. It is only when supposedly attractive opportunities elsewhere are brought to their attention and it is not too difficult to take advantage of these opportunities that a general exodus from poor areas may begin.

A second type of mobility within agriculture that to some degree may be regarded as normal is that of the movement of farm operators from farm to farm. In an agricultural system in which owned farms are held in fee simple absolute and in which there is a tradition favorable to the buying and selling of farm land, considerable movement of owners from farm to farm is to be expected. If in addition the tradition is one of exploitation, one may be fairly certain that the movement incident to the change of owners from farm to farm will be greater than is desirable for conservation purposes and that it will continue until the tradition has been definitely modified. Furthermore, in a system in which some farms are operated by tenants, some shifting of tenants from farm to farm is necessary to promote and maintain satisfactory landlord-tenant relations. Yet it seems clear that when a considerable percentage of tenants moves every year to a different farm, the volume of movement is more than is necessary to promote desirable landlord-tenant relations. Also, it may aggravate the serious problem of soil conservation.

A third type of mobility occurring in the farm population is that of tenure changes. Traditionally, our society is one of free and open classes. To keep these classes open and not only to permit but also to facilitate movement from one to another has been considered a necessary aim of democracy. The classes based upon occupation are generally designated as farm owners, tenants, croppers, and laborers. The normal vertical movement of workers up and down among these classes has been styled movement up and down the "agricultural ladder."

In years past the agricultural ladder has served as a road to farm ownership for many operators. Numerous investigations have showed that a considerable percentage of farm owners climbed from farm-reared boy to farm owner-operator via the hired-man and tenant stages. It is true that not all such owners stepped upon all the rounds going up; still, the utility of the "ladder" seemed apparent. But with the passing of time, it has gradually become more difficult to make the climb to the ultimate round of unencumbered ownership by means of agriculture alone. More and more farm ownership has passed into the hands of institutional agencies, such as banks and insurance companies, or into the hands of farm-reared persons who have risen by means of nonagricultural occupations to a financial competence sufficient to permit them to own farm land. The percentage of tenancy has grown steadily and with it the average age of tenants.[7] Not only does a smaller proportion climb beyond the round of tenancy, but it requires an increasing percentage of the working lifetime to accomplish the ascent. More and more farm owners tend to be the children of farm owners, while the children of tenants become tenants or drift into nonagricultural occupations as laborers.[8] During periods of economic distress the agricultural ladder may be used almost as much for descent as for ascent.[9] It is under such circumstances that farm tenants and croppers, struggling to improve their economic and social positions, fall victims to excessive mobility. Many eventually become habituated to frequent moves from farm to farm.[10] In this manner, shifting about at the same occupational level becomes a substitute for movement up the agricultural ladder. The effects upon the soil are devastating in the long run, while the effects upon the families of these chronic movers are undesirable. They become habituated to movement, to a low plane of living, and to a family life which is poorly adjusted to the community of residence. When the children become adults, they are ill-equipped to assume the responsibilities of citizenship.

With the disappearance of free or cheap land and the growth of urban unemployment, the potential farm laborer often has little choice but to accept whatever the agricultural industry has to offer him. The continued progress of farm mechanization tends to reduce his opportunities. Fruits, vegetables, and other specialty crops still offer considerable opportunity to the farm laborer, but the demand

[7] Turner, H. A., *A Graphic Summary of Farm Tenure*, Miscellaneous Publication No. 261, U. S. Department of Agriculture, Washington, D. C., December 1936, pp. 44–45.

[8] Beck, P. G. and Lively, C. E., *Movement of Open Country Population in Ohio, II. The Individual Aspect*, Bulletin 489, Ohio Agricultural Experiment Station, Wooster, Ohio, September 1931, pp. 13 and 46; and Hamilton, C. Horace, *Recent Changes in the Social and Economic Status of Farm Families in North Carolina*, Bulletin No. 309, North Carolina Agricultural Experiment Station, Raleigh, N. C., May 1937, pp. 74–77.

[9] Hamilton, C. Horace, *ibid.*, p. 88.

[10] Vance, Rupert B., *Human Factors in Cotton Culture*, Chapel Hill: University of North Carolina Press, 1929, pp. 134–135 and 308.

Farm Security Administration (Lange).

Seasonal Labor Attracts Many Migrants.

is highly seasonal and spotted in location. Hence, his earnings are low, his mode of living poor, his position in the community precarious, and much energy and time are spent in moving about from one area of employment to another. To even a greater degree than the farm tenant, the seasonal and casual farm laborer lacks community status and responsibilities.[11]

Although some movement of population within the occupation of agriculture must be regarded as normal and necessary as a means of making occupational adjustments and readjustments, the rate of occupational turnover is relatively low. To farm successfully requires highly specialized knowledge and the farm operator is usually trained by the apprenticeship method. The farm-reared child not only grows into the occupation but also lives among farmers occupationally segregated to a marked degree and is familiar with other occupations to a very limited extent. In addition to that he sometimes receives a considerable amount of formal agricultural training of a technical nature. Thus, his knowledge of the occupation represents an educational investment.

It follows that the supply of farmers is determined primarily by the number of farm-reared youth who select farming as a life work. But whatever the situation with respect to occupational selection among farm-reared youth, it is clear that in the past unguided migration has not been sufficiently effective to remove from the farms the surplus youth not needed in the farming industry.[12] Moreover, it is in the poorer agricultural areas where farming is already overcrowded that redundant population has been most pronounced. While the pull of apparent opportunity elsewhere is a powerful stimulus to migration, the reluctance of country people to migrate is such that a social policy which is calculated to adjust population to resources more effectively in overcrowded rural areas must rely upon some other means than the uncertain pull of distant cities.

MIGRATION AND AGRICULTURAL OPPORTUNITY

Viewing the farm population solely from the point of view of the number of workers necessary for commercial agricultural production,

[11] See, for example, Webb, John N., *The Migratory-Casual Worker*, Research Monograph VII, Division of Social Research, Works Progress Administration, Washington, D. C., 1937; Landis, Paul H., *Rural Immigrants to Washington State, 1932–1936*, Rural Sociology Series in Population, No. 2, Washington Agricultural Experiment Station, Pullman, Wash., July 1936; and Taylor, Paul S. and Vasey, Tom, "Contemporary Background of California Farm Labor," *Rural Sociology*, Vol. I, 1936, pp. 401–419.

[12] See Woofter, T. J., Jr., "Replacement Rates in the Productive Ages," *The Milbank Memorial Fund Quarterly*, Vol. XV, No. 4, 1937, pp. 348–354; and Lively, C. E., *Replacement Requirements of Gainful Workers in Agriculture in Ohio, 1930–1940*, Mimeograph Bulletin No. 109, Ohio State University and Ohio Agricultural Experiment Station, Columbus, Ohio, June 1938.

there are undoubtedly too many people living on farms.   Since the World War the market for agricultural products abroad has been greatly curtailed, and since 1929 the limited purchasing power of the nonfarm population has reduced its effective demand for food and fiber. Although a considerable proportion of the nonagricultural population is underfed from a nutritional standpoint, to make the diet adequate would require either sharp reductions in the cost of food or sharp increases in the incomes of the people.[13]   The outlook suggests, therefore, that if agricultural production is balanced with the present demand, there will be no sharp increase in commercial production within the immediate future.

The amount of cropland required to meet the probable demand for agricultural products in 1940 has been estimated at approximately 350 million acres.   Allowing another 50 million acres of land for crop failure and land lying fallow and 460 million acres for pasture lands, a total of 860 million acres of farm land is indicated for production in 1940.   This amounts to 87 percent of all land in farms and 84 percent of the arable land of the United States, whether included in farms or not.   According to these estimates[14] and in view of the trends toward a stationary population and more intensive cultivation, there is an adequate amount of farm land to meet the requirements for agricultural production for some time to come.

But although there is a sufficient supply of farm land in the United States for productive purposes, the quality of that land varies greatly from place to place.   Recently all arable land has been classified into four grades as follows:[15]

	Million acres
Grade 1 (Excellent)	101
Grade 2 (Good)	211
Grade 3 (Fair)	346
Grade 4 (Poor)	363
Total	1,021

Rough estimates indicate that about 90 percent of all arable land classified as "Excellent" is located in the Corn Belt, while about 75 percent of the 312 million acres classified as "Excellent" or "Good" is to be found in the Corn Belt, on its margin, and in Oklahoma and Texas.

It is recognized that because of its peculiar properties and because of geographical position and climatic factors, much of the poorer land

---

[13] National Resources Committee, *The Problems of a Changing Population, op. cit.*, pp. 114–115.

[14] National Resources Board, *A Report on National Planning and Public Works in Relation to National Resources and Including Land Use and Water Resources with Findings and Recommendations, Part II, Report of the Land Planning Committee,* Washington, D. C., 1934, pp. 126–127.

[15] *Ibid.*, p. 127.

is almost indispensable for productive purposes and should be improved as much as possible. Nevertheless, it should be remembered that as a long-time policy of conservation of agricultural resources, it is desirable to utilize land resources after the manner to which they are best adapted. Such a policy would result in a greater concentration of crop production upon the best agricultural land.

At present the farm population is not distributed in a manner determined only by productivity of the land resources. Estimates indicate that in 1930 at least two-thirds of the farm population was upon "Fair" or "Poor" farm land. Even when allowance for differences in type of farming is made, the variation in ratio of farm population to arable land is significant. In Iowa, the State possessing the largest block of first-grade land, there were 36 acres of arable land per capita of the farm population. Other States possessing much good land had similar acreages per capita. On the other hand, in some States where the major portion of the arable land is of third- and fourth-grade quality, the acreages per capita were much smaller. In some sections, notably in the Appalachian-Ozark Highlands, in the Lake States Cut-Over Area, and on the Great Plains, the land is now regarded as overpopulated from the standpoint of best use of the agricultural resources. In addition, large acreages are regarded as too poor and eroded for cultivation.[16]

Not only is much of the poorer farm land of the United States overpopulated from the standpoint of the best use of agricultural resources and from the standpoint of the possibility of realizing a reasonably satisfactory plane of living for the people on such lands, but also it would appear that a large proportion of these people is not needed on farms for purposes of commercial agricultural production. According to figures compiled from the 1930 Census one-half of the farms of the Nation produce little more than one-tenth of the commercial agricultural products. These farms are self-sufficing or part-time farms, or they operate upon such a small scale that they could all cease operations without reducing the volume of commercial farm products more than 11 percent. Without doubt the remaining 50 percent could expand operations sufficiently to compensate for the loss of these farms. Since these farms with low volume of commercial production are concentrated markedly in the poorer land areas, any such shift in operations would be a move in the direction of effecting a greater concentration of agricultural production upon the better lands.

Looking at the problem purely from the standpoint of productive possibilities, it seems probable that the least productive half of the present farm population could be removed from agriculture without

---

[16] Goodrich, Carter and Others, *Migration and Economic Opportunity*, Philadelphia: University of Pennsylvania Press, 1936, pp. 79, 156, and 243; and National Resources Board, *Report of the Land Planning Committee, op. cit.,* p. 127.

endangering the Nation's supply of food and fiber produced, except for that which they consume. There is scarcely any possibility of accomplishing such an end, however. Most of the people who live on farms know no other occupation or mode of life. Even if they were able to adapt themselves to other ways of living, urban industry has no place for them. Hence, it would be extremely difficult, circumstances as they are, to remove them from farming to any other occupation or situation in which they would be better off. In other words, the agricultural industry must reckon with an oversupply of farmers, and the commercial farmer must reckon with the marginal farmer, the subsistence farmer, and the part-time farmer, who stand ready to produce more for sale if the state of the market appears to warrant it.

When urban prosperity is the rule, the matter of overpopulation of the rural districts causes little concern because of the extensive migrations to urban occupations and because of the relatively high prices paid for farm products. But urban prosperity fluctuates. With the relatively high birth rate that prevails in the rural districts in general and upon the farms in particular, the failure of a large percentage of the rural natural increase to migrate cityward is soon reflected in a sharply increasing rural population. Too often these rapid rates of increase are to be found in the poorer land sections where the ratio of farm population to the land is already too high.

On the whole, the evidence appears adequate to warrant the conclusion that the future economic salvation of the American farm population under our present system does not lie merely in the direction of commercial farming. Already a large proportion, perhaps an increasing proportion, of the farm population dwells upon mediocre or poor land and conducts farming operations under conditions which place those people hopelessly out of the race for success by means of commercial production. Under present circumstances they can scarcely be expected to crowd into cities nor can they with confidence be settled elsewhere upon land under conditions that will with certainty improve their lot. Resettlement projects conducted upon a small scale and under certain circumstances may be successful in improving the lot of those resettled. Such treatment of the disadvantaged rural classes as a whole is impracticable, however. The gradual retirement of the poorest agricultural lands from cultivation and the removal of a share of the population will help, but, even so, it must be admitted that for the great majority of people farming on such lands economic and social improvement must come to them, if at all, where they are.

In formulating a policy for the future welfare of the farm population, therefore, it is well to remember that, although in the interests of conservation of agricultural resources it may be advisable further to concentrate commercial agricultural production upon the better lands, it does not follow that such concentration of production will necessarily be accompanied by a similar concentration of farm population. The trend toward mechanization of agricultural processes upon the better land and the birth rate differentials which occur in the farm population may prevent any such concentration in spite of the slight tendency for people to migrate more heavily from the poorer agricultural districts. It is well to remember also that when dealing with overpopulation in the poorer areas only certain alternative policies are possible. It is possible, first, to leave the people of these less favored districts alone in the hope that unguided migration will relieve the congestion of overpopulation. Unfortunately, the history of unguided migration does not offer evidence that this policy is likely to succeed. It is more likely to result in continued redundant population and a progressive decline in the plane of living of the people.

A second possible policy consists of attempting to relieve overpopulation by encouraging reduction in size of family and by stimulating heavy emigration. While birth rates may be reduced in these areas, a decreased birth rate does not become effective in reducing the number of gainful workers for nearly 20 years. Any relief within that time would have to come by means of heavier emigration. This in turn involves the obligation to assist the population in locating areas to which they may migrate with the probability of improving their situation.

A third possibility consists of using the combined knowledge of the sciences to enable the people of the so-called "overpopulated" areas to support themselves to better advantage where they now are. This could undoubtedly be done if the problem were approached from the standpoint of giving support to the local population rather than from the point of view of making commercial farmers. In such a program, part-time farming, a greater production of home-consumed products, the development of community industries for local consumption, and the expansion of service industries would all have a part. In any case, the encouragement of emigration should be a definite part of such policy in all areas where the birth rate appreciably outruns the requirements for maintaining a stationary population. By such means it may be possible to improve, or at least to maintain, the status of the large number of people who live upon the land but who have little or no chance of success as commercial farmers.

RELATION OF RURAL MIGRATION TO PUBLIC WORK PROGRAMS AND RELIEF

Although migration from one rural area to another and from rural areas to cities has been the chief method of adjusting population to resources in this country, the migration has been characterized by individuals moving independently of each other. Each individual has been free to make his own choice and to move from areas of lesser opportunity to areas of apparently greater opportunity. The fact that a large proportion of migrants to cities has been recruited from the relatively poorer areas has, even in prosperous times, made for difficulties of adjustment. These migrants, reared and educated in areas with meager and poor schools and other social facilities, have had to compete for jobs with individuals trained under more favorable circumstances. As a result they have tended to obtain the inferior and less secure positions. They have been more willing to live under substandard housing and sanitation conditions and frequently have contributed to the relief loads in the areas to which they have gone.

Even though the migration from 1920 to 1930 was extensive, amounting to more than 20 percent of the resident population in 1920 in some areas, it was not sufficient to accomplish needed adjustments between population and resources. Many of the less productive farmers were living on poor lands and in areas with meager resources, including those areas where exploitation had drastically reduced the resources available. Among these people levels of living were low and earnings precarious. Had there been any large-scale organization for public relief in the late 1920's, these areas would have been the scene of much of the activity of these organizations. A number of small voluntary agencies had begun to work in such areas, but their resources were clearly insufficient to cope with the need.

Since 1930 there has been both a considerable decline in the migration away from farms and some movement back to the land. This has led to an increase in farm population, with some tendency toward concentration in the areas with the poorest resources. It has resulted in the piling up of rural youth, which has in turn been the basis of much of the rural youth problem with which public relief agencies have been concerned. The prospects for migration from farms in the immediate future suggest that many of these young people who would have migrated since 1930 had conditions been more favorable may not have the opportunity of shifting later. Their problems now and in the future constitute a challenge to public agencies concerned with the welfare of rural people.

The retardation of migration after the beginning of the depression has had another serious effect upon relief needs in rural areas. The onset of the depression delivered the final blow to many struggling industries in areas where natural resources had been most completely exploited. Numerous surveys in areas formerly supporting forest industries have shown that since 1930 the sawmills have disappeared, and there are no prospects for resumption of forest operations. Similar conditions exist in a large number of mining areas and in areas depending on other rural industries as well. With alternative economic opportunities largely cut off, the migration normally to be expected under those circumstances did not occur. Stranded com-

Farm Security Administration (Mydans).

Rural Youth in Urban Slums.

munities appeared in many parts of the country. There was striking evidence of the role of migration in adjusting population to resources and of the need for public aid when "normal" processes of migration were interrupted or brought almost to a standstill. The reduction in the migration from rural areas since 1930 has been one of the most important factors in intensifying rural relief needs. Emergency programs have dealt with these needs, but the problems require long-time planning and basic attacks on fundamental causes which are not implicit in such programs.

Much attention has been given to the role of the back-to-the-land movement in relation to relief needs and relief policies. Before the establishment of the FERA in 1933, many urban areas had considered the possibility of a back-to-the-land movement as a relief measure, but it soon became clear that this was not likely to be successful. Even so, the idea has tended to persist. Although there had been a striking suburban trend before 1930 and this trend apparently continued after that date, many of the relief clients were not suited to the development of part-time or subsistence farms. In some areas, however, there was a movement to the land. This movement involved individuals and families whose resources had been largely exhausted. They sought shelter and the possibility of producing their own food and fuel in localities where little or no capital investment was required. Under the circumstances many of these efforts were doomed to failure, and relief agencies were called upon for assistance. The best agricultural land, that on which commercial farming has been most highly developed, experienced much less of the back-to-the-land movement than did poorer areas. In some localities, notably in those where rates of population growth were rapid, the combination of retarded migration and a back-to-the-land movement created serious population pressure and intensified relief needs.

During the depression years when the demand for urban industrial workers was markedly reduced, many prospective migrants looked about for other opportunities. The large majority of rural-urban migrants are available for unskilled work only and with the decline in opportunities for industrial employment an attempt was made to secure agricultural employment. The Pacific Coast States and the Southwest with their widely advertised climatic advantages and their need for seasonal unskilled agricultural workers proved extremely attractive. Families which had little or nothing to lose by leaving their earlier residences might find themselves no worse off by going to these Western States, and by the movement they might improve their condition. Severe droughts in the Great Plains stimulated some migration farther west. At the same time throughout the Great Plains and in parts of the Cotton Belt there was a rapid increase in the use of power machinery accompanied by displacement of farm families.

The volume of the movement to the West coast and other States was so great that the States were unable to absorb these migrants. Serious relief problems arose and continue—problems which the States alone have not been able to meet. Unless there is some striking reversal of the trend of migration to these States, public assistance will be needed for a long time to come. The recent migrants have little desire to go back to their earlier residences. Many of them have no facilities for returning and no alternative opportunities which would draw them back. Relief agencies are faced with the problem of facilitating their adjustment in their new residences, and even though there are some prospective large-scale developments which will make hitherto unused resources available, these are still far in the future.

The development of a Nation-wide work and relief program has had significant, though unmeasurable, effects upon the volume of rural migration. Prior to the widespread acceptance of public relief as an element of everyday life, residence and settlement laws probably had little effect upon the behavior of the average citizen, although requirements of residence as affecting eligibility for relief have been on the statute books of most States for many years. As long as public assistance was not an important element in the calculations of the average citizen, the fact that a continuous residence of 1 to 5 years might be required to establish eligibility for relief was hardly an item worth considering. In recent years, however, public relief has become a major fact in the lives of millions of persons, and the importance of residence requirements has been forcibly impressed upon them. These requirements undoubtedly have been a bar to some migration and may have served to prevent some desirable emigration from problem areas. Differences in policies of distributing relief also have undoubtedly affected currents of migration. Rumors of such differences may have been even more effective. Thus, reports in late 1933 and early 1934 indicated that in some areas there was a considerable shift from open country to villages because it was reputedly easier to secure CWA employment in villages. But there is little evidence that migrants have gone to large cities because of higher standards of relief. On the other hand, analysis of differential migration from certain severely affected areas suggests that areas with liberal relief policies were less likely to experience as much out-migration as those areas where relief policies were regarded as less liberal.

The establishment of a large-scale public work and relief program has obviously reduced the amount of migration, particularly the amount of aimless migration of those individuals and families for whom any change might be for the better and would certainly not entail any loss. The fact that a public agency was ready to assist people in distress enabled many to remain at their earlier residences and in some cases to reestablish themselves later. This result is not controverted by pointing out that in some areas relief policies may have served to postpone desirable long-time population adjustments. Analysis of the migrations from the drought areas indicates that in some of the most severely affected areas relief funds have served to retard fundamental adjustments in the agricultural economy which are now deemed to be necessary. In these and similar cases emergency funds have certainly alleviated immediate distress, but they might have contributed to long-time solutions had it been possible to put into effect more flexible policies of public assistance.

Since migration has played so large a role in American history, it is not surprising that the movement of people should be widely accepted as a major technique for the solution of many problems. Exhaustion of resources, stranded communities, settlement that was too dense for the Great Plains, population pressure in the Southern Appalachians, the rapid increase in numbers of rural youth—these are situations which appear to require migration from rural areas.

Promoting migration as a matter of public policy requires more careful analysis than this, however. It is comparatively easy to outline problem areas and to find that some of the people now living there should be encouraged to move elsewhere. But such a recommendation is obviously incomplete. Unless the analysis goes on to point out areas to which these migrants could go and to suggest how they may make the necessary adjustments, it has failed to meet the issue. The welfare of an area has meaning only in terms of the welfare of the people living there. To move people from a problem area without regard to this simple fact may involve the creation of problems as acute as those which were to have been solved. In all parts of the country relief agencies have had to deal with the results of migrations which were ill-advised, as judged by subsequent developments. The freedom of the individual to change his residence can be of major value in effecting adjustments if the individual can make the sound choices which this process assumes. In the process of adjusting population to resources, however, migration provides only one of the techniques, and in any specific situation others may be more efficient. In the work of relief agencies guided migration can be an effective part of the program, but other approaches to the rehabilitation of individuals and areas must also be used. Careful consideration of the alternatives may lead to the conclusion that a more efficient utilization of available resources would in many instances prove more effective than migration. It must be recognized that large-scale migration offers no panacea for meeting relief needs. Rather, the scale on which planned migrations are carried out is a significant element in their ultimate possibilities of success. In general, a combination of directed migration, reduced birth rates, and improvement of basic social and economic conditions within overpopulated areas seems to offer the soundest approach to solving the long-time problems of widespread rural destitution.

Appendixes

135

Appendix A

SUPPLEMENTARY TABLES

Table 1.—Counties of the United States by Percent Change in the Rural Population in Relation to the Average Change in the Total Rural Population,[1] by Geographic Division and State, 1900–1910, 1910–1920, and 1920–1930

Geographic division and State	Number of counties											
	1900–1910				1910–1920				1920–1930			
		Increase				Increase				Increase		
	Total	9.2 per-cent or more	Less than 9.2 per-cent	De-crease	Total	3.2 per-cent or more	Less than 3.2 per-cent	De-crease	Total	4.7 per-cent or more	Less than 4.7 per-cent	De-crease
United States	2,797	1,158	544	1,095	2,887	1,129	253	1,505	3,002	1,029	414	1,559
New England [2]	38	5	12	21	38	8	6	24	38	9	14	15
Maine	16	3	6	7	16	3	2	11	16	4	6	6
New Hampshire	—	—	—	—	...	—	—	—	—	—	—	—
Vermont	14	—	4	10	14	—	1	13	14	1	5	8
Massachusetts	—	—	—	—	—	—	—	—	—	—	—	—
Rhode Island	—	—	—	—	—	—	—	...	—	—	—	—
Connecticut	8	2	2	4	8	5	3	—	8	4	3	1
Middle Atlantic	143	30	34	79	143	39	12	92	143	58	21	64
New York	57	4	14	39	57	7	3	47	57	24	11	22
New Jersey	20	11	5	4	20	13	—	7	20	14	1	5
Pennsylvania	66	15	15	36	66	19	9	38	66	20	9	37
East North Central	435	71	86	278	436	93	33	310	436	93	56	287
Ohio	88	7	18	63	88	14	14	60	88	23	19	46
Indiana	92	2	15	75	92	7	2	83	92	16	11	65
Illinois	102	11	19	72	102	16	4	82	102	12	9	81
Michigan	83	28	19	36	83	21	4	58	83	25	9	49
Wisconsin	70	23	15	32	71	35	9	27	71	17	8	46
West North Central	582	201	84	297	606	224	65	317	618	133	124	361
Minnesota	82	24	21	37	86	57	11	18	86	6	27	53
Iowa	99	3	9	87	99	26	19	54	99	9	26	64
Missouri	114	13	16	85	114	14	6	94	114	12	6	96
North Dakota	39	33	2	4	49	29	4	16	53	16	17	20
South Dakota	53	41	6	0	61	39	6	16	68	28	19	21
Nebraska	90	40	18	32	92	37	11	44	93	22	18	53
Kansas	105	47	12	46	105	22	8	75	105	40	11	54

See footnotes at end of table.

Table 1.—Counties of the United States by Percent Change in the Rural Population in Relation to the Average Change in the Total Rural Population,[1] by Geographic Division and State, 1900–1910, 1910–1920, and 1920–1930—Continued

Geographic division and State	Number of counties											
	1900–1910				1910–1920				1920–1930			
	Total	Increase		De-crease	Total	Increase		De-crease	Total	Increase		De-crease
		9.2 per-cent or more	Less than 9.2 per-cent			3.2 per-cent or more	Less than 3.2 per-cent			4.7 per-cent or more	Less than 4.7 per-cent	
South Atlantic	500	222	144	134	515	247	52	216	536	204	56	276
Delaware	3	1	1	1	3	1	—	2	3	1	1	1
Maryland	23	4	9	10	23	4	4	15	23	8	3	12
Virginia	100	28	37	35	100	38	16	46	100	23	13	64
West Virginia	55	29	9	17	55	29	5	21	55	25	6	24
North Carolina	97	47	34	16	98	66	9	23	100	75	14	11
South Carolina	40	22	9	9	43	24	5	14	46	9	3	34
Georgia	137	60	37	40	146	62	12	72	155	36	9	110
Florida	45	31	8	6	47	23	1	23	54	27	7	20
East South Central	355	129	89	137	360	120	39	201	364	119	57	188
Kentucky	119	35	31	53	119	37	13	69	120	27	12	81
Tennessee	95	24	27	44	95	27	16	52	95	24	17	54
Alabama	66	34	16	16	67	35	7	25	67	25	15	27
Mississippi	75	36	15	24	79	21	3	55	82	43	13	26
West South Central	431	272	69	90	455	216	33	206	468	226	50	192
Arkansas	75	49	10	16	75	40	4	31	75	19	8	48
Louisiana	58	33	11	14	59	19	4	36	63	36	6	21
Oklahoma	55	25	18	12	76	37	3	36	77	33	8	36
Texas	243	165	30	48	245	120	22	103	253	138	28	87
Mountain	188	139	12	37	205	113	8	84	267	96	28	143
Montana	24	20	1	3	28	13	1	14	51	9	7	35
Idaho	21	19	1	1	23	8	—	15	44	12	3	29
Wyoming	13	11	—	2	14	7	1	6	21	12	2	7
Colorado	57	38	3	16	59	37	3	19	62	25	6	31
New Mexico	19	14	2	3	26	13	1	12	29	16	—	13
Arizona	13	12	—	1	13	11	—	2	14	10	1	3
Utah	27	15	4	8	27	20	2	5	29	8	6	15
Nevada	14	10	1	3	15	4	—	11	17	4	3	10
Pacific	125	89	14	22	129	69	5	55	132	91	8	33
Washington	36	33	2	1	38	17	3	18	39	21	4	14
Oregon	33	25	4	4	34	20	—	14	36	20	4	12
California	56	31	8	17	57	32	2	23	57	50	—	7

[1] The national averages for rural population increase were 9.2 percent for 1900–1910, 3.2 percent for 1910–1920, and 4.7 percent for 1920–1930.
[2] Exclusive of Massachusetts, New Hampshire, and Rhode Island.

Sources: Bureau of the Census, *Fourteenth Census of the United States: 1920*, Population Vol. I, 1921, tables 49 and 50, and *Fifteenth Census of the United States: 1930*, Population Vol. III, table 13, U. S. Department of Commerce, Washington, D. C., 1932.

Table 2.—Net Gain or Loss [1] Through Migration to the Rural Population [2] of the United States, by Geographic Division and State, 1920–1930 [3] (Estimated)

Geographic division and State	Rural population [4] 1920	Rural population [4] 1930	Increase or decrease, 1920–1930 Number	Increase or decrease, 1920–1930 Percent	Net gain or loss through migration, 1920–1930 Number	Net gain or loss through migration, 1920–1930 Percent of 1920 rural population
United States	51,742,600	54,185,200	+2,442,600	+4.7	−5,734,200	−11.1
New England	1,541,000	1,862,600	+320,700	+20.8	+145,500	+9.4
Maine	470,300	478,300	+8,000	+1.7	−40,600	−8.6
New Hampshire	163,800	193,000	+29,200	+17.8	+16,400	+10.0
Vermont	243,400	242,000	−1,400	−0.6	−23,500	−9.7
Massachusetts	202,900	419,900	+217,000	+106.9	+176,000	+86.7
Rhode Island	15,300	52,300	+37,000	+241.8	+30,600	+200.0
Connecticut	446,200	477,100	+30,900	+6.9	−13,400	−3.0
Middle Atlantic	5,615,100	5,894,300	+279,200	+5.0	−443,400	−7.9
New York	1,802,200	2,074,800	+272,600	+15.1	+98,100	+5.4
New Jersey	683,500	705,000	+21,500	+3.1	−50,100	−7.3
Pennsylvania	3,129,400	3,114,500	−14,900	−0.5	−491,400	−15.7
East North Central	8,466,100	8,542,400	+76,300	+0.9	−899,400	−10.6
Ohio	2,092,300	2,149,400	+57,100	+2.7	−181,300	−8.7
Indiana	1,454,100	1,449,200	−4,900	−0.3	−154,900	−10.7
Illinois	2,091,600	2,003,900	−87,700	−4.2	303,400	−14.5
Michigan	1,433,800	1,547,900	+114,100	+8.0	−78,900	−5.5
Wisconsin	1,394,300	1,392,000	−2,300	−0.2	−180,900	−13.0
West North Central	7,854,900	7,779,500	−75,400	−1.0	−1,100,800	−14.0
Minnesota	1,342,600	1,312,900	−29,700	−2.2	−207,400	−15.4
Iowa	1,535,400	1,498,800	−36,600	−2.4	−212,900	−13.9
Missouri	1,825,800	1,778,900	−46,900	−2.6	−261,900	−14.3
North Dakota	562,000	570,800	+8,800	+1.6	−92,200	−16.4
South Dakota	537,400	565,000	+27,600	+5.1	−63,700	−11.9
Nebraska	895,300	896,400	+1,100	+0.1	−122,900	−13.7
Kansas	1,156,400	1,156,700	+300	—	−139,800	−12.1
South Atlantic	9,746,000	10,188,100	+442,100	+4.5	−1,434,000	−14.7
Delaware	102,400	115,900	+13,500	+13.2	+2,500	+2.4
Maryland	584,200	661,100	+76,900	+13.2	−10,500	−1.8
Virginia	1,650,000	1,650,300	+300	—	−279,400	−16.9
West Virginia	1,102,300	1,246,600	+144,300	+13.1	−118,500	−10.8
North Carolina	2,089,600	2,383,900	+294,300	+14.1	−206,500	−9.9
South Carolina	1,408,700	1,383,300	−25,400	−1.8	−298,000	−21.2
Georgia	2,191,700	2,032,700	−159,000	−7.3	−510,600	−23.3
Florida	617,100	714,300	+97,200	+15.8	13,000	−2.1
East South Central	6,957,800	7,171,900	+214,100	+3.1	−1,097,200	−15.8
Kentucky	1,794,300	1,827,800	+33,500	+1.9	−313,300	−17.5
Tennessee	1,740,000	1,732,500	−7,500	−0.4	−316,000	−18.2
Alabama	1,856,500	1,921,300	+64,800	+3.5	−300,200	−16.2
Mississippi	1,567,000	1,690,300	+123,300	+7.9	−167,700	−10.7
West South Central	7,325,300	7,816,700	+491,400	+6.7	−922,700	12.6
Arkansas	1,473,900	1,484,200	+10,300	+0.7	−255,600	−17.3
Louisiana	1,181,300	1,281,400	+100,100	+8.5	−136,700	11.6
Oklahoma	1,498,100	1,585,900	+87,800	+5.9	−214,700	−14.3
Texas	3,172,000	3,465,200	+293,200	+9.2	−315,700	−10.0
Mountain	2,132,300	2,258,000	+125,700	+5.9	−258,900	−12.1
Montana	378,900	358,400	−20,500	−5.4	−71,000	−18.7
Idaho	314,700	317,200	+2,500	+0.8	−50,200	−16.0
Wyoming	137,300	156,300	+19,000	+13.8	−6,100	−4.4
Colorado	488,900	518,900	+30,000	+6.1	−50,400	−10.3
New Mexico	297,100	319,000	+21,900	+7.4	−43,600	−14.7
Arizona	217,800	288,100	+70,300	+32.3	+17,300	+7.9
Utah	235,400	243,200	+7,800	+3.3	−44,500	−18.9
Nevada	62,200	56,900	−5,300	−8.5	−10,400	−16.7
Pacific	2,103,200	2,671,700	+568,500	+27.0	+276,700	+13.2
Washington	610,400	681,700	+71,300	+11.7	−2,400	−0.4
Oregon	394,000	466,000	+72,000	+18.3	+22,800	+5.8
California	1,098,800	1,524,000	+425,200	+38.7	+256,300	+23.3

[1] Minus (−) indicates a loss.
[2] Includes only persons living in 1920 whose ages were reported.
[3] For method of computation see appendix B.
[4] Corrected for underenumeration of children under 5 years of age.

Table 3.—Net Gain or Loss [1] Through Migration to the Rural Population of the United States, by Geographic Division, State, and Residence, 1920–1930 [2] (Estimated)

Geographic division and State	Net gain or loss through migration, 1920–1930					
	Total rural		Rural-farm		Rural-nonfarm	
	Number	Percent of 1920 population	Number	Percent of 1920 population	Number	Percent of 1920 population
United States_____	−5,734,200	−11.1	−6,084,600	−19.3	+350,400	+1.7
New England_____	+145,500	+9.4	−69,800	−13.0	+215,300	+21.4
Maine_____	−40,600	−8.6	−39,200	−20.7	−1,400	−0.5
New Hampshire____	+16,400	+10.0	−10,600	−16.4	+27,000	+27.3
Vermont_____	−23,500	−9.7	−22,900	−18.3	−600	−0.5
Massachusetts_____	+176,000	+86.7	+13,200	+21.2	+162,800	+115.5
Rhode Island_____	+30,600	+200.0	+4,100	+77.1	+26,500	+266.8
Connecticut_____	−13,400	−3.0	−14,400	−15.9	+1,000	+0.3
Middle Atlantic_____	−443,400	−7.9	−349,000	−18.7	−94,400	−2.5
New York_____	+98,100	+5.4	−127,400	−16.2	+225,500	+22.2
New Jersey_____	−50,100	−7.3	−25,300	−18.4	−24,800	−4.5
Pennsylvania_____	−491,400	−15.7	−196,300	−20.8	−295,100	−13.5
East North Central_____	−899,400	−10.6	−969,900	−19.7	+70,500	+2.0
Ohio_____	−181,300	−8.7	−232,300	−20.4	+51,000	+5.4
Indiana_____	−154,900	−10.7	−181,200	−20.0	+26,300	+4.8
Illinois_____	−303,400	−14.5	−228,500	−20.8	−74,900	−7.5
Michigan_____	−78,900	−5.5	−158,300	−18.6	+79,400	+13.6
Wisconsin_____	−180,900	−13.0	−169,600	−18.4	−11,300	−2.4
West North Central____	−1,100,800	−14.0	−906,500	−17.5	−194,300	−7.3
Minnesota_____	−207,400	−15.4	−142,500	−15.9	−64,900	−14.6
Iowa_____	−212,900	−13.9	−165,000	−16.8	−47,900	−8.7
Missouri_____	−261,900	−14.3	−245,300	−20.2	−16,600	−2.7
North Dakota_____	−92,200	−16.4	−74,200	−18.7	−18,000	−10.9
South Dakota_____	−63,700	−11.9	−45,400	−12.5	−18,300	−10.6
Nebraska_____	−122,900	−13.7	−100,400	−17.1	−22,500	−7.3
Kansas_____	−139,800	−12.1	−133,700	−18.1	−6,100	−1.5
South Atlantic_____	−1,434,000	−14.7	−1,619,100	−25.0	+185,100	+5.6
Delaware_____	+2,500	+2.4	−9,900	−19.2	+12,400	+24.4
Maryland_____	−10,500	−1.8	−71,400	−25.5	+60,900	+20.0
Virginia_____	−279,400	−16.9	−265,400	−24.8	−14,000	−2.4
West Virginia_____	−118,500	−10.8	−105,300	−22.0	−13,200	−2.1
North Carolina_____	−206,500	−9.9	−242,400	−16.0	+35,900	+6.3
South Carolina_____	−298,000	−21.2	−343,700	−31.6	+45,700	+14.3
Georgia_____	−510,600	−23.3	−532,600	−31.3	+22,000	+4.5
Florida_____	−13,000	−2.1	−48,400	−17.2	+35,400	+10.5
East South Central_____	−1,097,200	−15.8	−1,036,400	−19.8	−60,800	−3.5
Kentucky_____	−313,300	−17.5	−346,000	−26.4	+32,700	+6.8
Tennessee_____	−316,000	−18.2	−273,400	−21.4	−42,600	−9.2
Alabama_____	−300,200	−16.2	−261,900	−19.4	−38,300	−7.5
Mississippi_____	−167,700	−10.7	−155,100	−12.1	−12,600	−4.4
West South Central____	−922,700	−12.6	−906,400	−17.3	−16,300	−0.8
Arkansas_____	−255,600	−17.3	−237,700	−20.6	−17,900	−5.6
Louisiana_____	−136,700	−11.6	−117,500	−14.8	−19,200	−5.0
Oklahoma_____	−214,700	−14.3	−197,500	−19.3	−17,200	−3.6
Texas_____	−315,700	−10.0	−353,700	−15.5	+38,000	+4.3
Mountain_____	−258,900	−12.1	−224,500	−19.4	−34,400	−3.5
Montana_____	−71,000	−18.7	−52,900	−23.3	−18,100	−11.9
Idaho_____	−50,200	−16.0	−43,300	−21.9	−6,900	−5.9
Wyoming_____	−6,100	−4.4	−6,300	−9.3	+200	+0.3
Colorado_____	−50,400	−10.3	−30,100	−11.3	−20,300	−9.1
New Mexico_____	−43,600	−14.7	−33,400	−20.7	−10,200	−7.6
Arizona_____	+17,300	+7.9	−9,900	−10.9	+27,200	+21.4
Utah_____	−44,500	−18.9	−47,200	−35.5	+2,700	+2.6
Nevada_____	−10,400	−16.7	−1,400	−8.9	−9,000	−19.4
Pacific_____	+276,700	+13.2	−3,000	−0.3	+279,700	+25.1
Washington_____	−2,400	−0.4	−12,000	−4.3	+9,600	+2.9
Oregon_____	+22,800	+5.8	−12,500	−5.9	+35,300	+19.5
California_____	+256,300	+23.3	+21,500	+4.3	+234,800	+38.9

[1] Minus (−) indicates a loss.
[2] For method of computation see appendix B.

Table 4.—Counties of the United States by Net Gain or Loss Through Migration to the Rural Population, by Geographic Division and State, 1920–1930 [1] (Estimated)

Geographic division and State	Gained rural population, 1920-1930				Lost rural population, 1920-1930				
	Total	Number of persons			Total	Number of persons			
		4,000 or more	1,000-3,999	Fewer than 1,000		Fewer than 1,000	1,000-1,999	2,000-3,999	4,000 or more
United States	517	113	201	203	2,542	450	639	893	500
New England	26	14	8	4	38	10	12	10	6
Maine	1	—	—	1	15	4	5	2	4
New Hampshire	7	1	5	1	3	3	—	—	—
Vermont	—	—	—	—	14	2	7	5	—
Massachusetts	12	8	2	2	—	—	—	—	—
Rhode Island	4	4	—	—	—	—	—	—	—
Connecticut	2	1	1	—	6	1	—	3	2
Middle Atlantic	37	16	15	6	106	17	16	23	50
New York	20	10	8	2	37	10	8	10	9
New Jersey	10	6	4	—	10	3	1	2	4
Pennsylvania	7	—	3	4	59	4	7	11	37
East North Central	48	14	18	16	388	52	91	171	74
Ohio	14	4	6	4	74	8	12	37	17
Indiana	7	2	3	2	85	14	30	35	6
Illinois	7	—	4	3	95	5	20	39	31
Michigan	16	8	4	4	67	13	16	31	7
Wisconsin	4	—	1	3	67	12	13	29	13
West North Central	53	3	12	38	567	88	206	228	45
Minnesota	1	—	—	1	86	3	35	39	9
Iowa	1	—	—	1	98	4	42	46	6
Missouri	5	2	2	1	109	4	16	69	20
North Dakota	1	—	—	1	52	6	31	15	—
South Dakota	14	—	4	10	55	22	24	9	—
Nebraska	9	—	2	7	84	25	35	20	4
Kansas	22	1	4	17	83	24	23	30	6
South Atlantic	78	13	38	27	477	76	114	134	153
Delaware	1	1	—	—	2	—	—	2	—
Maryland	4	3	—	1	10	2	5	8	4
Virginia	7	4	—	3	93	11	26	33	23
West Virginia	13	2	6	5	42	4	13	11	14
North Carolina	14	—	8	6	86	20	29	22	15
South Carolina	1	1	—	—	45	—	1	5	39
Georgia	9	—	8	1	152	22	31	45	54
Florida	29	2	16	11	38	17	9	8	4
East South Central	18	5	7	6	346	23	59	170	94
Kentucky	6	3	2	1	114	7	25	55	27
Tennessee	3	—	2	1	92	5	10	55	22
Alabama	1	—	1	—	66	1	5	23	37
Mississippi	8	2	2	4	74	10	19	37	8
West South Central	136	23	52	61	333	49	57	104	123
Arkansas	8	2	3	3	67	1	6	30	30
Louisiana	15	2	5	8	48	7	7	16	18
Oklahoma	16	3	5	8	61	2	17	16	26
Texas	97	16	39	42	157	39	27	42	49
Mountain	48	4	17	27	228	104	68	46	10
Montana	2	—	1	1	54	26	13	15	—
Idaho	7	—	2	5	37	9	19	9	—
Wyoming	8	—	3	5	15	11	3	1	—
Colorado	11	1	2	8	51	30	13	5	3
New Mexico	7	1	4	2	24	7	6	8	3
Arizona	9	2	4	3	5	1	1	1	2
Utah	1	—	1	—	28	11	10	5	2
Nevada	3	—	—	3	14	9	3	2	—
Pacific	73	21	34	18	59	31	16	7	5
Washington	15	2	10	3	24	12	5	4	3
Oregon	14	5	4	5	22	10	9	3	—
California	44	14	20	10	13	9	2	—	2

[1] For method of computation see appendix B.

Table 5.—Counties of the United States by Percent Net Gain or Loss Through Migration to the Rural Population, by Geographic Division and State, 1920–1930 [1] (Estimated)

Geographic division and State	Number of counties									
	Gained rural population, 1920–1930					Lost rural population, 1920–1930				
	Total	50 percent or more [1]	30–49 percent	10–29 percent	Less than 10 percent	Total	Less than 10 percent	10–19 percent	20–29 percent	30 percent or more
United States	517	81	66	169	201	2,542	485	1,170	673	214
New England	26	11	3	4	8	38	22	14	2	—
Maine	1	—	—	—	1	15	9	5	1	—
New Hampshire	7	—	1	2	4	3	3	—	—	—
Vermont	—	—	—	—	—	14	6	8	—	—
Massachusetts	12	7	2	1	2	—	—	—	—	—
Rhode Island	4	4	—	—	—	—	—	—	—	—
Connecticut	2	—	—	1	1	6	4	1	1	—
Middle Atlantic	37	1	4	20	12	106	46	32	18	10
New York	20	1	2	11	6	37	23	9	5	—
New Jersey	10	—	2	8	—	10	5	1	1	3
Pennsylvania	7	—	—	1	6	59	18	22	12	7
East North Central	48	1	8	13	26	388	87	203	84	14
Ohio	14	—	1	4	9	74	24	35	13	2
Indiana	7	—	3	1	3	85	24	49	10	2
Illinois	7	—	—	2	5	95	10	57	25	3
Michigan	16	1	4	6	5	67	14	18	29	6
Wisconsin	4	—	—	—	4	67	15	44	7	1
West North Central	53	8	3	13	29	567	61	377	109	20
Minnesota	1	—	—	1	—	86	7	62	14	3
Iowa	1	—	—	—	1	98	10	82	5	1
Missouri	5	1	1	1	2	109	6	49	47	7
North Dakota	1	—	—	—	1	52	3	40	8	1
South Dakota	14	4	—	4	6	55	5	44	5	1
Nebraska	9	—	—	4	5	84	12	51	19	2
Kansas	22	3	2	3	14	83	18	49	11	5
South Atlantic	78	12	6	27	33	477	87	169	158	63
Delaware	1	—	—	1	—	2	2	—	—	—
Maryland	4	—	1	2	1	19	4	11	4	—
Virginia	7	—	2	2	3	93	12	37	38	6
West Virginia	13	—	—	6	7	42	8	14	18	2
North Carolina	14	—	—	2	12	86	32	44	8	2
South Carolina	1	—	—	—	1	45	2	11	27	5
Georgia	9	1	—	5	3	152	18	32	58	44
Florida	29	11	3	9	6	38	9	20	5	4
East South Central	18	—	3	5	10	346	48	159	127	12
Kentucky	6	—	3	1	2	114	7	42	57	8
Tennessee	3	—	—	—	3	92	7	45	39	1
Alabama	1	—	—	1	—	66	8	38	18	2
Mississippi	8	—	—	3	5	74	26	34	13	1
West South Central	136	38	20	40	38	333	65	121	105	42
Arkansas	8	—	—	5	3	67	7	15	34	11
Louisiana	15	...	2	7	6	48	12	19	11	6
Oklahoma	16	1	—	5	10	61	9	21	21	10
Texas	97	37	18	23	19	157	37	66	39	15
Mountain	48	1	11	11	25	228	41	83	54	50
Montana	2	—	1	—	1	54	7	30	1	16
Idaho	7	—	—	4	3	37	2	12	17	6
Wyoming	8	1	—	2	5	15	5	7	2	1
Colorado	11	—	3	1	7	51	11	20	10	10
New Mexico	7	—	4	1	2	24	6	3	8	7
Arizona	9	—	2	2	5	5	1	1	2	1
Utah	1	—	—	—	1	28	3	7	13	5
Nevada	3	—	1	1	1	14	6	3	1	4
Pacific	73	9	8	36	20	59	28	12	16	3
Washington	15	—	1	10	4	24	12	2	8	2
Oregon	14	2	2	5	5	22	7	7	7	1
California	44	7	5	21	11	13	9	3	1	—

[1] For method of computation see appendix B.

Table 6.—Migrants Remaining on Farms, January 1, 1935, Who Lived in a Nonfarm Residence 5 Years Earlier, by Geographic Division and State

Geographic division and State	Migrants remaining on farms, January 1, 1935	Migrants as percent of total farm population, January 1, 1935
United States	1,995,253	0.3
New England	81,808	11.5
Maine	17,148	9.3
New Hampshire	11,206	14.7
Vermont	12,275	10.0
Massachusetts	20,356	12.5
Rhode Island	2,638	12.1
Connecticut	18,185	12.7
Middle Atlantic	195,881	10.3
New York	81,514	10.4
New Jersey	18,609	12.9
Pennsylvania	95,758	9.8
East North Central	414,604	8.7
Ohio	105,297	9.3
Indiana	74,518	8.7
Illinois	61,019	6.0
Michigan	110,413	13.1
Wisconsin	63,357	6.8
West North Central	279,008	5.5
Minnesota	49,676	5.4
Iowa	51,168	5.3
Missouri	81,958	6.9
North Dakota	11,562	3.0
South Dakota	12,950	3.6
Nebraska	23,299	4.0
Kansas	48,395	6.9
South Atlantic	264,773	4.3
Delaware	3,304	6.8
Maryland	11,570	4.8
District of Columbia	90	16.9
Virginia	40,053	3.8
West Virginia	47,150	8.4
North Carolina	50,227	3.1
South Carolina	32,510	3.4
Georgia	57,582	4.1
Florida	22,287	7.0
East South Central	214,067	4.0
Kentucky	61,326	4.7
Tennessee	59,400	4.5
Alabama	63,665	4.6
Mississippi	29,676	2.2
West South Central	266,909	5.0
Arkansas	51,763	4.4
Louisiana	31,186	3.6
Oklahoma	71,180	7.0
Texas	112,774	4.8
Mountain	114,166	9.6
Montana	15,674	8.0
Idaho	17,060	8.6
Wyoming	8,840	11.9
Colorado	26,920	9.7
New Mexico	24,745	13.1
Arizona	10,082	10.1
Utah	9,198	6.7
Nevada	1,647	10.7
Pacific	164,037	13.7
Washington	47,818	14.2
Oregon	45,141	18.1
California	71,078	11.7

Source: Bureau of the Census, *United States Census of Agriculture: 1935*, Vol. II, U. S. Department of Commerce, Washington, D. C., 1936, table XIII.

Table 7.—Farm Population, 1930, and Changes in Farm Population, 1930–1934,[1] by Region [2] and Area

Region and area	Percent of total farm population, 1930	Percent of Jan. 1, 1935, farm population which was not on farms in 1930	Percent of migrants to farms, 1930–1934	Percent change in farm population, 1930–1934	Percent increase in 1930 farm population because of migrants from nonfarm territory, 1930–1934	Percent change in farm population, exclusive of migrants from nonfarm territory, 1930–1934
UNITED STATES						
Total	100.0	6.3	100.0	+4.5	+6.6	−2.1
Nonproblem	75.2	6.2	73.4	+3.3	+6.4	−3.1
Problem [3]	24.8	6.5	26.6	+8.0	+7.0	+1.0
Less than 20 percent	10.6	6.3	10.8	+5.4	+6.6	−1.2
20–59 percent	12.1	6.7	13.5	+9.4	+7.3	+2.1
60 percent or more	2.1	6.4	2.3	+13.9	+7.3	+6.6
NORTHEAST						
Total	100.0	9.8	100.0	+15.1	+11.3	+3.8
Nonproblem	66.8	9.6	64.1	+13.4	+10.8	+2.5
Problem [3]	33.2	10.3	35.9	+18.5	+12.2	+6.3
Less than 20 percent	18.0	10.1	18.9	+17.3	+11.8	+5.5
20–59 percent	15.2	10.5	17.0	+19.8	+12.7	+7.2
60 percent or more	—	—	—	—	—	—
MIDDLE STATES						
Total	100.0	7.6	100.0	+5.0	+8.0	−3.0
Nonproblem	82.6	7.4	78.8	+3.6	+7.6	−4.0
Problem [3]	17.4	8.8	21.2	+11.4	+9.8	+1.6
Less than 20 percent	4.5	9.3	5.8	+9.9	+10.2	−1.1
20–59 percent	9.7	8.5	11.6	+12.8	+9.6	+3.2
60 percent or more	3.2	8.7	3.8	+10.2	+9.6	+0.6
NORTHWEST						
Total	100.0	6.0	100.0	−1.1	+5.9	−7.0
Nonproblem	84.5	6.3	89.2	−0.7	+6.2	−6.9
Problem [3]	15.5	4.3	10.8	−3.4	+4.1	−7.5
Less than 20 percent	10.4	4.0	6.7	−4.0	+4.0	−8.0
20–59 percent	5.0	4.8	4.0	−2.3	+4.7	−7.0
60 percent or more	0.1	4.8	0.1	+2.0	+4.9	−2.9
SOUTHEAST						
Total	100.0	3.9	100.0	+4.2	+4.1	+0.1
Nonproblem	65.7	3.6	60.0	+3.1	+3.7	−0.6
Problem [3]	34.3	4.5	40.0	+6.3	+4.8	+1.5
Less than 20 percent	14.3	3.9	14.1	+2.9	+4.1	−1.2
20–59 percent	17.1	4.9	22.1	+7.3	+5.3	+2.0
60 percent or more	2.9	4.6	3.8	+17.9	+5.4	+12.5
SOUTHWEST						
Total	100.0	6.0	100.0	+0.1	+6.0	−5.9
Nonproblem	93.8	6.0	93.5	−0.2	+6.0	−6.2
Problem [3]	6.2	6.0	6.5	+4.9	+6.4	−1.5
Less than 20 percent	1.0	3.7	0.6	−6.9	+3.4	−10.3
20–59 percent	4.4	6.6	5.1	+6.7	+7.0	−0.3
60 percent or more	0.8	6.9	0.8	+9.3	+6.1	+3.2
FAR WEST						
Total	100.0	13.7	100.0	+3.7	+14.2	−10.5
Nonproblem	68.1	14.2	70.5	+3.5	+14.7	−11.2
Problem [3]	31.9	12.6	29.5	+4.2	+13.1	−8.9
Less than 20 percent	22.7	11.5	19.3	+5.3	+12.1	−6.8
20–59 percent	7.6	14.8	8.4	+4.0	+15.4	−11.4
60 percent or more	1.6	17.7	1.8	−10.0	+15.9	−25.9

[1] Based upon tabulations from National Resources Committee, *Population Statistics: 1. National Data,* Washington, D. C., 1937, pp. 63–65.
[2] Regions are those used by Odum, Howard W., *Southern Regions of the United States,* Chapel Hill: University of North Carolina Press, 1936.
[3] Problem areas are those in which some or all of the farm land should be transferred to grazing, forests, or other conservational uses. The subclasses refer to the percent of farms which should be transferred.

Table 8.—Counties of the United States by Number of Children [1] Under 5 Years of Age per 1,000 Women 20 Through 44 Years of Age in the White Rural Population, by Geographic Division, State, and Residence, 1930

Geographic division and State	Rural-farm						Rural-nonfarm					
	Total counties	Children under 5 per 1,000 women 20–44					Total counties	Children under 5 per 1,000 women 20–44				
		Fewer than 440	440–659	660–879	880 or more	Unclassified[2]		Fewer than 440	440–659	660–879	880 or more	Unclassified[2]
United States	3,059	41	1,097	1,447	397	77	3,059	292	1,913	665	108	81
New England	64	4	44	14	1	1	64	4	55	5	—	—
Maine	16	—	13	2	1	—	16	—	13	3	—	—
New Hampshire	10	—	10	—	—	—	10	—	10	—	—	—
Vermont	14	—	3	11	—	—	14	—	12	2	—	—
Massachusetts	12	3	8	—	—	1	12	2	10	—	—	—
Rhode Island	4	—	3	1	—	—	4	—	4	—	—	—
Connecticut	8	1	7	—	—	—	8	2	6	—	—	—
Middle Atlantic	143	11	82	49	—	1	143	16	91	34	2	—
New York	57	6	44	6	—	1	57	9	45	3	—	—
New Jersey	20	5	15	—	—	—	20	6	14	—	—	—
Pennsylvania	66	—	23	43	—	—	66	1	32	31	2	—
East North Central	436	3	261	157	12	3	436	29	324	78	4	1
Ohio	88	2	63	23	—	—	88	4	64	18	2	—
Indiana	92	1	68	23	—	—	92	7	76	9	—	—
Illinois	102	—	86	16	—	—	102	14	84	4	—	—
Michigan	83	—	23	49	8	3	83	1	45	34	2	1
Wisconsin	71	—	21	46	4	—	71	3	55	13	—	—
West North Central	620	2	281	286	48	3	620	116	437	41	4	22
Minnesota	87	—	24	59	3	1	87	12	67	8	—	—
Iowa	99	—	67	32	—	—	99	26	72	1	—	—
Missouri	114	2	66	33	13	—	114	23	69	18	4	—
North Dakota	53	—	2	33	18	—	53	2	40	9	—	2
South Dakota	69	—	15	44	8	2	69	12	48	1	—	8
Nebraska	93	—	45	47	1	—	93	24	59	1	—	9
Kansas	105	—	62	38	5	—	105	17	82	3	—	3
South Atlantic	555	3	124	293	120	15	555	26	243	229	40	17
Delaware	3	—	3	—	—	—	3	—	3	—	—	—
Maryland	23	—	15	7	1	—	23	1	16	6	—	—
Virginia	100	3	35	52	9	1	100	4	43	37	12	4
West Virginia	55	—	8	24	23	—	55	—	4	34	17	—
North Carolina	100	—	9	51	39	1	100	1	40	50	8	1
South Carolina	46	—	8	31	7	—	46	1	23	22	—	—
Georgia	161	—	31	94	34	2	161	19	88	40	3	11
Florida	67	—	15	34	7	11	67	—	26	40	—	1
East South Central	364	—	49	214	101	—	364	22	182	118	34	8
Kentucky	120	—	27	51	42	—	120	2	63	34	16	5
Tennessee	95	—	13	63	19	—	95	5	39	34	16	1
Alabama	67	—	7	36	24	—	67	—	36	29	2	—
Mississippi	82	—	2	64	16	—	82	15	44	21	—	2
West South Central	469	—	78	303	66	22	469	30	311	103	4	21
Arkansas	75	—	1	49	25	—	75	2	44	29	—	—
Louisiana	63	—	3	46	14	—	63	—	33	25	3	2
Oklahoma	77	—	4	57	16	—	77	4	53	20	—	—
Texas	254	—	70	151	11	22	254	24	181	29	1	19
Mountain	276	2	71	126	49	28	276	19	171	56	20	10
Montana	56	1	16	36	1	2	56	7	44	2	—	3
Idaho	44	—	13	19	10	2	44	—	28	8	5	3
Wyoming	23	—	9	11	3	—	23	1	20	2	—	—
Colorado	62	—	21	31	2	8	62	4	48	6	2	2
New Mexico	31	—	3	16	11	1	31	2	10	16	3	—
Arizona	14	—	6	5	3	—	14	1	12	1	—	—
Utah	29	—	—	7	18	4	29	—	—	18	10	1
Nevada	17	1	3	1	1	11	17	4	9	3	—	1
Pacific	132	16	107	5	—	4	132	30	99	1	—	2
Washington	39	3	33	3	—	—	39	4	34	1	—	—
Oregon	36	2	33	1	—	—	36	4	32	—	—	—
California	57	11	41	1	—	4	57	22	33	—	—	2

[1] Number not corrected for underenumeration.
[2] Counties with fewer than 100 white women 20–44 years of age.

Source: Unpublished data from the Bureau of the Census, U. S. Department of Commerce, Washington, D. C.

Table 9.—Counties of the United States by Number of Children[1] Under 5 Years of Age per 1,000 Women 20 Through 44 Years of Age in the Colored Rural Population, by Geographic Division, State, and Residence, 1930

Geographic division and State	Rural-farm						Rural-nonfarm					
	Total counties	Children under 5 per 1,000 women 20–44					Total counties	Children under 5 per 1,000 women 20–44				
		Fewer than 440	440–659	660–879	880 or more	Unclassified[2]		Fewer than 440	440–659	660–879	880 or more	Unclassified[2]
United States	3,059	5	86	425	387	2,156	3,059	182	413	216	124	2,124
South Atlantic	555	3	21	171	177	183	555	48	214	128	27	138
Delaware	3	—	1	2	—	—	3	—	3	—	—	—
Maryland	23	—	2	8	8	5	23	—	7	10	3	3
Virginia	100	—	3	21	41	35	100	1	16	41	14	28
West Virginia	55	—	—	—	—	55	55	2	14	2	—	37
North Carolina	100	—	—	14	65	21	100	3	32	32	9	24
South Carolina	46	—	1	21	24	—	46	1	30	14	1	—
Georgia	161	1	5	91	38	26	161	22	73	25	—	41
Florida	67	2	9	14	1	41	67	19	39	4	—	5
East South Central	364	1	25	116	49	173	364	63	105	26	—	170
Kentucky	120	—	5	13	3	99	120	8	18	3	—	91
Tennessee	95	—	5	25	6	59	95	14	20	4	—	57
Alabama	67	—	1	43	14	9	67	7	39	12	—	9
Mississippi	82	1	14	35	26	6	82	34	28	7	—	13
West South Central	469	1	39	131	107	191	469	70	93	55	27	224
Arkansas	75	—	17	20	3	35	75	25	10	1	—	39
Louisiana	63	—	12	25	19	7	63	24	21	13	2	3
Oklahoma	77	—	2	18	29	28	77	1	12	16	5	43
Texas	254	1	8	68	56	121	254	20	50	25	20	139
Mountain	276	—	1	5	30	240	276	—	—	3	41	232
Montana	56	—	—	—	4	52	56	—	—	—	4	52
Idaho	44	—	—	—	—	44	44	—	—	—	—	44
Wyoming	23	—	—	—	1	22	23	—	—	—	1	22
Colorado	62	—	—	—	10	52	62	—	—	—	10	52
New Mexico	31	—	—	3	9	19	31	—	—	3	12	16
Arizona	14	—	1	2	6	5	14	—	—	—	14	—
Utah	29	—	—	—	—	29	29	—	—	—	—	29
Nevada	17	—	—	—	—	17	17	—	—	—	—	17
Pacific	57	—	—	2	24	31	57	1	1	4	29	22
California	57	—	—	2	24	31	57	1	1	4	29	22
Unclassified	1,338	—	—	—	—	1,338	1,338	—	—	—	—	1,338

[1] Number not corrected for underenumeration.
[2] Counties with fewer than 100 colored women 20-44 years of age.

Source: Unpublished data from the Bureau of the Census, U. S. Department of Commerce, Washington, D. C.

Table 10.—Counties of the United States by Number of Children [1] Under 5 Years of Age per 1,000 Women 20 Through 44 Years of Age in the Total Rural Population, by Geographic Division and State, 1930

Geographic division and State	Total counties	Children under 5 per 1,000 women 20–44				
		Fewer than 440	440–659	660–879	880 or more	Unclassified [2]
United States	3,059	36	1,401	1,397	218	7
New England	64	2	56	5	1	—
Maine	16	—	14	1	1	—
New Hampshire	10	—	10	—	—	—
Vermont	14	—	10	4	—	—
Massachusetts	12	1	11	—	—	—
Rhode Island	4	—	4	—	—	—
Connecticut	8	1	7	—	—	—
Middle Atlantic	143	13	89	40	1	—
New York	57	6	47	4	—	—
New Jersey	20	6	14	—	—	—
Pennsylvania	66	1	28	36	1	—
East North Central	436	2	310	119	5	—
Ohio	88	1	64	22	1	—
Indiana	92	1	77	14	—	—
Illinois	102	—	95	7	—	—
Michigan	83	—	31	49	3	—
Wisconsin	71	—	43	27	1	—
West North Central	620	4	400	187	28	1
Minnesota	87	—	54	32	1	—
Iowa	99	1	87	11	—	—
Missouri	114	3	70	35	6	—
North Dakota	53	—	10	32	11	—
South Dakota	69	—	33	28	7	1
Nebraska	93	—	68	24	1	—
Kansas	105	—	78	25	2	—
South Atlantic	555	1	112	373	69	—
Delaware	3	—	3	—	—	—
Maryland	23	—	16	5	2	—
Virginia	100	—	22	62	16	—
West Virginia	55	—	1	40	14	—
North Carolina	100	—	3	74	23	—
South Carolina	46	—	4	39	3	—
Georgia	161	1	26	123	11	—
Florida	67	—	37	30	—	—
East South Central	364	—	79	226	59	—
Kentucky	120	—	39	44	37	—
Tennessee	95	—	19	62	14	—
Alabama	67	—	4	57	6	—
Mississippi	82	—	17	63	2	—
West South Central	469	—	127	321	19	2
Arkansas	75	—	9	63	3	—
Louisiana	63	—	15	43	5	—
Oklahoma	77	—	13	62	2	—
Texas	254	—	90	153	9	2
Mountain	276	7	106	124	36	3
Montana	56	4	23	29	—	—
Idaho	44	—	23	14	7	—
Wyoming	23	—	15	8	—	—
Colorado	62	1	31	26	3	1
New Mexico	31	—	1	22	8	—
Arizona	14	—	2	10	2	—
Utah	29	—	—	13	15	1
Nevada	17	2	11	2	1	1
Pacific	132	7	122	2	—	1
Washington	39	—	38	1	—	—
Oregon	36	2	34	—	—	—
California	57	5	50	1	—	1

[1] Number not corrected for underenumeration.
[2] Counties with fewer than 100 women 20–44 years of age.

Source: Unpublished data from the Bureau of the Census, U. S. Department of Commerce, Washington, D. C.

Table 11.—Counties of the United States by Type of Net Migration,[1] 1920–1930, and Average [2] Fertility Ratio [3] of the Rural Population, 1930, by Geographic Division and State

Geographic division and State	Type of net migration					
	Absorption		Dispersion		Depopulation	
	Number of counties	Average fertility ratio	Number of counties	Average fertility ratio	Number of counties	Average fertility ratio
United States	517	627.9	994	714.4	1,548	671.6
New England	26	510.6	20	567.8	18	709.0
Maine	1	520.9	9	626.1	6	595.4
New Hampshire	7	541.7	—	—	3	551.9
Vermont	—	—	6	647.2	8	644.5
Massachusetts	12	500.4	—	—	—	—
Rhode Island	4	516.4	—	—	—	—
Connecticut	2	446.2	5	475.4	1	483.0
Middle Atlantic	37	504.9	42	596.0	64	634.6
New York	20	482.9	15	540.7	22	550.8
New Jersey	10	454.4	5	510.6	5	501.4
Pennsylvania	7	639.8	22	653.0	37	702.5
East North Central	48	613.0	101	614.0	287	621.3
Ohio	14	600.1	28	606.8	46	614.5
Indiana	7	623.0	20	590.8	65	586.9
Illinois	7	531.6	14	560.2	81	565.8
Michigan	16	660.4	18	656.4	49	726.1
Wisconsin	4	593.9	21	645.2	46	663.0
West North Central	53	699.4	204	669.6	363	605.3
Minnesota	1	684.7	32	648.8	54	641.9
Iowa	1	575.8	34	610.3	64	572.9
Missouri	5	621.0	13	732.4	96	610.1
North Dakota	1	1,055.5	32	786.5	20	715.0
South Dakota	14	777.0	34	660.5	21	623.5
Nebraska	9	662.4	31	634.7	53	589.7
Kansas	22	673.1	28	652.5	55	567.0
South Atlantic	78	663.3	202	790.3	275	747.3
Delaware	1	493.3	1	529.7	1	575.6
Maryland	4	580.9	7	668.0	12	668.4
Virginia	7	613.8	28	779.1	65	753.8
West Virginia	13	820.4	19	832.4	23	813.9
North Carolina	14	774.6	75	823.5	11	833.5
South Carolina	1	670.5	10	820.1	35	757.6
Georgia	9	576.6	44	771.9	108	742.0
Florida	29	595.1	18	715.6	20	668.4
East South Central	18	770.1	177	790.5	169	742.4
Kentucky	6	812.4	33	873.9	81	740.7
Tennessee	3	821.7	55	775.1	37	744.4
Alabama	1	739.4	41	793.4	25	778.5
Mississippi	8	722.8	48	748.5	26	709.8
West South Central	136	718.3	141	722.6	192	717.2
Arkansas	8	694.2	18	752.3	49	762.5
Louisiana	15	706.0	27	765.8	21	715.6
Oklahoma	16	724.1	25	738.6	36	753.7
Texas	97	721.2	71	692.9	86	676.4
Mountain	48	689.8	81	736.2	147	691.2
Montana	2	610.6	16	670.0	38	634.8
Idaho	7	630.4	8	778.6	29	710.0
Wyoming	8	623.3	10	647.4	5	637.8
Colorado	11	637.7	19	692.0	32	637.3
New Mexico	7	819.2	9	840.5	15	813.9
Arizona	9	788.3	2	721.6	3	758.2
Utah	1	837.2	13	920.0	15	898.2
Nevada	3	603.2	4	524.2	10	535.4
Pacific	73	528.0	26	539.7	33	541.3
Washington	15	542.1	10	528.4	14	562.9
Oregon	14	533.0	10	551.3	12	535.6
California	44	521.6	6	539.5	7	508.1

[1] For basis of classification of counties see ch. III, pp. 60–61
[2] Arithmetic mean.
[3] Children under 5 years of age per 1,000 women 20–44 years of age. Not corrected for underenumeration of children under 5 years of age.

Sources: Bureau of the Census, unpublished data and *Fifteenth Census of the United States: 1930*, Population Vol. III, tables 13 and 14, U. S. Department of Commerce, Washington, D. C.; and life tables through the courtesy of the Metropolitan Life Insurance Company.

Table 12.—Estimated Net Rural Migration, 1920–1930, and Selected Socio-Economic Factors in 99 Corn Belt Counties [1]

County and State	Percent estimated net rural migration, 1920–1930	Rank on specified factor — Rural migration, 1920–1930	Percent on relief, July 1934–June 1935 [3]	Farm plane of living index, 1930	Percent of gainful workers in agriculture, 1920	Income per gainful worker in agriculture, 1929	Fertility ratio, 1930	Percent of farm tenancy, 1920	Percent of 16- and 17-year olds in school, 1930	Value of farm machinery per farm, 193[0]	Percent population increase, 1920–1930	Percent population increase, 1910–1920	Classification by — Distance from city [3]	Land problem [4]
Putnam, Ill.	-37.8	1	17	91	91	72	70	23.5	66	34	1	37	1	2
Gallatin, Ill.	-30.9	2	13	4	40	2	47	72.5	95	96	2	7	1	2
Paulding, Ohio	-27.0	3	43	15	83	8	10	64	24	84	4	2	1	2
Boyd, Nebr.	-26.3	4	11	13	30	25	11	77	62	55	7	25	5	2
Cedar, Mo.	-24.9	5	14	2	3	1	90	97	84	99	3	4	5	2
St. Clair, Mo.	-21.9	6	38	3	5	3	28	90	88	97	6	27	2	2
Putnam, Ohio	-21.3	7	61	67	35.5	17	9	91	56	39	17.5	20	1	2
Pulaski, Ind.	-20.8	8	73	18.5	78.5	13	19	47.5	32.5	90	17.5	21	2	1
Brown, Ill.	-20.7	9	25	14	23	10	94	84	80.5	93	5	12.5	2	2
Benton, Mo.	-20.8	10	35	5	6	4	18	98	97	95	13	5	5	1
Franklin, Nebr.	-20.3	11	40	58	35	14	74	40.5	48.5	73	14.5	48	2	2
Schuyler, Ill.	-19.7	12	25	25	59	11	77	63	54.5	86	8	5	2	2
Parke, Ind.	-19.6	13	18	6	38		68	93	5	94	8	3	5	2
Jewell, Kans.	-19.5	14.5	32	18.5	17.5	32	63.5	55	6.5	75	11	11	5	2
Smith, Kans.	-19.5	14.5	28	11	39	38	82	59.5	22.5	80	17.5	46	5	2
Howard, Nebr.	-19.2	16	72	50	16	19	62	85	54.5	58	26	53.5	2	2
Greeley, Nebr.	-19.1	17	19	60	17.5	54	8	57.5	36	55.5	43	82	2	2
Mercer, Ill.	-18.5	18	39	92	31	52	83.5	36	72.5	63	10	37	5	2
Hickory, Mo.	-18.2	19.5	24	1	2	6	35	99	26	98	20	1	2	2
Frontier, Nebr.	-18.2	19.5	70.5	63	11.5	39	65	47.5	53	54	33.5	53.5	4	1
Scott, Ill.	-18.1	21	15	16	77	7	50	26	50	77	12	30	2	2
Hanson, S. Dak.	-18.1	22	3	42	4	44	23	8	30	19	59	52	4	2
Holt, Mo.	-17.5	23	36	33	41.5	9	81	81	20	83	14.5	44.5	2	2
Webster, Nebr.	-17.4	24	47	48	53.5	42	79.5	33	39	70	27	17	2	2
Polk, Nebr.	-17.2	25	85	88	40.5	85	61	20	61	37	28.5	62	1	2
Menard, Ill.	-17.2	25	82	84	93.5	45	93	29	92	66	17.5	18	2	2
Osceola, Iowa	-17.2	27.5	96	54	61	86	14	2	18	3	65	93	4	2
Ringgold, Iowa	-17.1	27.5	68	34	33	17	40	92	72.5	82	22.5	56	2	2
Iowa, Iowa	-17.1	29	91	93	74	71	73	82	19	29	25	59.5	4	2
Wabaunsee, Kans.	-16.7	30	41	38	29	93	34	78	72.5	76	32	12.5	2	2
Miner, S. Dak.	-16.3	31.5	1	39	9	29	41	25	93	30	48.5	91	4	2
Lyon, Iowa	-16.3	31.5	94	55	52	79	15	93	51.5	4	62	74	3	2
Warren, Ind.	-16.2	33	59	29	47	18	37	31.5	43.5	79	31	9	2	2
Valley, Nebr.	-16.1	34	50	87	63	57	49	67.5		53	39.5	67	5	2

See footnotes at end of table.

Table 12.—Estimated Net Rural Migration, 1920–1930, and Selected Socio-Economic Factors in 99 Corn Belt Counties [1]—Continued

County and State	Percent estimated net rural migration, 1920–1930	Rural migration, 1920–1930	Rank on specified factor										Classification by—	
			Percent on relief, July 1934–June 1935 [3]	Farm plane of living index, 1930	Percent of gainful workers in agriculture, 1930	Income per gainful worker in agriculture, 1929	Fertility ratio, 1930	Percent of farm tenancy, 1920	Percent of 16- and 17-year olds in school, 1930	Value of farm machinery per farm, 1930	Percent population increase, 1920–1930	Percent population increase, 1910–1920	Distance from city [3]	Land problem [4]
Sioux, Iowa	−16.0	35	79	78	69	84	6	5	96	14	75	73	3	2
Dixon, Nebr	−15.8	36	65	79.5	49.5	91	25	51.5	28	49	51	65	2	2
Cedar, Nebr	−15.6	37	45	81	30	73	13	14	90	32	74	77	3	2
Worth, Iowa	−15.5	38	93	51	60	22	57	50	48.5	21	38	96	4	2
Murray, Minn	−15.4	39	51	35	7	30	5	42	91	27	78	95	4	2
Louisa, Iowa	−15.3	40.5	76	74	76	58	12	79.5	12.5	40	33.5	33	2	2
Republic, Kans	−15.3	40.5	42	30	56	43	99	37.5	15.5	68	24	16	4	2
Antelope, Nebr	−15.2	42.5	99	56	24.5	67	33	44	40	61	66	83	4	2
Jackson, Minn	−15.2	42.5	89	37	14.5	61	43	46	87	25	64	87	4	2
Kearney, Nebr	−15.0	44.5	75	69.5	57.5	26	96	11.5	6.5	48	30	30	5	2
Carroll, Ind	−15.0	44.5	57	76	93.5	28	75	62	1	81	21	15	2	2
Nance, Nebr	−14.9	46	74	46.5	37.5	77	24	23.5	76	39	69.5	47	4	2
Hutchinson, S. Dak	−14.8	47	12	41	28	49	21	88	94	12	83.5	86	4	2
Charles Mix, S. Dak	−14.7	49	7	12	21.5	64	20	69.5	69	33	81	84	4	2
Thayer, Nebr	−14.7	49	23	72	84	90	44	22	42	50.5	48.5	32	5	2
Lac qui Parle, Minn	−14.7	49	6	26	14.5	24	27	43	66	17	60.5	58	5	2
Harlan, Nebr	−14.6	51	67	77	75	65	78	17	15.5	64	41	41	4	2
Kingsbury, S. Dak	−14.3	52	4	49	46	47.5	30	18.5	30	10	67.5	63	5	2
Benton, Ind	−14.1	53	70.5	79.5	88	62	69	3	2	57	46.5	40	4	2
Nemaha, Kans	−14.0	54	62	46.5	70	46	17	61	78	72	73	44.5	2	2
Turner, S. Dak	−13.8	55	29	68	45	74	58	40.5	75	11	69.5	79.5	3	2
Butler, Nebr	−13.7	56.5	98	65	55	50	53	49	51.5	16	57	34	3	2
Chase, Kans	−13.7	56.5	46	21	95	99	51	57.5	9	67	45	35	2	2
Grundy, Iowa	−13.5	58	92	95	53.5	81	92	4	79	6	50	75	2	2
Douglas, S. Dak	−13.4	59	2	43	13	37	16	76	99	36	87	85	4	2
Cottonwood, Minn	−13.3	60.5	55	23	37.5	47.5	29	51.5	77	23	76	94	5	2
Phillips, Kans	−13.3	60.5	22	8	57.5	31	91	65.5	60	88	43	8	3	2
Moody, S. Dak	−13.2	63	9	52	21.5	69	87	10	57	9	55	92	3	2
Jefferson, Kans	−13.2	63	48	20	31.5	20	79.5	95	10	92	36.5	23.5	1	2
Butler, Iowa	−13.2	63	80	40	67.5	34	55.5	16	85	35	57	71.5	2	2
Newton, Ind	−13.1	67.5	64	69.5	97	76	55.5	9	8	60	39.5	43	1	2
McCook, S. Dak	−13.1	67.5	8	44	43.5	55	31	15	59	22	85	71.5	3	2
Hayes, Nebr	−13.1	67.5	60	45	1	88	2	71	89	5	94	89	5	2
Renville, Minn	−13.1	67.5	20	27	24.5	33	38	74	66	13	67.5	54	5	2
Osage, Kans	−13.1	67.5	77	31	82	40	89	94	4	91	28.5	27	2	2

County														
Calhoun, Iowa	-13.1	67.5	84	90	85.5	87	88.5	6	17	8	60.5	70	2	2
Yellow Medicine, Minn.	-13.0	71.5	10	28	27	23	45	79.5	86	20	71	75.5	4	2
Hancock, Ill.	-13.0	71.5	58	64	95	15	97	75	22.5	87	22.5	22	3	2
Pottawatomie, Kans.	-12.9	73.5	34	24	80	56	90	89	21	78	52	15	3	2
Cedar, Iowa	-12.9	73.5	83	94	65	83	96	58	46.5	18	35	49	3	2
Pawnee, Nebr.	-12.7	75.5	44	75	34	35	67	53	34	69	53	14	5	2
Sherman, Nebr.	-12.7	75.5	21	22	10	16	23	69.5	80.5	71	82	78	2	2
Taylor, Iowa	-12.6	78	78	57	66	41	88	83	14	74	36.5	36	5	2
Adams, Iowa	-12.6	78	81	59	49.5	68	82	72.5	45	45	63	39	2	2
Woodford, Ill.	-12.6	78	86	99	89	53	86	11.5	62	46	43	30	1	2
Adair, Iowa	-12.2	80	66	83	43.5	75	76	31.5	32.5	38	46.5	50.5	1	2
Merrick, Nebr.	-12.1	81	90	61	87	95	71	58.5	3	52	57	68	2	2
Guthrie, Iowa	-11.8	82	53	71	78.5	59	59	45	35	50.5	54	61	1	2
Fremont, Iowa	-11.6	84	54	66	63	60	45	39	12.5	44	72	50.5	1	2
Humboldt, Iowa	-11.6	84	88	89	73	82	82	27	11	1	77	76	2	2
Boone, Nebr.	-11.6	84	30	85	31.5	66	26	37.5	82	55.5	91	81	4	2
Cuming, Nebr.	-11.2	86.5	95	97.5	19	98	26	54	98	7	89.5	53	2	2
Brule, S. Dak.	-11.2	86.5	5	17	72	21	63.5	87	41	41	88	90	5	2
Union, S. Dak.	-11.1	88	27	53	23	63	22	18.5	58	31	86	69	3	2
Ida, Iowa	-10.8	89	97	97.5	65	97	85	7	30	2	79	63	3	2
Thurston, Nebr.	-10.7	90	16	7	33	78	4	21	43.5	62	95	83	2	2
Atchison, Mo.	-10.3	91	49	82	41.5	70	45	28	46.5	47	83.5	33	2	2
Johnson, Nebr.	-10.3	92	31	62	71	27	63	35	72.5	43	80	3	5	2
Chase, Nebr.	-9.3	93	63	10	49.5	96	7	67.5	69	28	96.5	99	2	2
Furnas, Nebr.	-8.6	94.5	37	73	90	92	60	34	25	59	89.5	42	5	2
Doniphan, Kans.	-8.5	94.5	82	32	67.5	36	54	65.5	27	86	32	23.5	6	2
Dundy, Nebr.	-8.5	96	58	9	3	89	3	86	37	24	98	97	1	2
Kendall, Ill.	-7.5	97	69	96	96	51	96	13	64	18	93	27	5	2
Sarpy, Nebr.	-4.8	98	87	86	99	80	72	30	66	42	96.5	59.5	1	2
Cheyenne, Kans.	-1.6	99	33	36	11.5	94	1	96	83	28	99	98	5	2
Range	-37.8 to -1.6	58.6 to 1.5		65.6 to 221.6	79.8 to 39.3	$788 to $4,081	771.5 to 473.3	62.7 to 21.4	80.6 to 38.7	$1,792 to $224	-30.9 to +24.4	-19.5 to +36.7		
Average [5]	-14.7	12.04		158.4	60.7	$1,996	558.9	41.8	60.9	$1,037	-2.0	-1.1		

[1] Counties ranked on each factor, number one in each case being assigned to the first figure given in the "range."

[2] Based on 1930 population.

[3] Distance from city: 1=less than 50 miles from city of 100,000 or more; 2=50–99 miles from city of 100,000 or more; 3=less than 50 miles from city of 25,000–99,999; 4=50–99 miles from city of 25,000–99,999; 5=100 miles or more from city of 25,000–99,999.

[4] Land problem: 1=problem county; 2=nonproblem county.

[5] Median.

Table 13.—Estimated Net Rural Migration, 1920–1930, and Selected Socio-Economic Factors in 99 Appalachian-Ozark Counties [1]

County and State	Percent estimated net rural migration, 1920–1930	Rank on specified factor											Classification by—	
		Rural migration, 1920–1930	Percent on relief, July 1934–June 1935 [3]	Farm plane of living index, 1930	Percent of gainful workers in agriculture, 1930	Income per gainful worker in agriculture, 1929	Fertility ratio, 1930	Percent of farm tenancy, 1920	Percent of 16- and 17-year olds in school, 1930	Value of farm machinery per farm, 1930	Percent population increase, 1920–1930	Percent population increase, 1910–1920	Distance from city [3]	Land problem [4]
Carter, Mo.	-41.0	1	14	35	71	63	28	42	54	20.5	1	95	5	1
Searcy, Ark.	-38.7	2	69	5	15.5	15	43	52	8.5	69.5	2	39	4	1
Lee, Ky.	-38.3	3	8	86	64.5	7	18	51	7	93	4	91	4	1
Tucker, W. Va.	-36.0	4	25	9	98	59	48	97	6	48	3	9	2	1
Elliott, Ky.	-34.4	5	19	20	1	10	6	37.5	58	90	10	10	3	1
Menifee, Ky.	-33.6	6	7	7	3.5	21	11	60	86	86.5	12	23	2	1
Pushmataha, Okla.	-33.0	7	2	67	63	39.5	51	1	24.5	66	8	97	4	1
Franklin, Ark.	-32.5	8.5	38	1	57	73	87	4	4	60	91	21.5	3	2
Jackson, Ky.	-32.5	8.5	4	42.5	6	32	7	81	91	95	25	80	2	1
Swain, N. C.	-32.2	10	83	12	74.5	17	29	53	76	81	18	93	1	1
Powell, Ky.	-32.0	11	6	27.5	38	55	13	61.5	46	84	13	76	2	1
Butler, Ky.	-31.4	12	46	55	10	11	62	68	61.5	65	5	32	2	1
Hickman, Tenn.	-31.1	13	94	37.5	49	47	61	37.5	30	15.5	7	38	1	1
Reynolds, Mo.	-30.9	14	12	21	46	75	12	72	32	23	20.5	70	2	1
Gilmer, Ga.	-29.9	15	73	57	25	26	31	45	60	72	16.5	11.5	1	1
Grayson, Ky.	-29.4	16	76	36	26	42	60	71	45	78	11	45.5	2	1
Marion, Ark.	-29.1	17	30	13.5	22	50	75	18	2	50	16.5	42	4	2
Hancock, Tenn.	-28.7	18	77	85	5	41	22	20.5	69	63	37	36	1	1
Wirt, W. Va.	-28.2	19	36	40.5	45	85	50	82.5	43.5	51	9	2	3	1
Sevier, Tenn.	-28.0	20	93	37.5	41.5	69	52	11	47	39	31	50	1	2
Stewart, Tenn.	-27.6	21	75	71	28	76	55	76	68	41.5	27	40	2	1
Bollinger, Mo.	-26.8	22	57	75	19	71	64	67	78.5	18	19	29	2	1
Pope, Ill.	-26.6	23	55	52	37	60	97	12	51.5	35	6	5	2	1
Humphreys, Tenn.	-26.5	24	58	56	60	68	71	2	16	26.5	24	35	2	1
Perry, Tenn.	-26.0	25	71	51	39	51	72.5	34.5	12	15.5	32.5	7	2	1
Monroe, Ky.	-25.9	26	53	96	12	27	65	79	29	67.5	32.5	62.5	3	2
Craig, Va.	-25.5	27	81	59	54.5	94	91	44	1	2	14	6	3	1
Patrick, Va.	-25.5	28	92	3	14	66	21	10	42	43	39	37	2	2
Leslie, Ky.	-25.0	29	1	87	2	14	1	91	22	98	77	84	3	1
Floyd, Va.	-25.0	30	96	29	9	80	69	55	50	14	23	20	3	1
Casey, Ky.	-24.7	31	20	25	3.5	52	16	49	93	73	50	82	3	2
Lincoln, W. Va.	-24.5	32	16	72	49	29	10	84.5	63.5	92	53	26	3	1
Braxton, W. Va.	-24.2	33	44	42.5	59	70	38	23.5	72	56.5	42	64	3	2
Cumberland, Ky.	-23.7	34	13	30	7	45	45	23.5	83	74	47	79	2	1
Wayne, Ky.	-23.6	35	22	42.5	18	30.5	32	39	63.5	67.5	52	17.5	2	1
Dent, Mo.	-23.5	36	47	83	51	74	94	61.5	66	30	22	19	2	1

County	Value
Lumpkin, Ga.	−23.1
Hardin, Ill.	−23.0
Smith, Tenn.	−23.0
Pleasants, W. Va.	−23.0
Allen, Ky.	−22.7
Adair, Ky.	−22.6
Appomattox, Va.	−22.5
Nelson, Va.	−22.5
Wayne, Mo.	−22.3
Ohio, Ky.	−22.0
Buchanan, Va.	−22.0
Scott, Va.	−22.0
Crawford, Mo.	−21.6
Benton, Tenn.	−21.5
Scott, Tenn.	−21.1
White, Ga.	−21.0
Pocahontas, W. Va.	−21.0
Madison, N. C.	−20.6
Clay, Tenn.	−20.0
Decatur, Tenn.	−20.0
Ritchie, W. Va.	−19.7
Morgan, Tenn.	−19.5
Marion, Tenn.	−19.4
Alleghany, N. C.	−19.2
Fentress, Tenn.	−19.1
Rappahannock, Va.	−19.1
Martin, Ky.	−19.1
Gilmer, W. Va.	−19.0
Clinton, Ky.	−19.0
Laurel, Ky.	−18.3
Hardy, W. Va.	−17.4
Cherokee, N. C.	−17.3
Polk, Tenn.	−17.3
Page, Va.	−17.2
Iron, Mo.	−17.1
Franklin, Tenn.	−16.9
Cannon, Tenn.	−16.9
Grundy, Tenn.	−16.5
Lewis, Tenn.	−16.5
White, Tenn.	−16.5
Jefferson, Tenn.	−15.8
Clay, W. Va.	−15.8
Dade, Ga.	−15.8
Preston, W. Va.	−15.8
Barbour, W. Va.	−15.7
Giles, Va.	−15.7
Towns, Ga.	−15.4
Avery, N. C.	−14.2
Watauga, N. C.	−13.8

See footnotes at end of table.

Table 13.—Estimated Net Rural Migration, 1920–1930, and Selected Socio-Economic Factors in 99 Appalachian-Ozark Counties [1]—Continued

County and State	Percent estimated net rural migration, 1920–1930	Rank on specified factor											Classification by—	
		Rural migration, 1920–1930	Percent on relief, July 1934–June 1935 [5]	Farm plane of living index, 1930	Percent of gainful workers in agriculture, 1930	Income per gainful worker in agriculture, 1929	Fertility ratio, 1930	Percent of farm tenancy, 1920	Percent of 16- and 17-year olds in school, 1930	Value of farm machinery per farm, 1930	Percent population increase, 1920–1930	Percent population increase, 1910–1920	Distance from city [3]	Land problem [4]
Rowan, Ky.	-12.5	87	9	6	62	19	17	73	89	82.5	90	48.5	2	1
Lincoln, Ky.	-11.6	88	61	78	43	92.5	67	50	41	44	78	14	2	1
Adair, Okla.	-11.5	89	35	31	53	44	70	14	8.5	54.5	80	94	2	1
McCreary, Ky.	-10.6	90	27	22	90	4	8	58.5	97	96	96	—	2	1
Taney, Mo.	-9.7	91	10	63.5	61	79	84	47	19	45	81.5	8	3	2
Graham, N. C.	-9.6	92	45	11	74.5	25	14	19	61.5	94	92	58	1	1
Lee, Va.	-9.2	93	85	61	83	61.5	26	30	56	59	93	72	2	2
Delaware, Okla.	-9.0	94	15	49.5	23	83	37	29	3	19	85	89	2	1
Knott, Ky.	-7.5	95	31	4	33	13	2	40	31	99	97	78	4	1
Mitchell, N. C.	-5.9	96	82	68.5	66	20	24	84.5	84.5	85	95	1	2	2
Van Buren, Tenn.	+3.5	97	18	24	67	12	9	36	90	52.5	98	24	1	2
McDowell, N. C.	+4.5	98	84	48	96	28	85	33	96	54.5	94	90	3	1
Greenbrier, W. Va.	+10.0	99	63	91	95	91	77	90	21	5	99	71	4	1
Range	-41.0 to +10.0		73.0 to 5.8	5.8 to 99.0	91.0 to 25.4	$221 to $1,025	1,254.7 to 593.6	56.4 to 5.9	67.4 to 34.2	$391 to $25	-26.5 to +36.7	-34.6 to +73.1		
Average [4]	-21.5		24.3	29.5	63.6	$507	842.0	24.8	48.6	$125	-2.7	+0.3		

[1] Counties ranked on each factor, number one in each case being assigned to the first figure given in the "range."
[2] Based on 1930 population.
[3] Distance from city: 1=less than 50 miles from city of 100,000 or more; 2=50–99 miles from city of 100,000 or more; 3=less than 50 miles from city of 25,000–99,999; 4=50–99 miles from city of 25,000–99,999; 5=100 miles or more from city of 25,000–99,990.
[4] Land problem: 1=problem county; 2=nonproblem county.
[5] Median.

Table 14—Estimated Net Rural Migration, 1920–1930, and Selected Socio-Economic Factors in 99 Cotton Belt Counties [1]

County and State	Percent estimated net rural migration, 1920–1930	Rank on specified factor											Classification by—	
		Rural migration, 1920–1930	Percent on relief, July 1934–June 1935 [2]	Farm plane of living index, 1930	Percent of gain'ul workers in agriculture, 1930	Income per gainful worker in agriculture, 1929	Fertility ratio, 1930	Percent of farm tenancy, 1920	Percent of 16- and 17-year olds in school, 1930	Value of farm machinery per farm, 1930	Percent population increase, 1920–1930	Percent population increase, 1910–1920	Distance from city [3]	Land problem [4]
Chattahoochee, Ga.	−53.1	1	71	43	69	1	96	41	87	27	99	26	2	1
Taliaferro, Ga.	−39.1	2	47	19	21	5	54	13	62	69	1.5	43	2	1
Hancock, Ga.	−38.4	3	60	7	62	11	63	19	78	68	3	29	3	1
Perry, Ark.	−37.7	4	1	17.5	63	74	16	73	2	79	8	59	3	2
Madison, Ga.	−35.4	5	48	48	26	39	31	22	88	91.5	12	74	3	1
Fayette, Ga.	−35.5	6	19	41.5	9.5	31.5	47	21	73	87	6	52	2	1
Edgefield, S. C.	−35.1	8.5	41	93	50	18	27	24	35	33.5	14	9	2	1
McCormick, S. C.	−35.1	8.5	11	68.5	47.5	16.5	65	20	41	61.5	13	72.5	1	1
Franklin, Ga.	−35.1	8.5	50	72	30.5	44.5	52	40	61	96	11	65	3	2
Clay, Ala.	−35.0	8.5	77.5	97.5	45	35	34	74	9	48	4	57	2	2
Columbia, Ga.	−32.6	11	23	55	32	14	82	31	70	38	9	46	3	2
Henry, Ga.	−32.3	12	80	85	36	31.5	79	23	80	38	7	25	2	2
Lee, Ga.	−32.3	13	73	67	34	29.5	88	7	95	69	15	57	2	2
Saluda, S. C.	−31.7	14	12	97.5	20	55.5	37	46	11.5	5	16	14	2	1
Dawson, Ga.	−31.0	15	7	86	12	9.5	46	75	50	21	5	3	1	2
Issaquena, Miss.	−31.0	16.5	81	77	5	58	98	8	45.5	70	17	39.5	3	1
Hart, Ga.	−30.5	16.5	67.5	61	18	15	63	27	51	1	32	30.5	1	1
Bamberg, S. C.	−30.2	18	8	17.5	34.5	27.5	69	26	49	55.5	10	72.5	3	2
McDuffie, Ga.	−29.0	19	66	12	76	38	94	10	83	51	19.5	23	1	1
Franklin, Miss.	−27.7	20	13	78.5	91	65	70	65.5	25.5	95	19.5	34	1	3
Bleckley, Ga.	−26.4	21	37	44	80	11	77	34	98	28	18	6	3	2
Pointe Coupee, La.	−25.9	22	98	82	64.5	4	80	16.5	90	41	21	45	3	2
Hampton, S. C.	−25.8	23.5	6	20	85	87	87	50	63	13.5	33.5	91	4	2
Wheeler, Ga.	−25.7	23.5	49	41.5	69	21.5	8	45	79	4	22.5	82	4	1
Bibb, Ala.	−24.8	25	45	65.5	95	96	28	71	55.5	82	30	87	3	2
Turner, Ga.	−24.4	26	64	81	82	61	76	25	63	58	25	71	3	1
Grant, Ark.	−23.8	27	3	96	72	68	64	97	3	7	26	24	4	1
Douglas, Ga.	−23.4	28	28	83	75	41	43	52	94	56	41	35.5	3	2
Calhoun, S. C.	−23.4	28	4	64	25.5	91	49	33	52	67	36	47.5	1	2
Randolph, Ark.	−23.8	30	10	49	37.5	48.5	9	70	31	19.5	41	31	3	1
Hardin, Tenn.	−23.8	31	33	26.5	43	76	26	62	39.5	25.5	36	35.5	4	2
Emanuel, Ga.	−23.4	32.5	65	78.5	76	42.5	71	36	65	32	33.5	47.5	2	1
Murray, Ga.	−23.4	32.5	46	78.5	58	42.5	2	63	76.5	85.5	46	31	1	2
Jefferson, Ga.	−23.3	34.5	72	39	49	21.5	81	12	76.5	38	28.5	61	3	2

See footnotes at end of table.

Table 14.—Estimated Net Rural Migration, 1920–1930, and Selected Socio-Economic Factors in 99 Cotton Belt Counties ¹—Continued

County and State	Percent estimated net rural migration, 1920–1930	Rural migration, 1920–1930	Percent on relief, July 1934–June 1935[5]	Farm plane of living index, 1930	Percent of gainful workers in agriculture, 1930	Income per gainful worker in agriculture, 1929	Fertility ratio, 1930	Percent of farm tenancy, 1920	Percent of 16- and 17-year olds in school, 1930	Value of farm machinery per farm, 1930	Percent population increase, 1920–1930	Percent population increase, 1910–1920	Distance from city[3]	Land problem[4]
							Rank on specified factor						Classification by—	
Miller, Ga.	−23.3	34.5	31	35	22	85	12	42	96	75	39	89	4	2
Irwin, Ga.	−23.1	36	83	75	55	97	15	37	48	8.5	43.5	90	4	2
Cherokee, Ala.	−23.0	37	95	91.5	3	71	10	51	54	3	45	49	4	1
Gordon, Ga.	−22.4	38	56	59	83	72	72	61	57	19.5	40	75.5	2	1
Baker, Ga.	−22.3	39	67.5	13	14	51	11	15	89	63.5	37	54.5	1	1
Sharp, Ark.	−21.7	40	2	46	35	89	32	93	18	39.5	43.5	28	4	2
Fayette, Tenn.	−21.5	41	93	11	4	46	50	11	32	45.5	28.5	54.5	5	2
Lamar, Ala.	−21.1	42	96	91.5	13	25	6	80	19	77.5	55	51	1	2
Wilkinson, Miss.	−21.0	43	34	5	77.5	3	48	35	66	45.5	27	11	2	2
Wayne, Miss.	−20.9	44	29	26.5	81	16.5	4	94	36.5	39.5	53.5	58	3	2
Candler, Ga.	−20.8	45.5	26	70	70	90	56	55	82	95	48		4	1
Lowndes, Ala.	−20.8	45.5	92	4	6	8	67	4	13	82	24	7	4	2
Clay, Ark.	−20.7	47	21	47	73	92	73	68	58	53	58	84.5	2	1
Stewart, Ga.	−20.2	48	52	53.5	86	37	83	16.5	67	53	31	16	3	2
Warren, Ga.	−20.1	49	62	29	25.5	50	44	14	95	89	38	39	3	3
Avoyelles, La.	−19.5	50	94	51.5	54	47	45	59	55.5	75	53.5	50	4	2
Carroll, Miss.	−19.4	51.5	44	14	15	69	68	48	22	67	47	12	4	2
Telfair, Ga.	−19.1	51.5	59	41.5	89.5	63	74	67	72	67	50	84.5	2	2
Lamar, Miss.	−19.1	53.5	9	71	96	79	14	99	5	34.5	57	68	4	2
Covington, Miss.	−19.0	53.5	22	56.5	19	23	75	92	7	53	62.5	13	2	2
Wilkinson, Ga.	−18.3	55	36	33.5	89.5	29.5	40	53	92	91.5	42	79	1	1
Fayette, Ala.	−18.1	56	91	94.5	59	53.5	20	90	34	45.5	59.5	80.5	3	1
Jasper, Miss.	−18.0	57	27	62	42	33.5	55	84	17	65	61	40	2	2
Pickens, Ala.	−17.9	58	89	30.5	40	36	1	58	23	77.5	51	44	1	1
Winston, Ala.	−17.4	59	85	33.5	51	42.5	62	98	44	73	76	75.5	3	2
Choctaw, Ala.	−17.2	60	61	6	84	7	33	65.5	47	97	52	78	2	2
Benton, Miss.	−16.5	61	16	9	2	66	39	57	30	42.5	56	30	1	1
Shelby, Ala.	−15.8	62	32	88.5	98	73	91	76	59	8.5	64	41	3	2
Claiborne, Miss.	−15.6	63	17	36.5	53	6	61	29	24	15	35	5	3	2
Rankin, Miss.	−15.6	64.5	39	63	66	33.5	59	69	10	49.5	59.5	10	3	2
Crenshaw, Ala.	−15.5	64.5	90	33.5	56.5	57	22	64	64	82	66	35.5	4	2
Conecuh, Ala.	−15.4	66	82	23	39	11	84	79	36.5	61.5	67.5	83	3	2
Lonoke, Ark.	−15.4	67.5	57	68.5	46	98	21	43	25.5	10	63.5	88	3	2
Cleveland, Ark.	−14.9	67.5	5	73	27.5	80	42	85	20	62.5	69	20.5	4	2
Monroe, Ala.	−14.8	69	79	30.5	67	20	89	56	27	49.5	70	62.5	4	2
Lincoln, Ark.	−14.8	70	63	2	9.5	88	89	32	8	75	74	92	4	1
Sharkey, Miss.	−14.3	71	74	24	8	59	97	2	75	16.5	49	19	4	

County												Distance from city[3]	Land problem[4]
Henry, Ala.	−14.1	72	77.5	53.5	44	26	36	38	76.5	42.5	73	45.5	4	2
Evangeline, La.	−13.7	73	86	50	29	88	88	60	74	6	77	—	4	2
Schley, Ga.	−12.7	74	42	74	25.5	52	60	30	91	60	65	42	3	2
McNairy, Tenn.	−12.1	75.5	58	80	27.5	70	25	72	29	23	76	77	3	1
Smith, Miss.	−12.1	75.5	14	26.5	30.5	67	3	95	14	36.5	89	33	3	
Woodruff, Ark.	−11.5	77	35	17.5	68	93	78	9	28	24	72	64	3	2
Prentiss, Miss.	−11.4	78	24	60	4	75	57	54	16	9	81	53	2	1
Montgomery, N. C.	−10.8	79	20	99	92.5	62	35	88	43	12	86	33	2	2
Franklin, N. C.	−10.6	80	75	88.5	60	77	29	49	53	34.5	84.5	63	3	2
Caldwell, La.	−10.5	81	84	76	87.5	86	41	86	21	45.5	82	69.5	3	1
Montgomery, Ga.	−10.2	82	40	51.5	74	84	58	47	85	90	80	1	3	
Calhoun, Ga.	−9.7	83	55	36.5	71	64	92	6	97	57	67.5	17	4	2
Chester, Tenn.	−9.3	84	54	94.5	37.5	94	66	87	28	11	83	62.5	4	2
Newton, Miss.	−9.2	85	53	56.5	61	60	51	91	6	15	84.5	15	3	1
Jefferson Davis, Miss.	−8.9	86	18	21.5	7	78	19	83	1	71.5	88	38	3	2
Grant, La.	−8.8	87	25	58	97	48.5	86	77	15	59	79	18	3	1
Quitman, Ga.	−8.7	88	70	87	77.5	40	30	39	84	22	87	4	4	
Washington, Ala.	−7.6	89	38	65.5	92.5	19	17	96	69	55	90	37	4	1
Pickens, Ga.	−7.4	90	30	38	94	24	13	81	42	84	93	20.5	4	1
Polk, N. C.	−6.6	91	69	90	87.5	44.5	24	89	33	71.5	92	86	2	
Tunica, Miss.	−6.0	92	87	3	1	27.5	99	1	71	80	71	67	3	2
Greene, Ala.	−4.3	93	99	1	23.5	2	90	13	86	63	78	8	1	2
Tippah, Miss.	−3.5	94	15	45	11	53.5	23	73	11.5	29.5	94	90	2	1
Lake, Tenn.	−2.1	95	43	84	17	55.5	95	5	99	2	91	36	2	2
Leake, Miss.	+1.4	96	51	21.5	33	81	5	82	4	16.5	97	22	2	2
Richland, La.	+4.4	97	76	10	47.5	82	85	28	39.5	29.5	96	63	3	2
Tensas, La.	+10.5	98	97	8	62	95	93	3	60	32	95	2	3	2
West Carroll, La.	+22.4	99	88	15	56.5	99	13	44	45.5	32	98	64	3	2
Range	−53.1 to +22.4	32.5 to 0.1	14.4 to 35.4	90.7 to 15.0	$230 to $865	952.7 to 444.4	93.2 to 21.5	76.7 to 28.4	$251 6 to $867	−30.2 to +68.9	−53.3 to +31.7		
Average[5]	−19.5	9.21	21.5	74.4	$478	756.8	62.3	51.4	$125	−1.9	−2.9		

[1] Counties ranked on each factor, number one in each case being assigned to the first figure given in the "range."

[2] Based on 1930 population.

[3] Distance from city: 1 = less than 50 miles from city of 100,000 or more; 2 = 50–99 miles from city of 100,000 or more; 3 = less than 50 miles from city of 25,000–99,999; 4 = 50–99 miles from city of 25,000–99,999; 5 = 100 miles or more from city of 25,000–99,999.

[4] Land problem: 1 = problem county; 2 = nonproblem county.

[5] Median.

Table 15.—Counties of the United States by Percent of Gainful Workers 10 Years of Age and Over Engaged in Agriculture, by Geographic Division and State, 1930

Geographic division and State	Total counties	Percent of gainful workers engaged in agriculture				
		Less than 5	5–9.9	10–24.9	25–49.9	50 or more
United States	3,059	71	117	401	899	1,571
New England	64	9	9	35	10	1
Maine	16	—	2	11	3	—
New Hampshire	10	—	2	8	—	—
Vermont	14	—	—	6	7	1
Massachusetts	12	6	2	4	—	—
Rhode Island	4	1	1	2	—	—
Connecticut	8	2	2	4	—	—
Middle Atlantic	143	19	28	58	37	1
New York	57	6	7	24	20	—
New Jersey	20	7	4	8	1	—
Pennsylvania	66	6	17	26	16	1
East North Central	436	12	26	90	204	104
Ohio	88	7	4	23	42	12
Indiana	92	2	4	18	50	18
Illinois	102	1	8	15	55	23
Michigan	83	1	8	21	32	21
Wisconsin	71	1	2	13	25	30
West North Central	620	5	4	34	165	412
Minnesota	87	2	—	4	20	61
Iowa	99	—	1	10	34	54
Missouri	114	1	2	8	25	78
North Dakota	53	—	—	—	8	45
South Dakota	69	—	—	2	10	57
Nebraska	93	1	—	2	22	68
Kansas	105	1	1	8	46	49
South Atlantic	555	10	20	55	161	309
Delaware	3	—	1	—	2	—
Maryland	23	1	—	5	12	5
Virginia	100	1	2	5	36	56
West Virginia	55	2	8	10	20	15
North Carolina	100	1	1	7	25	66
South Carolina	46	—	—	2	12	32
Georgia	161	2	3	9	26	121
Florida	67	3	5	17	28	14
East South Central	364	3	7	11	65	278
Kentucky	120	2	3	5	21	89
Tennessee	95	—	2	2	23	68
Alabama	67	1	1	1	11	53
Mississippi	82	—	1	3	10	68
West South Central	469	5	11	29	109	315
Arkansas	75	—	—	3	6	66
Louisiana	63	—	1	6	18	38
Oklahoma	77	—	2	6	22	47
Texas	254	5	8	14	63	164
Mountain	276	5	7	49	90	125
Montana	56	1	1	6	16	32
Idaho	44	1	—	5	16	22
Wyoming	23	—	—	5	7	11
Colorado	62	3	—	12	18	29
New Mexico	31	—	—	5	12	14
Arizona	14	—	2	5	6	1
Utah	29	—	1	4	11	13
Nevada	17	—	3	7	4	3
Pacific	132	3	5	40	58	26
Washington	39	1	2	14	13	9
Oregon	36	1	1	6	20	8
California	57	1	2	20	25	9

Source: Bureau of the Census, *Fifteenth Census of the United States: 1930*, Population Vol. III, U. S. Department of Commerce, Washington, D. C., 1932, table 20.

Table 16.—Counties of the United States by Gross Farm Income [1] per Gainful Worker 10 Years of Age and Over Engaged in Agriculture, by Geographic Division and State, 1929

Geographic division and State	Total counties	Income per gainful worker engaged in agriculture				
		Less than $600	$600–$1,199.99	$1,200–$1,799.99	$1,800–$2,399.99	$2,400 or more
United States	[2] 3,059	704	916	794	420	224
New England	64	—	11	51	1	1
Maine	16	—	2	13	—	1
New Hampshire	10	—	1	9	—	—
Vermont	14	—	2	12	—	—
Massachusetts	12	—	3	9	—	—
Rhode Island	4	—	1	3	—	—
Connecticut	8	—	2	5	1	—
Middle Atlantic	143	1	38	91	11	2
New York	57	1	4	43	8	1
New Jersey	20	—	7	10	2	1
Pennsylvania	66	—	27	38	1	—
East North Central	436	5	190	194	46	1
Ohio	88	1	32	55	—	—
Indiana	92	1	39	45	7	—
Illinois	102	3	35	30	33	1
Michigan	83	—	62	21	—	—
Wisconsin	71	—	22	43	6	—
West North Central	620	7	112	208	189	104
Minnesota	87	—	28	44	15	—
Iowa	99	—	—	22	51	26
Missouri	114	6	70	35	1	2
North Dakota	50	—	2	40	11	—
South Dakota	69	1	2	31	34	1
Nebraska	93	—	1	16	41	35
Kansas	105	—	9	20	36	40
South Atlantic	555	295	230	27	3	—
Delaware	3	—	1	2	—	—
Maryland	23	—	14	9	—	—
Virginia	100	24	66	9	1	—
West Virginia	55	16	37	2	—	—
North Carolina	100	55	45	—	—	—
South Carolina	46	45	1	—	—	—
Georgia	161	127	34	—	—	—
Florida	67	28	32	5	2	—
East South Central	364	236	123	3	2	—
Kentucky	120	52	63	3	2	—
Tennessee	95	53	42	—	—	—
Alabama	67	59	8	—	—	—
Mississippi	82	72	10	—	—	—
West South Central	469	151	171	77	26	44
Arkansas	75	45	29	1	—	—
Louisiana	63	41	21	1	—	—
Oklahoma	77	12	36	22	3	4
Texas	254	53	85	53	23	40
Mountain	[2] 276	9	30	95	101	40
Montana	56	1	3	25	21	6
Idaho	44	—	3	8	24	9
Wyoming	23	—	—	3	14	6
Colorado	[2] 62	—	6	25	19	11
New Mexico	31	7	7	9	7	1
Arizona	14	1	3	6	4	—
Utah	29	—	6	13	7	3
Nevada	17	—	2	6	5	4
Pacific	132	—	11	48	41	32
Washington	39	—	4	18	5	12
Oregon	36	—	4	14	10	8
California	57	—	3	16	26	12

[1] Value of farm products sold, traded, or used by the operators' families in 1929 divided by the total number of persons engaged in agriculture as reported by the 1930 Census.
[2] Includes 1 county for which no data were available.

Sources: Bureau of the Census, *Fifteenth Census of the United States: 1930*, Population Vol. III, table 20, and Agriculture Vol. III, county table III, U. S. Department of Commerce, Washington, D. C.

Table 17.—Counties of the United States by Rural Plane of Living Index, by Geographic Division and State, 1930

Geographic division and State	Total counties	Rural plane of living index				
		Less than 50	50–99.9	100–149.9	150–199.9	200 or more
United States	3,059	870	811	741	513	124
New England	64	—	—	8	37	19
Maine	16	—	—	8	8	—
New Hampshire	10	—	—	—	10	—
Vermont	14	—	—	—	14	—
Massachusetts	12	—	—	—	—	12
Rhode Island	4	—	—	—	2	2
Connecticut	8	—	—	—	3	5
Middle Atlantic	143	—	2	42	61	38
New York	57	—	—	5	34	18
New Jersey	20	—	—	—	5	15
Pennsylvania	66	—	2	37	22	5
East North Central	436	2	107	172	125	30
Ohio	88	—	13	32	36	7
Indiana	92	1	29	42	18	2
Illinois	102	1	26	33	32	10
Michigan	83	—	30	34	15	4
Wisconsin	71	—	9	31	24	7
West North Central	620	24	94	276	218	8
Minnesota	87	—	17	34	35	1
Iowa	99	—	1	18	76	4
Missouri	114	19	38	53	3	1
North Dakota	53	—	12	38	3	—
South Dakota	69	5	12	29	23	—
Nebraska	93	—	3	31	57	2
Kansas	105	—	11	73	21	—
South Atlantic	555	336	178	29	8	4
Delaware	3	—	—	2	—	1
Maryland	23	—	12	5	4	2
Virginia	100	31	53	13	2	1
West Virginia	55	5	42	6	2	—
North Carolina	100	78	22	—	—	—
South Carolina	46	43	3	—	—	—
Georgia	161	148	11	2	—	—
Florida	67	31	35	1	—	—
East South Central	364	280	77	3	3	1
Kentucky	120	64	50	2	3	1
Tennessee	95	71	23	1	—	—
Alabama	67	64	3	—	—	—
Mississippi	82	81	1	—	—	—
West South Central	469	209	210	49	1	—
Arkansas	75	70	5	—	—	—
Louisiana	63	57	6	—	—	—
Oklahoma	77	25	44	8	—	—
Texas	254	57	155	41	1	—
Mountain	276	19	136	101	18	2
Montana	56	—	40	16	—	—
Idaho	44	—	15	25	4	—
Wyoming	23	—	9	14	—	—
Colorado	62	2	24	31	5	—
New Mexico	31	14	17	—	—	—
Arizona	14	2	11	1	—	—
Utah	29	1	12	7	8	1
Nevada	17	—	8	7	1	1
Pacific	132	—	7	61	42	22
Washington	39	—	2	17	19	1
Oregon	36	—	2	25	7	2
California	57	—	3	19	16	19

Sources: Bureau of the Census, *Fifteenth Census of the United States: 1930,* Population Vol. VI and Agriculture Vol. II, U. S. Department of Commerce, Washington, D. C.

Table 18.—Counties of the United States by Rural-Farm Plane of Living Index, by Geographic Division and State, 1930

Geographic division and State	Total counties	Rural-farm plane of living index				
		Less than 50	50–99.9	100–149.9	150–199.9	200 or more
United States	1 3,059	962	692	639	522	243
New England	64	—	—	1	17	46
Maine	16	—	—	1	12	3
New Hampshire	10	—	—	—	—	10
Vermont	14	—	—	—	4	10
Massachusetts	12	—	—	—	1	11
Rhode Island	4	—	—	—	—	4
Connecticut	8	—	—	—	—	8
Middle Atlantic	143	—	2	42	57	42
New York	57	—		6	32	19
New Jersey	20	—	—	—	3	17
Pennsylvania	66	—	2	36	22	6
East North Central	436	5	99	142	143	47
Ohio	88	—	11	23	41	13
Indiana	92	1	24	33	31	3
Illinois	102	4	20	26	34	18
Michigan	83	—	30	34	15	4
Wisconsin	71	—	14	26	22	9
West North Central	620	33	110	240	204	33
Minnesota	87	—	19	41	26	1
Iowa	99	—	—	11	62	26
Missouri	114	25	31	50	8	—
North Dakota	53	1	24	26	2	—
South Dakota	69	7	18	23	20	1
Nebraska	93	—	3	27	58	5
Kansas	105	—	15	62	28	—
South Atlantic	555	366	131	44	10	4
Delaware	3	—	2	—	—	1
Maryland	23	—	11	6	5	1
Virginia	100	37	45	15	2	1
West Virginia	55	13	33	7	1	1
North Carolina	100	85	14	1	—	—
South Carolina	46	46	—	—	—	—
Georgia	161	153	6	2	—	—
Florida	67	32	20	13	2	—
East South Central	364	298	58	6	2	—
Kentucky	120	75	38	5	2	—
Tennessee	95	78	16	1	—	—
Alabama	67	65	2	—	—	—
Mississippi	82	80	2	—	—	—
West South Central	469	234	168	51	12	4
Arkansas	75	73	2	—	—	—
Louisiana	63	53	8	2	—	—
Oklahoma	77	37	34	6	—	—
Texas	254	71	124	43	12	4
Mountain	1 276	26	120	92	24	13
Montana	56	2	36	17	1	—
Idaho	44	—	15	21	6	2
Wyoming	23	—	16	7	—	—
Colorado	1 62	3	23	27	7	1
New Mexico	31	16	13	2	—	—
Arizona	14	2	6	5	1	—
Utah	29	2	6	8	5	8
Nevada	17	1	5	5	4	2
Pacific	132	—	4	21	53	54
Washington	39	—	2	5	18	14
Oregon	36	—	1	13	17	5
California	57	—	1	3	18	35

1 Includes 1 county for which no data were available.

Sources: Bureau of the Census, *Fifteenth Census of the United States: 1930*, Population Vol. VI and Agriculture Vol. II, U. S. Department of Commerce, Washington, D. C.

Table 19.—Estimated Net Migration of the Rural Population of the United States, 1920–1930, Using 2 Methods, by Geographic Division and State

Geographic division and State	Net rural migration, 1920–1930		Difference	
	First method [1]	Second method [2]	Number	Percent
United States	−5,734,200	−5,633,300	100,900	1.8
New England	+145,500	+133,100	12,400	8.5
Maine	−40,600	−44,500	3,900	9.6
New Hampshire	+16,400	+14,500	1,900	11.6
Vermont	−23,500	−25,800	2,300	9.8
Massachusetts	+176,000	+174,900	1,100	0.6
Rhode Island	+30,600	+29,600	1,000	3.3
Connecticut	−13,400	−15,600	2,200	16.4
Middle Atlantic	−443,400	−425,500	17,900	4.0
New York	+98,100	+83,500	14,600	14.9
New Jersey	−50,100	−16,100	34,000	67.9
Pennsylvania	−491,400	−492,900	1,500	0.3
East North Central	−899,400	−927,900	28,500	3.2
Ohio	−181,300	−190,200	8,900	4.9
Indiana	−154,900	−160,400	5,500	3.6
Illinois	−303,400	−309,400	6,000	2.0
Michigan	−78,900	−84,200	5,300	6.7
Wisconsin	−180,900	−183,700	2,800	1.5
West North Central	−1,100,800	−1,112,900	12,100	1.1
Minnesota [3]	−207,400	−208,300	+900	0.4
Iowa	−212,900	−217,400	4,500	2.1
Missouri	−261,900	−266,500	4,600	1.8
North Dakota	−92,200	−90,200	2,000	2.2
South Dakota [3]	−63,700	−62,800	900	1.4
Nebraska	−122,900	−124,000	1,100	0.9
Kansas	−139,800	−143,700	3,900	2.8
South Atlantic	−1,434,000	−1,364,500	69,500	4.8
Delaware	+2,500	+2,300	200	8.0
Maryland	−10,500	−8,900	1,600	15.2
Virginia	−279,400	−266,400	13,000	4.7
West Virginia	−118,500	−116,100	2,400	2.0
North Carolina	−206,500	−190,100	16,400	7.9
South Carolina	−298,000	−282,400	15,600	5.2
Georgia [3]	−510,600	−492,500	18,100	3.5
Florida [3]	−13,000	−10,400	2,600	20.0
East South Central	−1,097,200	−1,067,800	29,400	2.7
Kentucky	−313,300	−310,600	2,700	0.9
Tennessee	−316,000	−308,300	7,700	2.4
Alabama	−300,200	−288,700	11,500	3.8
Mississippi	−167,700	−160,200	7,500	4.5
West South Central	−922,700	−890,100	32,600	3.5
Arkansas	−255,600	−250,900	4,700	1.8
Louisiana	−136,700	−130,300	6,400	4.7
Oklahoma	−214,700	−210,700	4,000	1.9
Texas [3]	−315,700	−298,200	17,500	5.5
Mountain	−258,900	−255,900	3,000	1.2
Montana [3]	−71,000	−70,100	900	1.3
Idaho	−50,200	−49,200	1,000	2.0
Wyoming [3]	−6,100	−6,000	100	1.6
Colorado	−50,400	−52,000	1,600	3.2
New Mexico [3]	−43,600	−42,900	700	1.6
Arizona	+17,300	+18,600	1,300	7.5
Utah	−44,500	−43,700	800	1.8
Nevada	−10,400	−10,600	200	1.9
Pacific	+276,700	+278,200	1,500	0.5
Washington	−2,400	−1,400	1,000	41.7
Oregon	+22,800	+22,300	500	2.2
California	+256,300	+257,300	1,000	0.4

[1] State total calculated with a 10.25-year survival factor applied by 5-year age groups to rural-farm and rural-nonfarm population of each State. See appendix B for method of computation.
[2] State total calculated with a 10.25-year survival factor applied by 10-year age groups to rural population of each county. See appendix B for method of computation.
[3] Containing counties that changed boundaries or were organized between 1920 and 1930.

Appendix B

METHODOLOGICAL NOTES

1. ESTIMATES OF NET RURAL MIGRATION, 1920–1930

To ESTIMATE net rural migration, 1920–1930, calculations were based upon the census enumerations of 1920 and 1930. To correct for the underenumeration of children under 5 years of age, in both 1920 and 1930, 5 percent was allowed for all white children and 11 percent for colored children in the North, 13.5 percent in the South, 8 percent in the West, and 13 percent in the United States as a whole.[1] Survival factors were applied to the 1920 population to determine the number of survivors in 1930 had there been no migration.[2] The results were compared with the population enumerated in 1930, and the differences were attributed to migration. The estimated net rural migration was based upon those persons living in 1920 with no attempt made to estimate the net migration of children born after the 1920 Census enumeration. Because of the differences in degree of completeness of the census reports on population for the various political subdivisions, it was necessary to use different methods for counties from those used for the United States as a whole and for the individual States.

United States as a Whole and the Individual States

Since for the Nation as a whole and for the individual States both the 1920 and 1930 rural populations were tabulated by age groups, a *forward* method of estimating net migration, beginning with the rural

---

[1] Whelpton, P. K., "Geographic and Economic Differentials in Fertility," *The Annals of the American Academy of Political and Social Science*, Vol. 188, November 1936, pp. 37–55.

[2] The life tables used were made available through the courtesy of the Metropolitan Life Insurance Company.

population of 1920, was used.   A type illustration will make the steps clear:

Data given:
    1920 rural population _ 1, 000
    1930 rural population _   850
    Children under 10 years of age in 1930_ _ _ _ _ _ _ _ _ _ _ _   200
Calculations:
    Total survivors in 1930 of 1920 population (1,000 x survival factor) _   900
    Survivors in 1930 of 1920 population and living in county (850–200) _   650
    Net survivors of migrants (900–650) _ _ _ _ _ _ _ _ _ _ _ _ _   250
    Deaths:
        To 1920 population _ _ _ _ _ _ _ _ _ _ _ _ _ _ _ _ _ _ _   100

        To nonmigrants $\left(\frac{650}{900}\times 100\right)$ _ _ _ _ _ _ _ _ _ _ _ _ _ _ _   72

        To migrants (100–72) _ _ _ _ _ _ _ _ _ _ _ _ _ _ _ _ _ _   28
        One-half deaths to migrants _ _ _ _ _ _ _ _ _ _ _ _ _ _ _   14
    Net loss from migration (250+14)_ _ _ _ _ _ _ _ _ _ _ _ _ _ _   264

The above example indicates the procedure when a net loss from migration occurred.   A similar procedure was followed when a net gain from migration occurred.   It was assumed that migration was not selective with respect to death rates and that the net result of migration was distributed evenly throughout the decade.   Therefore, one-half of the deaths occurring to migrants were charged to the area of origin and one-half to the area of destination.

Counties of the United States

For estimating net rural migration by counties the above procedure had to be modified somewhat.   In 1920 the rural population of counties was not tabulated by age and hence the *forward* method of calculation could not be used.   A *backward* or reverse method was followed instead.   By this procedure the example cited above takes the following form:

Data given:
    1920 rural population _ 1, 000
    1930 rural population _   850
    Children under 10 years of age in 1930 _ _ _ _ _ _ _ _ _ _ _ _   200
Calculations:
    Survivors of 1920 population still living in area (850–200) _ _ _ _ _ _   650

    1920 base of 650 survivors: $\dfrac{650}{\text{survival factor}}$ _ _ _ _ _ _ _ _ _ _   722

    Potential migrants (1,000–722) _ _ _ _ _ _ _ _ _ _ _ _ _ _ _   278
    Deaths:
        To 1920 population _ _ _ _ _ _ _ _ _ _ _ _ _ _ _ _ _ _ _   100
        To nonmigrants (722–650) _ _ _ _ _ _ _ _ _ _ _ _ _ _ _ _   72
        To migrants (100–72) _ _ _ _ _ _ _ _ _ _ _ _ _ _ _ _ _ _   28
        One-half deaths to migrants _ _ _ _ _ _ _ _ _ _ _ _ _ _ _   14
    Net loss from migration (278–14) _ _ _ _ _ _ _ _ _ _ _ _ _ _ _   264

Survival Factors

The life table used in estimating deaths of the white rural population was computed by the Metropolitan Life Insurance Company on the basis of the death registration States of 1930. Using this table, which gives slightly higher survival rates than for the United States as a whole, survival rates for 10.25 years [3] were developed by 5-year age groups. These were used for estimating deaths by States and for the United States as a whole. In making county estimates survival factors based upon 10-year age groups were used for calculating the number of potential migrants by the *backward* method. Since the 1920 age distribution of the rural population was not available by counties, the number of migrant deaths was estimated by using a composite survival factor for all ages.

For estimates by race two survival factors were used, white and colored. Colored races other than Negro were grouped with Negroes for survival purposes. Since no rural Negro life table was available, one was constructed by assuming that rural-urban differences in Negro mortality were proportional to rural-urban differences in white mortality. The white and colored survival rates for 10.25 years used to estimate deaths for the intercensal period, 1920–1930, are given in table A.

Table A.—Survival Rates in the Rural Population, by Age and Color, 1920–1930

Age, 1920	Number of survivors in 1930 per 1,000 persons in 1920	
	White rural population	Colored rural population
Under 5 years	969. 6	952. 2
5–9 years	980. 4	970. 2
10–14 years	979. 4	941. 5
15–19 years	970. 5	911. 6
20–24 years	964. 9	894. 2
25–29 years	961. 1	879. 3
30–34 years	955. 4	863. 5
35–39 years	945. 1	835. 9
40–44 years	928. 7	803. 4
45–49 years	902. 4	758. 8
50–54 years	860. 5	711. 0
55–59 years	792. 5	661. 1
60–64 years	694. 5	594. 5
65–69 years	560. 3	505. 8
70–74 years	397. 5	405. 7
75–79 years	242. 4	286. 0
80–84 years	120. 9	189. 0
85 years and over	42. 0	90. 4

These survival factors were combined in the weighted proportions of the two racial groups in 1930 in the rural-farm and rural-nonfarm populations by age groups. The biracial net migration was then estimated for the rural-farm and rural-nonfarm populations separately

---

[3] To take account of the fact that the 1920 Census was taken as of January 1, and the 1930 Census as of April 1.

and the results added to obtain the net rural migration. This procedure was followed for States and for the United States as a whole, except that in States where the colored races amounted to less than 5 percent of the total in either the rural-farm or rural-nonfarm population, white survival factors alone were used.

For counties only net rural migration could be estimated. Here the racial combination was handled somewhat differently. The States were classified with respect to the percent of colored population in 1930. In the 25 Northern and Western States having less than 5 percent colored in the total rural population, only white survival factors were used for all counties. In the remaining 23 Southern and Western States all counties were classified according to the percent of colored in the rural population in 1930. For counties with less than 5 percent, survival factors based upon the rural population of Missouri were used since it had about 3 percent colored in 1930. For counties having 5–9 percent colored, survival factors based upon the rural population of Kentucky were used, and so on to Mississippi which served for those counties having 40–49 percent colored. Counties with 50–59 percent colored were treated with a survival factor weighted to 55 percent Negro and 45 percent white assuming an even age distribution for the two racial groups. Counties with 60–69 percent colored were treated with a survival factor weighted to 65 percent colored and 35 percent white, and counties with 70–79 percent colored were treated with a survival factor weighted to 75 and 25 percent, respectively.

Reliability of County Estimates of Net Migration as Compared With State Estimates

The estimates of net rural migration by States may be regarded as sufficiently reliable to indicate general trends inasmuch as they check closely with the estimates for the United States as a whole. Their reliability rests chiefly upon the completeness of the census enumerations, the accuracy of these enumerations by age, and the reliability of the estimates of mortality. The estimates of mortality are based upon careful computations by 5-year age groups weighted for white and colored elements. The county estimates, however, are based upon less precise estimates of mortality. Furthermore, in a number of individual counties, chiefly suburban in nature, the estimates did not appear reasonable. Such counties were Kings, Wash.; Maricopa, Ariz.; and Bergen, N. J. Finally, in a number of States where county boundaries had changed importantly during the decade or new counties had been created, the estimates for two or more counties had to be made as one and the average result assigned to each. This introduces further error.

Appendix table 19, p. 162, compares the estimates by States and by counties. Although the estimates of total net migration for the United States obtained by the two methods are surprisingly similar., there are glaring differences in certain States. These sharp differences arise from the unusual results obtained in a few counties.

2. APPLICATION OF A NET REPLACEMENT QUOTA TO INDICATE GROWTH IN A POPULATION

As an illustration of the application of a net replacement quota to indicate growth in a population if there is no migration, the computation for the native white rural-farm population is given below (table B). The ratio of children under 5 years of age to women 20–44 years of age in the rural-farm population in 1930 was 752, as given by Whelpton.[4] This indicates a net replacement of 71 percent in one generation. By using survival rates as computed for rural whites by the Metropolitan Life Insurance Company and assuming that at the end of each 5-year period the ratio of children to women is the same, the increase during a 30-year period will amount to 77 percent.

Table B.—Native White Rural-Farm Population in 1930 and Estimated for 1960, by Age and Sex

Age	Native white rural-farm population, 1930		Estimated native white rural-farm population, 1960	
	Male	Female	Male	Female
Total	12,559,000	11,252,000	21,453,000	20,648,000
Under 5 years	1,364,000	1,316,000	2,713,000	2,617,000
5–9 years	1,541,000	1,473,000	2,500,000	2,417,000
10–14 years	1,563,000	1,455,000	2,273,000	2,201,000
15–19 years	1,485,000	1,257,000	2,057,000	1,994,000
20–24 years	1,055,000	871,000	1,766,000	1,710,000
25–29 years	748,000	694,000	1,488,000	1,450,000
30–34 years	682,000	676,000	1,200,000	1,231,000
35–39 years	717,000	702,000	1,413,000	1,370,000
40–44 years	665,000	626,000	1,404,000	1,330,000
20–44 years	—	*3,569,000*	—	*7,097,000*
45–49 years	629,000	562,000	1,299,000	1,125,000
50–54 years	577,000	477,000	891,000	761,000
55–59 years	481,000	374,000	606,000	586,000
60–64 years	382,000	282,000	512,000	537,000
65–69 years	284,000	201,000	475,000	503,000
70–74 years	208,000	143,000	359,000	375,000
75–79 years	112,000	82,000	244,000	249,000
80–84 years	47,000	40,000	132,000	128,000
85–89 years	15,000	16,000	49,000	46,000
90–94 years	3,000	4,000	11,000	11,000
95 years and over	1,000	1,000	1,000	1,000

3. METHOD USED IN COMPUTING COUNTY PLANE OF LIVING INDEX

The rural-farm plane of living index was based upon six factors which were available in the 1930 Census for each county of the United States. They included the following:

1. Average value of farm dwelling.
2. Percent of farms reporting telephones.
3. Percent of farms reporting automobiles.

---

[4] Whelpton, P. K., *op. cit.*

4. Percent of farms reporting electricity.
5. Percent of farms reporting running water.
6. Percent of farms reporting radios.

For each of these six factors the arithmetic mean for the United States was obtained. For each factor the position of each county was then computed as a percent of the mean. This gave six relatives for each county. Giving each factor the weight of one, these six relatives were averaged to obtain the average relative position of each county in terms of the mean for the United States.

Only two of the above factors were available for the rural-nonfarm population, average value of dwelling and percent of families reporting radios. To get the average value of the dwelling it was necessary to convert rental value into actual value by assuming the yearly rental to be equal to 10 percent of the value of the dwelling. Rented and owned dwelling values were then combined in weighted proportions for each county. The same procedure was used with the two factors as was used with the six rural-farm factors in order to secure the rural-nonfarm plane of living index by counties.

The rural plane of living index was devised by combining the rural-farm and rural-nonfarm indices, weighted according to the proportions of rural-farm and rural-nonfarm population in the respective counties in 1930.

4. RURAL POPULATION MOBILITY FIELD SURVEYS

In order to provide more detailed data on rural population movements and the characteristics of migrants than are available from census data, special studies have been carried on in eight States—Arizona, Iowa, Kentucky, Maryland, North Carolina, North Dakota, Ohio, and South Dakota—since the beginning of 1935. Within each State the selection of the sample areas and the size of the sample were determined by local needs, interests, and resources. In some cases the sample was considered representative of rural areas of the State in general. In others the survey was limited to some significant situation within the State. However, schedules and instructions to enumerators were identical and editing and tabulating of schedules were centralized. To this extent the data from the several surveys are comparable, and the scattered studies have shown considerable uniformity in their results.

Data on mobility were secured for the period from January 1, 1928, to January 1, 1935, or January 1, 1926, to January 1, 1936, in the various States. Only changes in residence of a relatively permanent nature were included. In order to eliminate short-distance movements, unimportant from the standpoint of the person's integration with the social organization of the community, recorded migrations were arbitrarily limited to those which involved a change of residence from one minor civil division to another.

In each interview information was secured concerning all members of the household and all living children of the head of the household, regardless of their whereabouts at the time of the survey. In most instances the members of the family who were still in the survey area were able to give the desired information concerning those who had left, including a statement concerning their residence and employment on January 1, 1929, as well as at the time of the survey. Thus, the field surveys yielded information concerning two types of movement with reference to the survey areas: (1) the in-migration of persons who were there when schedules were taken and (2) the out-migration of adult children of persons who were still in the areas.

In Iowa, North Carolina, North Dakota, Ohio, and South Dakota the sample areas were enumerated completely. In Kentucky and Maryland the rural population mobility schedule was alternated with a standard of living schedule, resulting in a 50 percent sample. The survey was also carried on in Arizona but the schedules were received too late for inclusion in the present report. Excluding Arizona, approximately 22,000 cases were enumerated.

COUNTIES AND TOWNSHIPS [5] SURVEYED

State and county	Township	State and county	Township
Arizona:		Maryland:	
Graham		Garrett	
Maricopa		Somerset	
Yuma		North Carolina:	
Iowa:		Avery	
Allamakee	{ Center	Haywood	
	{ Jefferson	North Dakota:	
	{ Bellair	Burke	Leaf Mountain
	Douglas	Divide	De Witt
	Franklin		{ Beach
Appanoose	Lincoln	Golden Valley	{ Elk Creek
	Pleasant	McKenzie	Charbon
	{ Sharon	Morton	Flasher
Black Hawk		Mountrail	Fertile
Boone		Sioux	Morristown
Buena Vista	(Sioux Rapids)	Slope	{ Crawford
Calhoun	Lake Creek		{ Independent
Cass	Franklin	Ward	Freedom
Cerro Gordo		Williams	Missouri Ridge
Clay	Lincoln	Ohio:	
Decatur		Adams	
Humboldt	Grove	Ashtabula	
Iowa	Hilton	Medina	
Keokuk	Plank	Morgan	
Madison	Monroe	Muskingum	
Marshall	Marion	Union	
O'Brien		Van Wert	
Poweshiek	Pleasant	Warren	
Story	Indian Creek	South Dakota:	
Union		Custer	
Webster	Elkhorn	Edmunds	
Wright	{ Dayton	Haakon	
	{ Norway	Kingsbury	
Kentucky:		Tripp	
Magoffin		Turner	
Morgan			

[5] Where townships are not specified, the entire county was included in the survey.

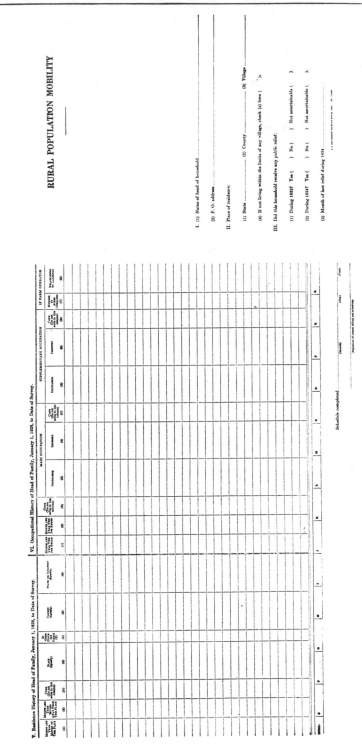

RURAL POPULATION MOBILITY

I. (1) Name of head of household ....

(2) P. O. address ....

II. Place of residence:

(1) State .... (2) County .... (3) Village ....

(4) If not living within the limits of any village, check (x) here ( )x

III. Did this household receive any public relief:

(1) During 1933? Yes ( ) No ( ) Not ascertainable ( )

(2) During 1934? Yes ( ) No ( ) Not ascertainable ( )

(3) Month of last relief during 1934 ....

IV. Members of Household and All Living Children of Head of Household

Schedule No. _____

Line No.	
1	Relationship to head.
2	Sex (M. or F.)
3	Color or race and nativity
4	Marital status (S., M., Wid., Sep., Div.)
5	Age at first marriage
6	Was person attending school? (Yes or No)
7	Last year of school completed
8	Age
	Answer For All Persons 16 Years Old Or Over
9	Residence: Longest continuous: This county
10	This State
11	Total: This county
12	This State
13	Place where reared: Place (specify)
14	County (specify)
15	State or country (specify)
16	Number of years at that place
17	Number of years spent on farm, ages 8 to 20
18	If employed: Occupation
19	Industry
A	Code
20	If not employed, or employed at work relief: Month and year last regular employment ended
21	Last regular employment: Occupation
22	Industry
B	Class
23	Residence Jan. 1, 1939: Place (specify)
24	County (specify)
25	State or country (specify)
26	Was person employed Jan. 1, 1939? (Yes or No)
27	Occupation
28	Industry
C	Code
29	Was person in this household Jan. 1, 1935? (Yes or No)
30	Residence Jan. 1, 1935: Place (specify) County (specify)
31	State or country (specify)
32	If child has ever left home, give age at leaving

Appendix C

LIST OF TABLES

TEXT TABLES

173

SUPPLEMENTARY TABLES

Appendix D

SELECTED BIBLIOGRAPHY

Anderson, W. A., *Living Conditions Among White Land-Owner Operators in Wake County*, Bulletin No. 258, North Carolina Agricultural Experiment Station, Raleigh, N. C., June 1928.
————, *Mobility of Rural Families. I*, Bulletin 607, Cornell University Agricultural Experiment Station, Ithaca, N. Y., June 1934.
————, *Mobility of Rural Families. II*, Bulletin 623, Cornell University Agricultural Experiment Station, Ithaca, N. Y., March 1935.
———— and Loomis, C. P., *Migration of Sons and Daughters of White Farmers in Wake County, 1929*, Bulletin No. 275, North Carolina Agricultural Experiment Station, Raleigh, N. C., June 1930.
Asch, Berta and Mangus, A. R., *Farmers on Relief and Rehabilitation*, Research Monograph VIII, Division of Social Research, Works Progress Administration, Washington, D. C., 1937.

Baker, O. E., *A Graphic Summary of the Number, Size, and Type of Farm, and Value of Products*, Miscellaneous Publication No. 266, U. S. Department of Agriculture, Washington, D. C., 1937.
Beck, P. G. and Forster, M. C., *Six Rural Problem Areas, Relief—Resources—Rehabilitation*, Research Monograph I, Division of Research, Statistics, and Finance, Federal Emergency Relief Administration, Washington, D. C., 1935.
———— and Lively, C. E., *Movement of Open Country Population in Ohio, II. The Individual Aspect*, Bulletin 489, Ohio Agricultural Experiment Station, Wooster, Ohio, September 1931.
Breithaupt, L. R., *Preliminary Data Concerning an Immigrant Family Survey in Oregon, January 1930 to November 1936*, Circular of Information No. 164, Oregon Agricultural Experiment Station, Corvallis, Oreg., January 1937.
———— and Hoffman, C. S., *Preliminary Information Concerning Immigration into Rural Districts in Oregon, January 1933 to June 1936*, Circular of Information No. 157, Oregon Agricultural Experiment Station, Corvallis, Oreg., August 1936.
Brunner, Edmund deS. and Lorge, Irving, *Rural Trends in Depression Years*, New York: Columbia University Press, 1937.
————, Hughes, Gwendolyn S., and Patten, Marjorie, *American Agricultural Villages*, New York: George H. Doran Company, 1927.

Clark, Dan E., "The Westward Movement in the Upper Mississippi Valley During the Fifties," in Schmidt, Louis Bernard and Ross, Earle Dudley, *Readings in the Economic History of American Agriculture*, New York: The Macmillan Company, 1925.

Creamer, Daniel B., *Is Industry Decentralizing?* Philadelphia: University of Pennsylvania Press, 1935.

────── and Swackhamer, Gladys V., *Cigar Makers—After the Lay-Off*, Report No. L–1, National Research Project, Works Progress Administration, Philadelphia, Pa., December 1937.

Dickins, Dorothy, *Occupations of Sons and Daughters of Mississippi Cotton Farmers*, Bulletin No. 318, Mississippi Agricultural Experiment Station, State College, Miss., May 1937.

Dodson, L. S., *Living Conditions and Population Migration in Four Appalachian Counties*, Social Research Report No. III, U. S. Department of Agriculture, Farm Security Administration and Bureau of Agricultural Economics, Washington, D. C., October 1937.

Eugenics Survey of Vermont, *Selective Migration From Three Rural Vermont Towns and Its Significance*, Fifth Annual Report, Burlington, Vt., September 1931.

Farm Population Estimates, January 1, 1938, U. S. Department of Agriculture, Bureau of Agricultural Economics, Washington, D. C., June 16, 1938.

Farm Tenancy, Report of the President's Committee, National Resources Committee, Washington, D. C., February 1937.

Fedde, Margaret and Lindquist, Ruth, *A Study of Farm Families and Their Standards of Living in Selected Districts of Nebraska, 1931–1933*, Research Bulletin 78, Nebraska Agricultural Experiment Station, Lincoln, Nebr., July 1935.

Galpin, Charles J. and Manny, T. B., *Interstate Migrations Among the Native White Population as Indicated by Differences Between State of Birth and State of Residence*, U. S. Department of Agriculture, Bureau of Agricultural Economics, Washington, D. C., October 1934.

Gee, Wilson and Corson, John J., *Rural Depopulation in Certain Tidewater and Piedmont Areas of Virginia*, Institute Monograph No. 3, The Institute for Research in the Social Sciences, University of Virginia, Charlottesville, Va., 1929.

Gillette, John Morris, *Rural Sociology*, Third Edition, New York: The Macmillan Company, 1936.

Goodrich, Carter and Others, *Migration and Economic Opportunity*, Philadelphia: University of Pennsylvania Press, 1936.

────── , Allin, Bushrod W., and Hayes, Marion, *Migration and Planes of Living, 1920–1934*, Bulletin No. 2, Study of Population Redistribution, Philadelphia: University of Pennsylvania Press, 1935.

Hamilton, C. Horace, *Recent Changes in the Social and Economic Status of Farm Families in North Carolina*, Bulletin No. 309, North Carolina Agricultural Experiment Station, Raleigh, N. C., May 1937.

────── , *Rural-Urban Migration in North Carolina, 1920 to 1930*, Bulletin No. 295, North Carolina Agricultural Experiment Station, Raleigh, N. C., February 1934.

Hart, Hornell N., *Selective Migration as a Factor in Child Welfare in the United States*, First Series No. 53, Vol. 1, No. 7, University of Iowa, Iowa City, Iowa, September 1921.

Hathway, Marion, *The Migratory Worker and Family Life*, Chicago: University of Chicago Press, 1934.

Heberle, Rudolf and Meyer, Fritz, *Die Groszstädte im Strome der Binnenwanderung*, Leipzig: S. Hirzel, 1937.

Hill, George W., *Rural Migration and Farm Abandonment*, Research Bulletin Series II, No. 6, Division of Research, Statistics, and Finance, Federal Emergency Relief Administration, Washington, D. C., June 1935.

Hoag, Emily F., *The National Influence of a Single Farm Community*, Bulletin No. 984, U. S. Department of Agriculture, Washington, D. C., December 1, 1921.

Jerome, Harry, *Migration and Business Cycles*, New York: National Bureau of Economic Research, Inc., 1926.

Kiser, Clyde Vernon, *Sea Island to City*, New York: Columbia University Press, 1932.

Klineberg, Otto, *Negro Intelligence and Selective Migration*, New York: Columbia University Press, 1935.

Kumlien, W. F., McNamara, Robert L., and Bankert, Zetta E., *Rural Population Mobility in South Dakota*, Bulletin 315, South Dakota Agricultural Experiment Station, Brookings, S. Dak., January 1938.

Landis, Paul H., *Rural Immigrants to Washington State, 1932–1936*, Rural Sociology Series in Population, No. 2, Washington Agricultural Experiment Station, Pullman, Wash., July 1936.

Lewis, Edward E., *The Mobility of the Negro*, New York: Columbia University Press, 1931.

Lively, C. E., *Replacement Requirements of Gainful Workers in Agriculture in Ohio, 1930–1940*, Mimeograph Bulletin No. 109, Ohio State University and Ohio Agricultural Experiment Station, Columbus, Ohio, June 1938.

——— and Almack, R. B., *A Method of Determining Rural Social Sub-Areas With Application to Ohio*, Bulletin No. 106, Parts I and II, Ohio Agricultural Experiment Station and Social Research Section, Farm Security Administration, Region III, Columbus, Ohio, January 1938.

——— and Beck, P. G., *Movement of Open Country Population in Ohio, I. The Family Aspect*, Bulletin 467, Ohio Agricultural Experiment Station, Wooster, Ohio, November 1930.

——— and Foott, Frances, *Population Mobility in Selected Areas of Rural Ohio, 1928–1935*, Bulletin 582, Ohio Agricultural Experiment Station, Wooster, Ohio, June 1937.

Lorimer, Frank and Osborn, Frederick, *Dynamics of Population*, New York: The Macmillan Company, 1934.

McCormick, T. C., *Comparative Study of Rural Relief and Non-Relief Households*, Research Monograph II, Division of Social Research, Works Progress Administration, Washington, D. C., 1935.

Mathews, Lois Kimball, *The Expansion of New England*, Boston: Houghton Mifflin Company, 1909.

Melvin, Bruce L., *Rural Youth on Relief*, Research Monograph XI, Division of Social Research, Works Progress Administration, Washington, D. C., 1937.

Migratory Labor in California, California State Relief Administration, San Francisco, Calif., 1936.

Moore, H. E. and Lloyd, O. G., *The Back-to-the-Land Movement in Southern Indiana*, Bulletin 409, Indiana Agricultural Experiment Station, Lafayette, Ind., April 1936.

National Resources Board, *A Report on National Planning and Public Works in Relation to National Resources and Including Land Use and Water Resources With Findings and Recommendations, Part II, Report of the Land Planning Committee*, Washington, D. C., 1934.

National Resources Committee, *Population Statistics, 1. National Data,* Washington, D. C., 1937.

————, *Population Statistics, 3. Urban Data,* Washington, D. C., 1937.

————, *The Problems of a Changing Population,* Washington, D. C., May 1938.

Odum, Howard W., *Southern Regions of the United States,* Chapel Hill: University of North Carolina Press, 1936.

Oyler, Merton, *Cost of Living and Population Trends in Laurel County, Kentucky,* Bulletin No. 301, Kentucky Agricultural Experiment Station, Lexington, Ky., March 1930.

Paxson, Frederic L., "Frontier," *Encyclopaedia of the Social Sciences,* Vol. 6, pp. 500–503.

Purcell, Richard J., "Connecticut in Transition 1775–1818," in Schmidt, Louis Bernard and Ross, Earle Dudley, *Readings in the Economic History of American Agriculture,* New York: The Macmillan Company, 1925.

Rankin, J. O., *Nebraska Farm Tenancy,* Bulletin 196, Nebraska Agricultural Experiment Station, Lincoln, Nebr., October 1923.

————, *The Nebraska Farm Family,* Bulletin 185, Nebraska Agricultural Experiment Station, Lincoln, Nebr., February 1923.

Rosenberry, Lois Kimball Mathews, *Migrations from Connecticut After 1800,* Historical Publication LIV, Tercentenary Commission of the State of Connecticut, Yale University Press, 1936.

Rossiter, William S., *Increase of Population in the United States, 1910–1920,* Census Monograph I, U. S. Department of Commerce, Bureau of the Census, Washington, D. C., 1922.

Sanders, J. T., *The Economic and Social Aspects of Mobility of Oklahoma Farmers,* Bulletin No. 195, Oklahoma Agricultural Experiment Station, Stillwater, Okla., August 1929.

Schuler, E. A., *Social Status and Farm Tenure—Attitudes and Social Conditions of Corn Belt Farmers,* Social Research Report No. IV, U. S. Department of Agriculture, Farm Security Administration and Bureau of Agricultural Economics, Washington, D. C., April 1938.

Scott, Emmett J., *Negro Migration During the War,* New York: Oxford University Press, 1920.

Segner, Freda P., *Migrant Minnesota,* Works Progress Administration, St. Paul, Minn., November 1936.

Sorokin, Pitirim, *Social Mobility,* New York: Harper and Brothers, 1927.

———— and Zimmerman, Carle C., *Principles of Rural-Urban Sociology,* New York: Henry Holt and Company, 1929.

————, Zimmerman, Carle C., and Galpin, Charles J., *A Systematic Source Book in Rural Sociology,* Vol. III, Minneapolis: University of Minnesota Press, 1932.

State and Special Censuses Since 1930, U. S. Department of Commerce, Bureau of the Census, Washington, D. C., May 29, 1937.

Stauber, B. R., *The Farm Real Estate Situation, 1935–36,* Circular No. 417, U. S. Department of Agriculture, Bureau of Agricultural Economics, Washington, D. C., October 1936.

Taeuber, Conrad and Taylor, Carl C., *The People of the Drought States,* Research Bulletin Series V, No. 2, Division of Social Research, Works Progress Administration, Washington, D. C., 1937.

Taylor, Carl C., Wheeler, Helen W., and Kirkpatrick, E. L., *Disadvantaged Classes in American Agriculture*, Social Research Report No. VIII, U. S. Department of Agriculture, Farm Security Administration and Bureau of Agricultural Economics, Washington, D. C., April 1938.

Taylor, Paul S., *Power Farming and Labor Displacement in the Cotton Belt, 1937*, Parts 1 and 2, Serial No. R. 737, U. S. Department of Labor, Bureau of Labor Statistics, Washington, D. C., 1938.

Thomas, Dorothy S., *Research Memorandum on Migration Differentials*, Bulletin 43, Social Science Research Council, New York, 1938.

Thompson, Warren S., *Ratio of Children to Women, 1920*, Census Monograph XI, U. S. Department of Commerce, Bureau of the Census, Washington, D. C., 1931.

————, *Research Memorandum on Internal Migration in the Depression*, Bulletin 30, Social Science Research Council, New York, 1937.

———— and Whelpton, P. K., *Population Trends in the United States*, New York: McGraw-Hill Book Company, Inc., 1933.

Thornthwaite, C. Warren, *Internal Migration in the United States*, Philadelphia: University of Pennsylvania Press, 1934.

Truesdell, Leon E., *Farm Population of the United States*, Census Monograph VI, U. S. Department of Commerce, Bureau of the Census, Washington, D. C., 1926.

Turner, Frederick Jackson, *The Frontier in American History*, New York: Henry Holt and Company, 1920.

Turner, H. A., *A Graphic Summary of Farm Tenure*, Miscellaneous Publication No. 261, U. S. Department of Agriculture, Washington, D. C., December 1936.

Vance, Rupert B., *Human Factors in Cotton Culture*, Chapel Hill: University of North Carolina Press, 1929.

————, *Research Memorandum on Population Redistribution Within the United States*, Bulletin 42, Social Science Research Council, New York, 1938.

Vasey, Tom and Folsom, Josiah C., *Survey of Agricultural Labor Conditions*, U. S. Department of Agriculture, Farm Security Administration and Bureau of Agricultural Economics, Washington, D. C., 1937.

Warren, G. F. and Pearson, F. A., *The Agricultural Situation*, New York: John Wiley and Sons, Inc., 1924.

Webb, John N., *Migrant Families*, Research Monograph XVIII, Division of Social Research, Works Progress Administration, Washington, D. C., 1938.

————, *The Migratory-Casual Worker*, Research Monograph VII, Division of Social Research, Works Progress Administration, Washington, D. C., 1937.

————, *The Transient Unemployed*, Research Monograph III, Division of Social Research, Works Progress Administration, Washington, D. C., 1935.

Webb, Walter Prescott, *Divided We Stand*, New York: Farrar & Rinehart, Inc., 1937.

————, *The Great Plains*, Boston: Ginn and Company, 1931.

Whetten, N. L. and Devereux, E. C., Jr., *Studies of Suburbanization in Connecticut, 1. Windsor*, Bulletin 212, Storrs Agricultural Experiment Station, Storrs, Conn., October 1936.

Williams, Faith M. and Others, *Family Living in Knott County, Kentucky*, Technical Bulletin No. 576, U. S. Department of Agriculture, Washington, D. C., August 1937.

Wilson, Harold Fisher, *The Hill Country of New England, Its Social and Economic History, 1790–1930*, New York: Columbia University Press, 1936.

Woofter, T. J., Jr., *Landlord and Tenant on the Cotton Plantation*, Research Monograph V, Division of Social Research, Works Progress Administration, Washington, D. C., 1936.

Young, E. C., *The Movement of Farm Population*, Bulletin 426, Cornell University Agricultural Experiment Station, Ithaca, N. Y., March 1924.

Zimmerman, Carle C. and Frampton, M. E., *Family and Society*, New York: D. Van Nostrand Company, Inc., 1935.

ARTICLES IN PERIODICALS

Baker, O. E., "Rural and Urban Distribution of the Population in the United States," *The Annals of the American Academy of Political and Social Science*, Vol. 188, November 1936, pp. 264–279.
———, "Rural-Urban Migration and the National Welfare," *Annals of the Association of American Geographers*, Vol. XXIII, No. 2, 1933, pp. 59–126.
Beecroft, Eric and Janow, Seymour, "Toward a National Policy for Migration," *Social Forces*, Vol. 16, 1938, pp. 475–492.

Cance, Alexander E., "The Decline of the Rural Population in New England," *Quarterly Publications of the American Statistical Association*, Vol. XIII, New Series, No. 97, 1912, pp. 96–101.

Dorn, Harold F. and Lorimer, Frank, "Migration, Reproduction, and Population Adjustment," *The Annals of the American Academy of Political and Social Science*, Vol. 188, November 1936, pp. 280–289.

Galpin, Charles J., "Returning to the Farm," *National Republic*, Vol. XVI, April 1929, pp. 20–21.
Gee, Wilson and Runk, Dewees, "Qualitative Selection in Cityward Migration," *The American Journal of Sociology*, Vol. XXXVII, 1931, pp. 254–265.

Hamilton, C. Horace, "The Annual Rate of Departure of Rural Youths From Their Parental Homes," *Rural Sociology*, Vol. I, 1936, pp. 164–179.
Hoffman, Charles S., "Drought and Depression Migration into Oregon, 1930 to 1936," *Monthly Labor Review*, Vol. 46, No. 1, 1938, pp. 27–35.

Leybourne, Grace G., "Urban Adjustments of Migrants From the Southern Appalachian Plateaus," *Social Forces*, Vol. 16, 1937, pp. 238–246.
Lively, C. E., "Note on Relation of Place-of-Birth to Place-Where-Reared," *Rural Sociology*, Vol. 2, 1937, pp. 332–333.
———, "Spatial and Occupational Changes of Particular Significance to the Student of Population Mobility," *Social Forces*, Vol. 15, 1937, pp. 351–355.
———, "Spatial Mobility of the Rural Population With Respect to Local Areas," *The American Journal of Sociology*, Vol. XLIII, 1937, pp. 89–102.

Ravenstein, E. G., "The Laws of Migration," *Journal of the Royal Statistical Society*, Vol. LII, 1889, pp. 241–305.
Reed, Lowell, Jr., "Population Growth and Forecasts," *The Annals of the American Academy of Political and Social Science*, Vol. 188, November 1936, pp. 159–166.
Rowell, Edward J., "Drought Refugee and Labor Migration to California in 1936," *Monthly Labor Review*, Vol. 43, No. 6, 1936, pp. 1355–1363.

Satterfield, M. Harry, "The Removal of Families from Tennessee Valley Authority Reservoir Areas," *Social Forces*, Vol. 16, 1937, pp. 258–261.

Smith, T. Lynn, "Recent Changes in the Farm Population of the Southern States," *Social Forces*, Vol. 15, 1937, pp. 391–401.

Spengler, Joseph J., "Migration Within the United States," *The Journal of Heredity*, Vol. 27, 1936, pp. 2–20.

Taeuber, Conrad and Hoffman, Charles S., "Recent Migration from the Drought Areas," *Land Policy Circular*, U. S. Department of Agriculture, Farm Security Administration, Division of Land Utilization, Washington, D. C., September 1937, pp. 16–20.

———— and Taeuber, Irene B., "Short Distance Interstate Migrations," *Social Forces*, Vol. 16, 1938, pp. 503–506.

Taylor, Paul S. and Vasey, Tom, "Contemporary Background of California Farm Labor," *Rural Sociology*, Vol. I, 1936, pp. 401–419.

———— and ————, "Drought Refugee and Labor Migration to California, June–December 1935," *Monthly Labor Review*, Vol. 42, No. 2, 1936, pp. 312–318.

Trimble, William J., "The Influence of the Passing of the Public Lands," *Atlantic Monthly*, Vol. CXIII, June 1914, pp. 755–767.

Truesdell, Leon E., "Trends in Urban Population," *The Municipal Year Book*, 1937, pp. 129–136.

Wakefield, Richard and Landis, Paul H., "Types of Migratory Farm Laborers and Their Movement into the Yakima Valley, Washington," *Rural Sociology*, Vol. 3, 1938, pp. 133–144.

Wehrwein, George S. and Baker, J. A., "The Cost of Isolated Settlement in Northern Wisconsin," *Rural Sociology*, Vol. 2, 1937, pp. 253–265.

Whelpton, P. K., "Geographic and Economic Differentials in Fertility," *The Annals of the American Academy of Political and Social Science*, Vol. 188, November 1936, pp. 37–55.

Wilhelm, Donald, "Exodus, 1933," *New Outlook*, Vol. 161, No. 9, 1933, pp. 43–45.

Woofter, T. J., Jr., "Replacement Rates in the Productive Ages," *The Milbank Memorial Fund Quarterly*, Vol. XV, No. 4, 1937, pp. 348–354.

————, "The Natural Increase of the Rural Non-Farm Population," *The Milbank Memorial Fund Quarterly*, Vol. XIII, No. 4, 1935, pp. 311–319.

Zimmerman, Carle C., "The Migration to Towns and Cities. II," *The American Journal of Sociology*, Vol. XXXIII, 1927, pp. 105–109.

————, Duncan, O. D., and Frey, Fred C., "The Migration to Towns and Cities. III," *The American Journal of Sociology*, Vol. XXXIII, 1927, pp. 237–241.

Index

INDEX